Bilingualism
and
Cognition

Bilingualism
and
Cognition

Informing Research, Pedagogy, and Policy

❧

Eugene E. García

José E. Náñez, Sr.

AMERICAN PSYCHOLOGICAL ASSOCIATION

WASHINGTON, DC

KH

Published by
American Psychological Association
750 First Street, NE
Washington, DC 20002
www.apa.org

To order
APA Order Department
P.O. Box 92984
Washington, DC 20090-2984
Tel: (800) 374-2721; Direct: (202) 336-5510
Fax: (202) 336-5502; TDD/TTY: (202) 336-6123
Online: www.apa.org/pubs/books
E-mail: order@apa.org

In the U.K., Europe, Africa, and the Middle East, copies may be ordered from
American Psychological Association
3 Henrietta Street
Covent Garden, London
WC2E 8LU England

Typeset in Goudy by Circle Graphics, Inc., Columbia, MD

Printer: Maple-Vail Book Manufacturing Group, York, PA
Cover Designer: Berg Design, Albany, NY

The opinions and statements published are the responsibility of the authors, and such opinions and statements do not necessarily represent the policies of the American Psychological Association.

Library of Congress Cataloging-in-Publication Data

García, Eugene E., 1946-
Bilingualism and cognition : informing research, pedagogy, and policy / by : Eugene E. García and José E. Náñez Sr.
    p. cm.
  Includes bibliographical references.
  ISBN-13: 978-1-4338-0879-1
  ISBN-10: 1-4338-0879-X
  1. Bilingualism in children—United States. 2. Language acquisition. 3. Education, Bilingual—United States. I. Náñez, José E. II. Title.

  P115.5.U5G39 2011
  404'.20830973—dc22
                                    2010048206

British Library Cataloguing-in-Publication Data

A CIP record is available from the British Library.

Printed in the United States of America
First Edition

doi: 10.1037/12324-000

6/8/12

CONTENTS

Bilingualism
and
Cognition

INTRODUCTION

There is a growing need among researchers, educators, policymakers, and students for a book that makes the case for joining cognitive psychology and neuroscience with applied educational research to better inform bilingual research, pedagogy, and policy. Failure to engage interdisciplinary research on bilingual cognitive and linguistic processes that may enhance students' second language acquisition may perpetuate bilingual schoolchildren's lag in academic performance (e.g., in reading; see Chapter 8 of this volume) relative to their monolingual English-speaking peers.

This volume focuses on describing bilingual cognitive and language development processes; identifying and discussing research-informed bilingual education methods; and models and stating best practices for implementation of the methods and models to inform bilingual research, pedagogy, and policy. This focus is timely. The creation of the new Center for Early Care and Education Research: Dual Language Learners (CECER-DLL), funded by the U.S. Department of Health and Human Services, Administration for Children and Families, attests to the continued need on the part of educators and policymakers for research on dual-language learners' (emergent bilinguals'; see Epilogue) cognitive and linguistic development (see Chapters 3, 6, 7), as well as the urgent nature of this research. According to the CECER-DLL director,

> The main goal of conducting these [literature] reviews is to determine the state of, and gaps in knowledge related to the early care and education of young DLLs [dual language learners] which will help us in the process of developing a research agenda for the CECER-DLL, and at the same time will inform researchers, practitioners and policy makers at large. (D. C. Castro, personal communication, June 2, 2010)

The timeliness and consistent historical relevance of the topic is further illustrated by the creation and the implantation of federal intervention programs such as No Child Left Behind (2001) and the Bilingual Education Act (1968, 1974, 1978, 1984, 1988, 1994), as well as reports such as the National Literacy Panel on Language Minority Children and Youth (August & Shanahan, 2006). For example, data from the cognitive psychology side as presented in Part I of this volume show that children who are proficient bilinguals acquire specific cognitive benefits that serve them well in applied learning situations (see Chapter 3).

While reports to federal, state, and private agencies and programs continue to focus concern on emergent bilinguals' lag in academic performance, a peek into the chapters in this volume should make readers who support high-quality bilingual education glad to know that over the past 50 years many studies have concluded that *balanced-proficient bilinguals* (i.e., individuals who speak two languages at a high proficiency level) enjoy numerous cognitive benefits over monolinguals (e.g., Chapters 3 and 7). This general historical finding continues to be supported by current research, including the most recent meta-analysis (Adesope, Lavin, Thompson, & Ungerleider, 2010), which shows that the bulk of the data from more than 60 studies continue to show a positive relationship between bilingualism and cognition.

INTENDED AUDIENCE FOR THIS VOLUME

The primary intended audience of this volume consists of a broad spectrum of researchers/experts, administrators, policymakers, and teachers with an interest in cognition and language development, especially as they relate to emergent bilingual children. Readers who are familiar with cognitive or language development processes or both may choose to skip this introduction, read it as a refresher, or go directly to the synopses of the chapters below to get a flavor of the chapter contents. They may choose to read Part I to update and refresh their memory regarding the content of Chapters 1 through 4, or they may go to Part II, where information that may be less familiar to them, concerning how to best serve the educational needs of emergent bilingual children, is discussed in detail. Experts in applied education research, teaching, and policy may wish to review Part II and focus on the less familiar information in Part I. The secondary intended audience consists of readers who are novices or less informed about the fields of cognition and language development and educational research, which includes but may not be limited to students and laypersons. In any case, we highly recommended that readers read the volume in its entirety, to benefit from the extensive literature reviews of the most current information on cognitive and language development in monolinguals and bilinguals, as well as the relationship between cognition and language, with specific emphasis on best-practice-informed bilingual education.

COMPOSITION OF THE VOLUME

An interesting and challenging goal we set for this volume is how to assist the intended audiences to use the integrated information provided to develop a whole-child (cognitive/brain, individual/behavior, and sociocultural) approach to the enhancement of bilingual education. This volume is also designed to meet a growing need for a book like this, to join cognitive psychology and neuroscience with applied educational research to better inform research, pedagogy, and policy. To accomplish these goals, we have formatted the volume into two parts: Part I focuses on cognitive and language development in monolingual and bilingual children and psychometrics, and Part II analyzes the research on education circumstances, pedagogy, and policies that best serve the educational needs of bilingual children. There is a natural flow between the chapters, and together Parts I and II are designed to assist students and professionals interested in bilingual education and research to find empirical and applied research solutions to achieve positive pedagogical outcomes and policies for educating emergent bilingual children. This organizational scheme serves the purpose well. Specifically, Part I addresses cognitive and language development in monolingual children (Chapters 1–2), setting the stage for discussion of bilingual development in these areas (Chapter 3). Chapter 4 addresses psychometric issues in bilingual research. As a whole, the chapters in Part I are designed to provide a solid foundation for launching discussion of how the information in Part II can be applied for enhancing academic settings (Chapters 5 and 6), pedagogy (Chapter 7), and informing policymakers' decisions (Chapter 8).

Thus, Part I is designed to provide a structurally sound springboard for the in-depth discussion of the applied topics in Part II. The two parts together present a comprehensive view of bilingual children's cognitive and linguistic abilities that serve them well in applied learning settings. Therefore, bilingualism serves as the bridge connecting the topics addressed in the two parts. Bilingualism also serves as the agent for unifying the fields of cognitive psychology, neuroscience, and education through collaborative research and weaves the topics covered in both parts in a seamless manner.

RELATIONSHIP BETWEEN COGNITIVE PSYCHOLOGY AND EDUCATION: A HISTORICAL PERSPECTIVE

As the "science of mind and behavior," psychology allowed a transition from earlier post hoc philosophical descriptive discussion of topics such as the proverbial question of nature versus nurture influences on human cognitive and physical development and behavioral outcomes to the systematic exploration of such topics through the scientific method. Through a prospective empirical research approach, psychology allowed scientific exploration of the behavior–mind interaction in areas such as language acquisition and cognitive processes in general and specifically in bilinguals (addressed in Part I) for the first time.

Psychology's evolution as a scientific discipline is a relatively recent historical event. The discipline was launched when Wilhelm Wundt in 1875 set up a room to demonstrate sensation and perception principles. William James also established a psychology demonstration laboratory at Harvard University in the same year. Stanley Hall (1891) is recognized as the first developmental psychologist for his initiation of systematic exploration of the children's thought processes (Shaffer & Kipp, 2007). The work of developmental psychologists such as Hall served as an early natural link between the fields of education and psychology. Edward Thorndike was the first educator assigned to the discipline of psychology with his appointment at Columbia University, where he conducted scientific research on education. William James was instrumental in establishing educational psychology as well, by bringing the scientific method to bear on research on pedagogical methods and ideas (Charles, 1987; Hilgard, 1996). Horace Mann was the founder of the American public education system (Cremin, 1957; Filler, 1965). In 1737, as the first secretary of the Massachusetts State Board of Education, Mann campaigned to establish a publicly supported school system in Massachusetts, a system that evolved into the present U.S. public education system.

This brief historical account serves as a reminder that the disciplines of cognitive psychology and education enjoyed early common bonds through developmental and educational psychology. However, cognitive psychology, with its emphasis on the study of behavior and the brain as a goal unto itself, remained strongly focused on the conduct of research in the laboratory setting. By its nature, such research favors the removal of the individual from the natural learning environment to the laboratory, where environment and experience are systematically manipulated to isolate factors that reveal a better understanding of what develops, when it develops, why it develops, and how it develops, with little consideration of how these factors may affect the learner in applied learning environments. Neuroscience has enhanced our knowledge of what goes on in the human brain. It is hoped that cognitive psychologists and neuroscientists will combine their efforts to better understand the observed differences in brain function and structure between bilinguals and monolinguals. Such collaboration also has the potential to reveal what the changes mean for behavioral and cognitive processing in bilinguals. An understanding of the basic effects of learning on cognitive processes that is achieved by observing the learner exclusively in the laboratory or neuroimaging room comes at the expense of decreased generalizability to the behavior of the child in broader ecological settings like the classroom, where many largely uncontrollable environmental factors vie for the learner's attention.

Faced with the broader issues of learning and pedagogy in the dynamic, cluttered classroom environment, education researchers have generally opted to focus their investigations in a more applied realm. Although naturalistic observation affords greater generalizability from an ecological perspective, identifying and isolating precise causes is less likely through this method (i.e., gains in generalizability may be achieved at the expense of scientific predictive power). These differences in research focus moved the disciplines of cognitive psychology and education in separate directions with regard to the study of human learning and cognition. Over the years, the disciplines became separate research repositories for the study of related issues; substantive collaborative research is still largely lacking.

Given the historically separate research foci of the two disciplines, this volume makes a strong case for bringing the fields' research foci closer in order to develop interdisciplinary approaches and applications for answering questions regarding what and how. We attempt to do this by exploring what the child's cognitive structures and processes are, as well as how they function in the developing individual (the main focus of Part I), with the intent of enhancing researchers' understanding of how these affect children, especially emergent bilinguals, in applied settings (discussed extensively in Part II).

Although research collaboration between the disciplines of interest does occur to some extent, such collaboration could definitely be greater in quantity and scope. One way to move toward this end is to build on the appreciation shared by researchers from different fields that the process of learning two or more languages is much more complex than merely adding a second language to an existing (first) one, which is like building a puzzle whose completion is always limited to the sum of the parts. Rather, bilingual mastery results in cognitive plasticity and power (discussed in Part I) that generalize to benefit the learner in other areas of cognition and in applied learning environments (discussed in Part II). That is, the outcome is significantly greater than the sum of the parts. Collaborative research on what the parts are and how they fit together to affect completion of the evolving puzzle is a natural place to begin.

As greater knowledge is gained through collaborative cognitive and educational research, the puzzle will evolve, suggesting new research directions and opportunities. For example, the continued development and refinement of neuroimaging technology, along with improvements in psychometric and methodological approaches to the study of bilingual cognitive processes, will likely take researchers into a new realm of understanding how processes such as cognition and language are related in bilinguals. We join with other researchers who have diligently engaged in conducting unbiased, methodologically strong cognitive and bilingual research with applied educational goals in mind in calling for the conduct of bilingual research using the best research methods, practices, and research tools available (e.g., August & Hakuta, 1997; Bialystok, 1997, 2000, 2001; Bialystok, Majumder, & Martin, 2003; Cummins, 1976, 1981b; Hakuta, 1990; Kuhl, 2004; Kuhl, Conboy, Padden, Nelson, & Pruitt, 2005). Bilingual education stands to benefit directly from collaborative research endeavors on the topics of bilingual and cognitive development.

There is a growing acknowledgment in psychology and neuroscience that bilingualism is associated with functional (Kim, Relkin, Lee, & Hirsch, 1997), structural (Mechelli et al., 2004), and cognitive (Adesope et al., 2010; Bialystok, Craik, Klein, & Viswanathan, 2004; Bialystok et al., 2005; Chee et al., 2000) changes in the human brain. Education researchers should apply such findings to the design of experimental educational settings for bilingual children, in order to examine questions such as how simultaneous (early bilingualism; birth to 3–5 years) and sequential (late bilingualism; second-language learning significantly after first language acquisition [i.e., after 5 years of age]) bilingual acquisition correlate with the child's learning processes and academic performance in the classroom. The possibilities for designing and conducting such collaborative research are considerable.

Education researchers seek to understand the functioning of the child's brain in the classroom learning environment; educational psychologists seek to teach children how to think, learn, and problem solve in and out of the classroom setting; and cognitive psychologists and neuroscientists seek to understand the child's brain at the structural and functional levels. Linking the disciplines through collaborative research shows great promise for successfully mining the wealth of scientific knowledge regarding cognitive and learning processes in emergent and fully bilingual children, as well as in children in general.

There is a growing sense among educators, administrators, and policy-makers that past education research on applied topics such as reading, math, and bilingualism has not taken full advantage of cognitive psychologists' and neuroscientists' laboratory discoveries concerning the mental processes, functions, and structures involved in perceptual learning and neural plasticity. Such professionals are increasingly realizing that encouraging basic and applied scientists to join their research efforts and resources can significantly enhance our understanding of the workings of children's minds in the learning situations in which they spend the bulk of their waking hours during the school year. To accomplish this goal, however, political influence must be applied to fund collaborative interdisciplinary research to identify, evaluate, and implement education policy, procedures, and practice based on outcomes of best-practice-informed pedagogical research. This case is made in Chapter 3 (Part I) and is significantly expanded on in Chapters 5 to 8 (Part II), in which applied educational and policy issues are discussed at length and recommendations for improved bilingual research and education are presented.

A major part of this volume concerns understanding the bilingual child's cognitive and linguistic developmental processes at the level of the brain (Part I) and informing pedagogy and policy (Part II). In the latter areas, expanded collaboration will result in the establishment of a solid bilingual research and education agenda for informing local, state, and national policy regarding how best to educate bilingual children to ensure that they are adequately prepared to contribute to America's continued intellectual and economic leadership in an increasingly technological, multicultural, multilingual, and global environment.

It is our sincere hope that this book will make a significant contribution to the emerging appreciation that by engaging in collaborative interdisciplinary scientific endeavors, scholars can achieve greater understanding of the mental processes involved in cognition/intelligence and bilingual processes to a significantly greater extent than can be accomplished through separate research streams. Such a research agenda will lead to better understanding of the whole child at the level of the brain (plasticity/malleability), the individual (behavior/performance), and the group (social/cultural interactions). The challenge then will be to find ways to most effectively apply the newly acquired knowledge to benefit bilingual children as they interact in their daily learning environments.

DEMOGRAPHICS

The demographic data provided in this section serve to support the call for increasing collaborative research on the relationship between cognitive and linguistic processes with the goal of providing enhanced bilingual education for emergent bilingual students. The timeliness of such research is critical because of the rapid growth of ethnic minority groups in general and particularly of Latino groups in the United States, since the demographic shifts described below have been accompanied by rapid growth in the number of children from non-English or limited-English-speaking homes.

Migration and Growth Patterns Among U.S. Minorities

Migration patterns and demographics among U.S. ethnic, racial, and cultural groups have been changing rapidly. Therefore, one goal of this volume is to stress the urgency of gaining research-based knowledge to assist professional educators, administrators, and policymakers in their quest to define and implement maximally effective bilingual education practices and policies. To do this, collaborative research attention needs to be focused on developing best-practice, research-informed, bilingual education models to help such students gain English proficiency while enhancing their home language ability as well (see Part II).

Minority populations in the United States, especially Latino and some Asian/Pacific Islander groups, have increased dramatically in recent decades. Every time a new U.S. census or demographic think-tank report is released, the message that America is becoming a significantly more diverse nation is reinforced. The Brookings Institution's report, *Diversity Spreads Out: Metropolitan Shifts in Hispanic, Asian, and Black Populations Since 2000* (Frey, 2006), makes the point very clearly. The report reveals not only that the United States is undergoing a rapid transition ethnically but also that the geographic distribution of racial/ethnic/cultural groups is continuously changing. For example, the following excerpts from the report describe American demographic shifts since the 2000 census:

- "The fastest growing metro areas for each minority group in 2000–2004 are no longer unique but closely parallel the fastest growing areas in the nation."
- "Minorities contributed the majority of population gains in the nation's fastest-growing metropolitan areas and central metropolitan counties from 2000–2004."
- "A strong multi-minority presence characterized 18 larger 'melting pot' metro areas, and 27 large metro areas now have 'majority minority' child populations."
- "Because the nation's child population is more racially diverse than its adult population, in nearly one-third of all metro areas, including Washington, D.C., Chicago, Phoenix, and Atlanta, fewer than half of all people under age 15 are white."

- "The wider dispersal of minority populations signifies the broadening relevance of policies aimed at more diverse, including immigrant, communities." (Frey, 2006, p. 1)

The U.S. Census Bureau (2006) report contains a variety of data on the diversification of America and serves as the source for reports such as the Brookings Institution's series cited here. The Brookings Institution data also show that nine out of the 10 fastest-growing U.S. metropolitan areas between 2000 and 2004 experienced significantly greater growth in minority than White populations, ranging from an astonishing 94%, 93%, and 91% minority growth for McAllen–Edinburg–Pharr, Texas; Bakersfield, California; and Stockton, California, respectively, to 58% in Sacramento–Roseville, California. Overall, the percentage growth of the Latino population has outpaced that of all other groups in eight of the 10 major metropolitan areas.

Latino and Bilingual Demographics

The statistics documenting rapid increases in the number, diversity, and migration patterns among U.S. minorities are accompanied by an even greater increase in the growth of non-English-speaking and bilingual groups, especially among Latinos and new Asian/Pacific Islander immigrant groups. The U.S. Census Bureau (2006) report estimates that well over 1 million children live in U.S. homes where a language other than English is spoken exclusively, is the dominant language, or is spoken on a regular basis. These children are often referred to as *limited English proficient*, among other labels. Given that such children experience two interacting languages, García (2008) referred to them as *bilingual*. However, García noted that this does not mean that bilingual children, including those categorized via ethnic or cultural language groups, constitute homogeneous cultural or language proficiency groups. García pointed out that coupled with the use of different definitions of student identification, differences in identification measures themselves, and differences in statistical methods for generalizing from sample size to actual population size, estimates of children from bilingual homes range from 2.5 million to 4.6 million, that is, approximately 7% to 10% of U.S. students overall and growing.[1] Latino groups continue to spread throughout the United States and

---

[1] Various labels have been used in the literature to refer to second-language learners. Throughout this book, we refer to children learning two languages as *bilingual*, with the understanding that such children vary in proficiency and balance between their two languages at any given time in the acquisition process. We use the term *emergent bilinguals* for those in the process of acquiring, but not yet proficient in, a second language, and we use the term *balanced-proficient bilinguals* for those possessing complete mastery of two languages. This is the practice unless the children are referred to otherwise in published reports, books, or the research literature we quote. We use *Latino* as the preferred term when referring to groups of Hispanic heritage.

have or approach majority status in some major population centers, especially in the western and southwestern United States. Significant expansion among Latinos has recently occurred in southern states (e.g., Florida, Georgia, Tennessee) as well as in some midwestern states (e.g., South Dakota).

The phrase "demography is destiny" is applicable to the present circumstances in bilingual education. Two useful reports outlining the demography of bilingual students are *The New Demography of America's Schools* by demographer Randy Capps and colleagues (Capps et al., 2005) at the Urban Institute, and *Children in Immigrant Families: Looking to America's Future* by Donald Hernandez and his colleagues (Hernandez, Denton, & Macartney, 2008) at the University at Albany, State University of New York. These reports use the U.S. Census Bureau (2000) data to describe the ethnic, linguistic, economic, domestic, educational, and geographic (including their origins and destinations) characteristics among immigrant children and families. Although the data the authors analyzed and interpreted in these reports are a decade old, the information provided is useful to project the future demographic characteristics of the U.S. student body. Certainly, Census 2010 will shed further light and in some cases correct misguided projections based on 2000 data. Until then, however, these reports continue to be helpful tools in orienting our understanding of the future challenges and opportunities for educators serving children of immigrant origins who learn English as a second language.

Currently, at least one in five children ages 5 to 17 in the United States has a foreign-born parent (Capps et al., 2005), and many, though not all, of these children learn English as their second language. It is important to note that bilingual students and children from immigrant families (i.e., a child with at least one foreign-born parent) are not synonymous populations, but certainly they are closely related. Most children from immigrant households are considered English learners at some point in their lives. Yet a majority (74%) of school-age children (5–17 years) from immigrant families speak English exclusively or very well according to the Census 2000 data.

The overall child population speaking a non-English native language in the United States rose from 6% in 1979 to 14% in 1999 (National Clearinghouse for English Language Acquisition, 2006), and the number of language-minority students in K–12 schools was recently estimated to be over 14 million (August & Shanahan, 2006). The representation of bilinguals in U.S. schools is highest in early education. This is because bilingual children tend to develop oral and academic English proficiency by third grade. The bilingual share of students from prekindergarten to Grade 5 rose from 4.7% to 7.4% from 1980 to 2000, whereas the bilingual share of students in Grades 6 to 12 rose from 3.1% to 5.5% during the same time period (Capps et al., 2005). Young bilinguals (ages 0–8 years), therefore, have been the fastest growing student population in the United States over the past few decades, due primarily to increased rates in (legal and illegal) immigration as well as high birth rates among immigrant families (Hernandez et al., 2008).

Although the majority of emergent bilingual children come from Spanish-speaking immigrant families, these children represent many national origins and more than 350 languages. In 2000, more than half of bilinguals came from Latin American immigrant families (Capps et al., 2005). Mexico led the way with nearly 40% of children from immigrant families (Hernandez et al., 2008), and Spanish was the native language of some 77% of bilinguals nationally during the 2000–2001 school year (Hopstock & Stephenson, 2003). Following Mexico, the Caribbean, East Asia, and Europe (combined with Canada and Australia) each accounts for 10% to 11% of the overall population of children from immigrant families; Central America, South America, Indochina, and West Asia each accounts for 5% to 7% of the total; and the former Soviet Union and Africa account for 2% to 3% each. At least three in four children in immigrant families are born in the United States (Capps, 2001), although U.S. nativity is higher among elementary-age children of immigrant families than among those attending secondary schools (Capps et al., 2005).

Just as immigrant families are settling in new destinations in response to labor demands (Zúñiga & Hernández-León, 2005), bilingual students increasingly attend school in districts and states that served few to no bilingual children in the 1980s and previous decades. Although immigrant families continue to be concentrated in California, Texas, New York, Florida, Illinois, and New Jersey (Capps et al., 2005), several other states have witnessed rapid increases in their immigrant populations. Indeed, seven states experienced over 100% increases in the number of children from immigrant families attending pre-K to fifth grade from 1990 to 2000, including Nevada, North Carolina, Georgia, Nebraska, Arkansas, Arizona, and South Dakota (from greatest to lesser percentage increases; Capps et al., 2005). During the 1990s, Nevada, Nebraska, and South Dakota saw increases of 354%, 350%, and 264% in their bilingual populations, respectively. This has led several school districts and states to frantically search out, identify, and provide educational resources to children learning English as a second language.

Latinos: From Invisible Minority to Ethnic/Cultural Prominence

The changing ethnic group and language demographics in the United States noted in the previous section provide a clear view of the evolution of Latinos from an invisible sector of the U.S. population, historically subsumed within the "White" category in the census, to a prominently visible sector of the nation's population. As early as the 1970 census, the category "Spanish Heritage" was incorporated (see U.S. Census Bureau, 1970, Table 190), recognizing the significant growth in the Latino population in the United States.

The National Population Projection from the U.S. Census Bureau (2008) estimated that people of "Hispanic Origin" (of any race) will number approximately 49,726,000 by 2010, up from 22.3 million listed in the 1990 census. The actual number of Latinos is likely significantly higher because they may be underrepresented in the census tabulations due to low participation and distrust of census (i.e., government) personnel. Among Latinos, 29.2 million are listed under the category "U.S. Residents of Mexican Origin," constituting 64% of the Latino population (U.S. Census Bureau, 2007), up from the nearly 60% of the Hispanics reported by Ramirez (2004). (See Chapter 5 of this volume for a detailed discussion of some of the challenges the increased demographics of school-age Latino students present for bilingual classroom education.) In sum, the demographic shifts discussed here have resulted in a significant growth in the numbers of emergent bilingual children in U.S. classrooms, making interdisciplinary collaborative research on best-practice-driven bilingual educational practice and policy essential.

CHAPTER SYNOPSES

Parts I and II of this volume are designed with the specific goal of helping students and professionals who are interested in bilingual education and research to find empirical and applied research solutions that will, we hope, lead to positive pedagogical outcomes and policies for educating bilingual children. As mentioned earlier, overarching goals for this book include (a) to state the case for strengthening research collaboration between the disciplines of cognitive psychology, neuroscience, and education; (b) to refresh and enhance the educated reader's knowledge of children's cognitive and language development processes, as well as educate undergraduate and graduate students preparing for careers in education, cognitive psychology, or neuroscience; and (c) to provide readers greater insight into the cognitive processes associated with successful pedagogy for improving educational achievement, with specific focus on bilingual children, a rapidly growing sector of the American population. This is especially expedient, given that bilingual children tend to come from ethnic groups that are experiencing a significant lag in academic success relative to European American and some Asian American groups.

Part I (Chapters 1–4)

Chapter 1 provides an extended review of language and cognitive development among monolingual children. Chapter 2 discusses the major theories and theoretical approaches that have, over time, sought to address language and cognitive development in monolinguals. Together, these two chapters build a solid foundation for providing the reader with a detailed review of language and cognitive development and address important questions also raised in Chapter 3 regarding language and cognition in bilinguals. For example, what is the nature (i.e., negative, neutral, or positive) of the correlation between bilingualism and cognition? Some of the major issues of contention between supporters and opponents of bilingual education are explored (e.g., English immersion vs. two-way-immersion education for emergent bilingual children in the classroom; heritage language–second language transfer; effectiveness of all-day vs. half-day kindergarten; cost-effectiveness of bilingual vs. monolingual early education programs). In Chapter 3, the reader will find that high-quality bilingual education programs, taught by well-trained bilingual teachers, are cost-effective and produce the best results for helping emergent bilingual children make the transition to balanced-proficient bilinguals in a timely fashion. Together, the first three chapters address questions such as: What are the similarities or differences between bilingual and monolingual linguistic and cognitive processes? Are there cognitive advantages, for example, in problem-solving abilities, mental reaction time, verbal and nonverbal IQ, and metacognition, that accrue to monolinguals relative to bilinguals? In other words, does bilingualism result in decreases in such areas because of cognitive overload or heritage language interference in acquisition of second language, and what other factors might play a role?

In Chapter 4, we address some psychometric issues historically. What have been some of the major issues of contention between researchers in the area of IQ testing and intelligence? Where does the field currently stand, and what should future direction(s) be? For example, the long-standing debate between psychometricians concerning the relationships between IQ and intelligence, with "Jensonians" (who believe ethnic cultural group differences in IQ/intelligence have a genetic basis) on one side and environmentalists (who consider intelligence to be mostly environmentally based) on the other, is brought up to date in this chapter. We conclude that the Jensonian–environmentalist debate is a tired one, and we propose the use of neuroscience approaches to take educational, cognitive, behavioral, and psychophysical-based bilingualism research to the level of the brain and neural networks. For aspiring researchers in the area of bilingualism, Chapter 4 also raises psychometric issues of importance in the areas of bilingualism and cognition and provides a list of the major instruments that have been used to conduct such research with monolinguals and bilinguals over time, along with a list of researchers and studies that have used the different instruments.

Part II (Chapters 5–8)

Part II focuses on the educational circumstances of bilingual students in the United States, their educational achievement, the conceptual basis for educational interventions related to their schooling, the specific instructional practices in addressing their bilingual character, and the federal and state policies that have been generated in response to such bilingual issues. Chapter 5 builds on the demographic information provided in this introduction regarding demographic shifts and growth among minority students and their families by presenting an overview of the educational attributes of this growing population of students in the United States. Achievement gaps have been the norm for this population ever since researchers have become concerned with measuring achievement outcomes. These gaps are visible at every level of the educational pipeline. However, they should not be understood simply as related only to the linguistic character of the population; more appropriately, these gaps must be seen as the result of an interaction of related variables, such as the quality of education minority students receive, the educational capital they bring to the educational enterprise, and their immigrant status.

Chapter 6 highlights the conceptual/theoretical interface of cognitive, linguistic, and cultural parameters as they relate to educational interventions for bilingual students. The particular "best fit" of sociocultural theory raises the notion that overall development and learning are best understood as an interaction of cognitive and linguistic factors operating continuously in sociocultural contexts. Chapter 7 addresses best-practices and successful strategies for educating bilingual children. Teaching and learning that recognize and respond to the cognitive and linguistic resources of bilingual students best serves these students in terms of academic achievement and overall educational well-being. Those strategies and programmatic approaches, such as dual language programs, are reviewed. Chapter 8 provides a detailed analysis of state and federal policies that have been generated in recognition that these students lag behind others. Particular policies related to potential solutions have been addressed by federal and state courts as well as national and state legislative entities. They have generated a class of students with specific legal treatments that differ from nonbilingual children. And they can be characterized as conceptually antagonistic/restrictive with regard to what is known about the intersection of cognition and bilingualism in many circumstances.

I

FOUNDATIONS

Part I provides the essential theoretical and research background on cognitive and language development and bilingual psychometrics to promote detailed discussion of relevant topics in the applied fields of bilingual education, pedagogy, and policy addressed in Part II.

1

LANGUAGE AND COGNITIVE DEVELOPMENT

This chapter informs readers about language and cognitive developmental processes in general (i.e., in monolinguals). A dual purpose is to set the stage for understanding the language and cognitive development theories in Chapter 2 and to build a solid foundation for understanding language and cognitive processes in bilinguals in Chapter 3. The emergence of language and cognitive development can be discussed separately or together. In either case, the two processes are inextricably intertwined, melding in a symbiotic fashion. Thus, although language and cognition are discussed under separate headings in this chapter, we consider the two processes individually or together, according to the topic of linguistic development being discussed.

LANGUAGE DEVELOPMENT

Numerous textbooks (e.g., Berk, 2008; Berko Gleason & Bernstein Ratner, 2008; Shaffer & Kipp, 2010) provide extended discussions of the topics of language and cognitive development (Chapter 1, this volume) and the theories of language and cognitive development (Chapter 2, this volume). We model this chapter in their fashion, discussing the numerous classic studies presented in those volumes while incorporating the newest literature available.

Although there are a number of theories of language development, it should be noted from the start that no current theory on its own can account for the complex process of language acquisition. Language is an exclusively human communicative process; no other organism on earth has evolved a communication system as intricate or dynamic. As a process that is unprecedented among other organisms, language affords humans the ability to communicate personal and shared sociocultural experiences. As Corballis (2009) noted,

> Languages gained grammatical complexity perhaps driven by the evolution of episodic memory and mental time travel, which involve combinations of familiar elements—Who did what to whom, how, where, and why? Language is thus adapted to allow us to share episodic structure, whether past, planned, or fictional, and so increase survival fitness. (p. 19)

Pinker (1994, cited in Pinker, 2007, p. 28) eloquently stated his view of the importance of language relative to developmental processes: "Pride of place must go to language—ubiquitous across the species, unique in the animal kingdom, inextricable from social life and from the master of civilization and technology, devastating when lost or impaired."

Many researchers believe that language and cognitive development are intertwined. Both are emergent processes that involve brain structures and functions as a result of interaction with environmental (e.g., exposure to speech) and psychosocial (social interaction within the culture or group) experiences. Pinker (2007) made a strong case for the interaction between language and cognitive development: "Language . . . reflects the way we grasp reality. . . . It is . . . a window into human nature" (p. xiii).

Nonhuman Species

Achieving the speech side of language is no easy task. In fact, it is impossible for nonhuman species. To reinforce the fact that verbal language (speech) is unique to humans, we briefly review the extensive animal literature here. The resounding conclusion is that all attempts by humans to teach a variety of nonhuman species to talk have failed.

Obviously, animals communicate, but their communication is nowhere near as elaborate as that of humans. Terrace et al. (1979) cited research showing that various species use species-specific communication modes. For example, there are birds that rigidly sing one song for mating, one song for alarm, and a separate song marking territories and defense (Thorpe, 1961); bees are known to communicate the presence and quality of food sources (Frisch & Lindauer, 1956); and sticklebacks have distinctive courtship behaviors (Tinbergen,

1951). However, none of these animals possess the intellectual ability to produce speech as it is observed in humans.

Apes possess significantly greater intellectual ability than horses, birds, bees, fish, and other animals. Not surprisingly, the most successful studies reported in the literature used great apes as subjects because apes are the closest to humans genetically, intellectually, behaviorally, and socially. Although several researchers have shown some success in teaching rudimentary language symbol use to apes, and apes have shown the cognitive ability to comprehend some aspects of human language, they fall far short of acquiring speech.

Attempts by those who hoped to "talk with the animals" have failed for a number of reasons. Key among them is the species difference in structure and function of the larynx and mouth; humans evolved fine control of the structures that allow for vocal speech (Enard, Przeworski, et al., 2002). There is also at least one mutated gene (FOXP2) that leads to language impediments by impacting speech and language neural systems in affected individuals (Enard, Przeworski, et al., 2002; Liegéois et al., 2003) and differs between humans and apes. Therefore, as noted by Brakke and Savage-Rumbaugh (1995),

> Part of the difficulty in assessing language skills in apes arises from the fact that they do not speak. Even if they possessed all of the cognitive requisites for language, the structure of their vocal apparati would not permit articulate speech (Duchlin, 1990; Lieberman, 1991). (p. 121)

Apes are simply not biologically equipped to vocalize in the same way as humans. Taking these biological differences into account, a number of researchers have used nonspeech training methodology in their interspecies language communication research (R. A. Gardner & Gardner, 1969; Premack, 1976; Rumbaugh, 1977). The initial success reported by Premack and the Gardners led to similar efforts by other researchers. However, their success was limited. For example, Terrace (1987) and his team set out to raise a chimpanzee in a manner much like raising a human infant. They attempted to teach American Sign Language to the baby chimpanzee, amusingly named Nim Chimsky. Terrace's and earlier researchers' initial results generated much excitement: It appeared, at least for a brief period, that the gap between ape and human communication would be bridged, providing humans a peek into the ape mind and society.

While writing his book, *Nim, a Chimpanzee Who Learned Sign Language*, Terrace (1987) made a significant discovery upon careful, detailed, slow-motion review of video recordings of Nim's signing. It became clear to him that Nim was merely imitating the gestures presented by his human trainers. From his review of the projects undertaken earlier by Premack, the Gardners, and other researchers, Terrace concluded that there was no evidence that Nim or any of the apes trained by other researchers were capable of generating their own sentences. "None of those projects produced positive results" (Terrace, 1987, p. v).

Even under the exhaustive training programs carried out by his trainers, Nim was not able to move from imitating his teachers' communicative gestures and symbols to learning to use the symbols to generate nonimitative, novel sentences, a process that is easily accomplished by human toddlers with normal language acquisition ability and exposure to language. Terrace et al. (1979) summed up his findings: "By age three, a child stops imitating its parents' utterances; by four, Nim's imitations grew to 54 percent" (p. 72). Terrace concluded that besides lack of the physical apparati to produce speech, apes also lack the cognitive ability to acquire language. Chief among the reasons they are incapable of learning language through symbols or gestures is their limited cognitive ability relative to humans.

Terrace et al. (1979) stated that human language contains two "levels of structures, the word and the sentence" (p. 891). While apes may use symbols as words or learn to sign words and simple word combinations, they are incapable of using the words to generate novel sentences, a task that young humans with normal language development can do with relative ease.

Several years after terminating the Nim project, Terrace visited Nim. During the visit, Nim produced some of the signs he had learned while in training. Terrace (1987) concluded that his failed wish to hold meaningful conversation with Nim "defined all too clearly an unbreachable gulf between man and animals" (p. xiii).

Brakke and Savage-Rumbaugh (1995) were not convinced by Terrace's conclusion; they proposed that there may be species differences in apes' approximations of human speech. From interacting with both *Pan paniscus* (bonobo pygmy chimps) and *Pan troglodytes* ("regular chimps"), Savage-Rumbaugh and her collaborators noted that the former appeared to have greater ease with language-learning tasks. Perhaps one type of ape has greater ability to learn to use symbols for communication than others. Savage-Rumbaugh and her colleagues reared an infant bonobo they named "Panbanisha" and an infant chimpanzee they named "Panpanzee" in a manner similar to that experienced by human infants. The bonobo exhibited greater comprehension of the trainers' symbols and oral speech. Brakke and Savage-Rumbaugh concluded that bonobos seem to experience language acquisition characteristics similar to those of normal human infants up to 2½ years of age, albeit at a slower rate.

It is clear from the research cited here that evolution demarcated language-learning potential between humans and apes, who are believed to have shared "neural prerequisites for basic language acquisition" (Lieberman, 1991, p. 138) for millenia, with changes benefiting humans occurring within the last 6 to 8 million years. Brakke and Savage-Rumbaugh (1995) cited several studies indicating that an increased function of the frontal lobe may have played a significant role in providing humans cognitive advantages over apes (Diamond, 1991; Goldman-Rakic, 1987). Humans possess greater volume in frontal lobe tissue than apes (Passingham, 1982). From an evolutionary perspective, "the same systems that appear to be limiting the chimpanzee's attention, memory, processing and integration of information may have allowed humans to proceed beyond the limits currently observed in bonobos" (Passingham, 1982, p. 140).

However, current studies do show some interesting similarities between apes and humans. For example, in summarizing the findings of previous research, Lyn (2007) noted that bonobos have shown the greatest facility and success in language acquisition, which includes English comprehension similar to that of human infants at 2 1/2 years of age, and understanding and using more than 200 lexigrams on a keyboard. Linguistic errors that are made more often than expected by chance are indicators that, like humans, bonobos possess the ability to form mental representations at the symbolic level and do not learn only through operant conditioning (Terrace, 1987).

There is unequivocal evidence that for genetic reasons, apes and other animals are extremely unlikely to develop human-style language. Specifically, there is an interesting new line of neuroimaging and DNA extraction and examination research that points to differences in genetic mutation at the *FOXP2* gene between animals such as mice, monkeys, and apes, and humans that may account for why humans and not other organisms evolved spoken language (Enard, Przeworski, et al., 2002; Krause, Croft, & James, 2007; Liégéois et al., 2003). The mutation is said to predate the common ancestor of modern humans and Neanderthals, which existed about 300,000 to 400,000 years ago. (See the Evolutionary Theory section of Chapter 2 for a more detailed discussion of the *FOXP2* gene and its effects on speech and language.)

In summary, the animal literature shows that while apes may possess some basic language encoding and production abilities using symbols, they are not very successful at more complex tasks, such as language generalization and use of symbols beyond that of normal 2 1/2-year-old humans. Some of the limitations are due to biological differences between ape and human linguistic structures and function. The evidence is just as strong for cognitive limitations in apes; restrictions in spontaneous language production and generalization are major lines of demarcation between ape and human language development. Thus, for the foreseeable future, it is unlikely that humans and apes will engage in meaningful speech- or sign-based conversation.

Humans

Unlike other organisms, human infants with normal linguistic development ability routinely master the complex process of language acquisition. Provided with the physical and brain/cognitive structures to produce language and opportunities for sociolinguistic interaction with other humans, they achieve language proficiency within a relatively short time span, in what appears to be an almost automatic process. How infants accomplish this formidable task continues to be a mystery, however (Kuhl, 2004).

Prelinguistic Phase: Fetuses and Infants

Research dating back to the early 20th century documented that human fetuses and infants are sensitive to environmental auditory stimuli (Sontag & Wallace, 1935). Later research using a variety of methods, including "classical conditioning, habituation, and exposure to learning, reveal that the fetus does have a memory" (Hepper, 1996, p. 16). Other studies showed that newborns possess recognition memory for music they were exposed to prenatally and for sounds they were familiarized with during Week 30 of gestation (Johansson, Wedenberg, & Westin, 1992). Saffran, Loman, and Robertson (2000) reported that 7-month-olds exhibit memory for musical experiences presented 2 weeks prior. Several other studies also provide support for prenatal auditory sensitivity. One of these (Kisilevsky, 2003) documented differential fetal responding (heart rate acceleration or deceleration) when a passage was read by the mother or a stranger, respectively. DeCasper, Lecanuet, Busnel, Granier-Deferre, and Maugeais (1994) reported that fetuses exhibit decreased heart rate (a sign of relaxation and attending) to a recording of a children's rhyme previously recited by their mothers, whereas no heart rate change was observed to an audio recording of a different rhyme.

The above-mentioned studies demonstrate that humans are born primed and most likely hard-wired to respond to musical and language sounds (e.g., words, rhymes, passages). The findings indicate that prenatal auditory experiences lay the foundation for subsequent language acquisition, especially if the sounds are common in the mother's spoken language (Moon, Cooper, & Fifer, 1993). The findings represent convincing evidence that infants are active gatherers of linguistic information from the beginning and constitute early evidence that sensitivity and attention to the language(s) the child will eventually acquire occur very early in linguistic and cognitive development (Eimas, Siqueland, Jusczyk, & Vigorito, 1971; Kuhl, 2004).

Neonates' initial attempts at oral communication consist of crying to express needs. Although early crying is similar across situations, astute caregivers become efficient at differentiating their newborns' cries in reference to their physical needs and desire for reciprocal interaction (hungry cry → feeding) and emotional states or desire for social interaction (tired cry → holding and rocking). This early communicative mode changes rather quickly; by "22 months the children had multiple linguistic ways of performing many communicative functions" (Hoff, 2005, pp. 260–261). During this time in prelinguistic development, infants with normal hearing ability are also actively involved in the process of laying a solid vocal foundation in preparation for acquisition of spoken language.

Whereas infants reach language development stages at different individual rates, they acquire speech-decoding ability in the same sequence. Shaffer and Kipp (2010) cited research showing that normal-hearing newborns are sensitive to differences in speech sounds. For example, Sansavini, Bertoncini, and Giovanelli (1997) found evidence that infants only a few days old show sensitivity to stress patterns and rhymes when exposed to multisyllable words. There is also evidence that newborns are better than adults at discriminating phonemes from different languages. According to Saffran and Thiessen (2003) and Werker and Desjardins (1995), in the process of language development, the ability to distinguish phonemes outside the native language(s) is lost.

During this prelinguistic development phase, infants engage in cooing and making random (gurgling) sounds (Oller & Eilers, 1988). Shaffer and Kipp (2010) pointed to research showing that prelinguistic infants also use a variety of methods in their attempts to communicate with adults. Infants actively seek to learn the "tune" of their native language(s). Also, infants younger than 6 months of age seem to enjoy the "noise making" of prelanguage exchanges; that is, they vocalize at the same time adults are speaking to them (Rosenthal, 1982). After that age, they engage in turn-taking, for example, pausing and listening intently while adults speak, babbling when the adult pauses, and listening for adult responses to them. These attempts at verbal communication are accompanied by hand and facial gestures between 8 and 10 months of age (Acredolo & Goodwyn, 1990).

During the first year of life, infants begin to demonstrate eagerness for greater verbal interaction. At approximately 3 to 4 months, they engage in the expression of repetitive consonant–vowel vocalizations (e.g., *baba, papa*; K. Bloom, 1998). As they mature and with increased vocal interactions with "expert" speakers, infants increase such behavior, which is thought to lead to development of brain connections that allow them to more closely approximate real speech (K. Bloom, 1998).

At around 6 to 9 months, infants transition to babbling and spend much time using and "practicing" longer consonant–vowel repetitions (e.g., *bababab, papapapa*; K. Bloom, 1998; I. Taylor, 1990). There is strong evidence that cooing and babbling are prewired prespeech abilities that all infants possess. Even deaf and blind infants coo and babble at the appropriate age (Hoff-Ginsberg, 1997). However, according to Shaffer and Kipp (2010), numerous researchers (Eilers & Oller, 1994; Oller & Eilers, 1988) have reported that due to the lack of required environmental language exposure and stimulation they fall behind hearing babies in generating adult-like language sounds, at about 6 months of age.

However, deaf babies do exhibit manual babbling that is similar to oral babbling in syllable structure that parallels oral babbling development (Petitto & Marentette, 1991; Petitto, Holowka, Sergio, & Ostry, 2001). Specifically, infants who were sign-exposed, but reared by deaf parents, engage in hand babbling whose rhythm is distinct from random hand motions also produced by hearing infants at this age (Petitto et al., 2001). Petitto, Zatorre, Gauna, Nikelski, Dostie, and Evans (2000) neuroimaging work also shows that the superior temporal gyrus (previously identified to function specifically in processing speech and sound) is involved in deaf adults' sign language production. According to Petitto et al., this demonstrates that language and speech are not interchangeable concepts. That is, speech is used in vocal communication, whereas language can be vocal or signed. Petitto et al.'s work demonstrates that sign language meets all the requirements for what has traditionally been labeled language. Thus, cooing, babbling, and signing constitute prespeech universals that serve the purpose of preparing infants for transitioning to the language production stage.

By 13 months, toddlers show understanding of words used by their mother to refer to objects (Thomas, Campos, Shucard, Ramsay, & Shucard, 1981). By this age, infants are well on their way to understanding that specific words are used to refer to specific objects that they are familiar with. Shaffer and Kipp (2010) cited Oviatt's (1980) findings that between 12 and 17 months of age, infants exhibit understanding of nouns and verbs they produce on their own and that are used regularly by older speakers, indicating that during this phase of development, language comprehension appears before language production. Research also shows that although infants younger than 11 months of age experience difficulty understanding language such as speech in the form of commands by adults, between 12 and 17 months of age they understand the referents and actions of many nouns and verbs that they do not yet produce in their early speech (Oviatt, 1980). Shaffer and Kipp believed this indicates that comprehension precedes production in infants' language development.

Verbal Language Acquisition Phase: Infants and Toddlers

Infants' first words appear at approximately 1 year of age and mark the initiation of the language acquisition phase, which is ushered in by development of holophrasic speech (Kosslyn & Rosenberg, 2006). During this phase of language development, holophrases (i.e., infants' use of single words to convey a complete, meaningful statement) become part of the infant's language repertoire (for a detailed discussion, see Bochner & Jones, 2003; Dominey, 2005).

With this developmental milestone arrives a significant sociolinguistic and cognitive leap, as the toddler begins using words to replace babbling and hand signals to convey needs and desires to those around much more effectively. Bates, O'Connell, and Shore (1987) noted, "you know your child is no longer an infant when she tells you about her day, reconstructs Little Red Ridinghood almost intact, and talks about needs and feelings that you had to guess about just a few short months ago" (p. 149). The toddler's first one-word statements are geared toward common daily occurrences, for example, obtaining desired objects such as toys and food or making specific events happen or reoccur.

Language development becomes progressively more complex and sophisticated as the toddler's words are sequenced into longer strings to eventually produce articulate declarative statements, ask questions, and make requests. Interestingly, such an increase is also observed in the complexity of deaf children's language (gestures).

For example, Goldin-Meadow and Mylander (1990a) observed 10 young deaf children

> who have not had access to any conventional linguistic input but who have otherwise experienced normal social environments. The children . . . are deaf with hearing losses so severe that they cannot naturally acquire spoken language, and whose hearing parents have chosen not to expose them to sign language. In previous work, we demonstrated that, despite their lack of conventional linguistic input, the children developed spontaneous gesture systems which were structured at the level of the sentence, with regularities identifiable across gestures in a sentence, akin to syntactic structure. (p. 527)

The children ranged from 1 year 4 months to 4 years 1 month at the start of the observations to 2 years 6 months and 5 years 9 months, respectively, at the termination of observations. Goldin-Meadow and Mylander (1990b) stated that hand gestures serve much like the verbalizations that normal-hearing children produce. These findings were supported by detailed observation of signing development in "David," one of the original 10 children observed by Goldin-Meadow and Mylander. An interesting conclusion from the observations is that although David used input from his mother (i.e., the mother's gestures and other communicative behavior; Goldin-Meadow & Mylander, 1990b) in his communication attempts, there was also significant input on his part; that is, the child plays an active role in gestural development (Goldin-Meadow & Mylander, 1990a). From their observations, the authors concluded the following:

> The fact that David could fashion rudiments of a morphological system out of the noisy and limited input available to him suggests that some aspects of linguistic analysis may be guided by factors internal to the child. At the very least, our data suggest that children will seek structure at the word level when developing systems for communication, and that they will recruit whatever input is available—conventional or otherwise—in order to develop that structure. (Goldin-Meadow & Mylander, 1990b, pp. 559–560)

More recent observations of deaf children's signing behavior and development provide corroborative evidence for the early findings by researchers such as Goldin-Meadow and Mylander. The newer findings show that the developmental sequence of "homesigning" is similar to the progression from holophrases to two-word and multiple-word sentences in normal hearing children, specifically, single-gesture, two-gesture, and ultimately multiple-gesture statements (Lust, 2006).

The focus soon becomes perfecting language development through the acquisition of progressively more complex language features required to understand exceptions to language rules (e.g., use of the irregular verb in English; go → goed; hit → hitted) and sentence forms (e.g., use of the passive sentence form in English; "Bill kicked the ball" → "The ball was kicked by Bill") that are not common in everyday speech. However, this is not necessarily true for all languages. For example, the Inuits' language focuses on the use of passives, likely resulting in the observation that such statements are produced earlier by Inuit children than by native English speakers (Berk, 2008).

Shaffer and Kipp (2010) stated that development of early speaking ability is initially a slow process, with infants acquiring single words at a time (L. Bloom, 1973). Things change very quickly; by the time toddlers reach 18 to 24 months, their language acquisition rate increases to 10 to 20 words per week (Reznick & Goldfield 1992). Research cited by Shaffer and Kipp (2010) shows a dramatic increase in language production that is sometimes referred to as the *naming explosion* because as they continue to develop cognitively, toddlers realize that many words refer to objects, places, animals, and people, leading to rapid development of pairing of words with their referents (e.g., Ganger & Brent, 2004; Reznick & Goldfield, 1992). In accordance with the hypothesis that language comprehension precedes production, by 2 years of age, the typical child produces some 200 words and understands a much greater number (Benedict, 1979; Nelson, 1973; Shaffer & Kipp, 2010).

The language learning process is driven by development of the language structures and components that make up the complex, sometimes culture-specific language production rules. In the English language, these include the following: *Phonology*, the rules for production and use of basic units of sound; *morphology*, the rules for using sounds to create meaningful words; *syntax*, the rules of grammar that "specify how words are combined to form sentences"; *semantics*, "the study of words and their meaning"; and, *pragmatics*, "the study of how people use language to communicate effectively" (Kail, 2010, p. 278). Each of these structures and components of language is discussed in some detail in the following pages; however, space limitations preclude in depth discussion here. (See Berk, 2008; Bohannon & Bonvillian, 2008; and Shaffer & Kipp, 2010 for in depth discussions of these language elements).

Phonological Development.   Phonological development is a rapidly occurring process as the 1½-year-old infant's immature word pronunciation increasingly becomes guided by phonological rules that allow the infant's "words" to progressively approximate correct adult pronunciation (Shaffer & Kipp, 2010). When words are multisyllabic, for example, *shampoo,* infants tend to initially produce the stressed syllable only (*poo*) and not the unstressed syllable (*sham*). Infants also tend to replace "an ending consonant syllable with a vowel (saying 'appo' for 'apple') (Ingram 1986; Lewis, Antone, & Johnson, 1999)" (in Shaffer & Kipp, 2010, p. 402). Similar errors are made by infants universally, and the observed resistance to correction attempts by adults makes it likely that biological factors, specifically the infant's immature vocal track, may partially account for this type of speech (Shaffer & Kipp, 2010). However, there are individual differences in this developmental process, and children's speech becomes more uniform with experience and vocal tract maturation during the preschool years. By age 4 to 5 years, most children's phonological ability (word pronunciation) is similar to that of adults (Ingram, 1986).

Morphology.   In the area of morphology, we look at the morpheme

> the smallest unit of meaning in a language; it cannot be broken into any smaller parts that have meaning unto themselves. Words can consist of one or more morphemes. Free morphemes are those that can stand alone—words such as hit or cat. Bound morphemes cannot stand alone; they must always be attached to free morphemes as a suffix or prefix (e.g., *ing, ed,* and *un*). Derivational morphemes are bound morphemes that can be used to change a word into another part of speech; for example, *ness* changes the adjective sad into the noun *sadness*. Other bound morphemes do not change a word's meaning but merely modify it to indicate such aspects as tense, person, number, case, and gender. English does not contain many of these inflections; other languages, such as Greek, Italian, and French, are more inflected languages and contain many of these morphemes attached to their verbs. (Kelley, Jones, & Fein, 2004, p. 196)

Semantic Development.   One way that children learn the meaning of words is through *fast mapping,* the process of pairing a word and an object (Shaffer & Kipp, 2010; K. M. Wilkinson & Mazzitelli, 2003). Children begin fast mapping early in language development. For example, 13- to 15-month-olds engage in fast mapping (Schaefer & Plummert, 1998; Woodward, Markman, & Fitzsimmons, 1994). Between the ages of 18 and 20 months, for fast mapping to occur, infants must attend to the object or event labeled by a new word at the same time as the adult who introduced the word (Baldwin et al., 1996). But by 24 months of age, joint attention is no longer required for fast mapping (Moore, Angelopoulos, & Bennett, 1999). Preschool-age children exhibit significant fast-mapping skills (K. M. Wilkinson, Ross, & Diamond, 2003).

The phonological naming explosion and fast-mapping processes follow a developmental sequence that is most likely due to the child's cognitive development process. Shaffer and Kipp (2010) cite a study by Dapretto and Bjork (2000) that reported that 24-month-olds, who are well into the naming explosion and fast-mapping phases, performed significantly better than 14-month-olds on a task that required naming of objects that had been placed into a box while the children watched. This indicates that the advanced cognitive abilities of the older children improved their retrieval memory abilities relative to the younger, less cognitively advanced children.

Fast mapping is a powerful heuristic for assisting young children to understand and learn the meanings of new words and their referents. However, fast mapping may be related to two errors that children make during the early stages of language development (Shaffer & Kipp, 2010). In one case, the child can make an *overextension* error (Mandler, 2004; McDonough, 2002; Samuelson, 2002) by applying a word for an object or animal (e.g., *kitty*) to refer to similar objects or animals with four legs and fur. Alternatively, children can also make *underextension* errors (Jerger & Damian, 2005), where a higher category word, such as *cookie*, is misapplied to refer to only one type of cookie. Shaffer and Kipp (2010) described a study by Akhtar, Carpenter, and Tomasello (1996) indicating that by 2 years of age, young children possess the cognitive ability to use social and contextual cues in their linguistic interactions with adults.

Syntactical Development. *Syntactical bootstrapping* is a method that children use to infer whether a novel word refers to an object itself, an action, or an attribute of the referent (Shaffer & Kipp, 2010). That is, by observing word use within a sentence, toddlers can make inferences about the meaning of a word. Shaffer and Kipp (2010) cited research by M. Taylor and Gelman (1988) and Waxman and Markow (1998) demonstrating toddlers' syntactical inferencing abilities.

Pragmatics. Shaffer and Kipp (2010) noted that toddlers and children must also learn the pragmatic or socioculturally agreed-upon communication rules of their language to better understand the relationship between words and the objects or actions they refer to, as well as the intended meaning of the words (especially novel words) in the speaker's interactions with others. Pragmatic rules differ by language group within and between cultures (Kelley, Jones, & Fein, 2004); in some languages (e.g., English and Spanish), word order is important in determining conveyed meaning or whether meaning is conveyed at all. Word order may affect not only meaning but also the perceived consequences conveyed by statements. However, this is not the whole story. Sometimes word order (grammar) may be perfect, but the conveyed meaning (semantics) is meaningless, as demonstrated by Chomsky's (1957) famous examples: "Colorless green ideas sleep furiously," which is grammatically correct but meaningless in English, while "Fastly dinner eat, ballgame soon start" conveys meaning in English (is semantically correct and understandable) but is grammatically incorrect (cited in Kosslyn & Rosenberg, 2007, p. 330). Thus, to understand the intended message, language learners must attend to the pragmatics of the statements they hear, such as the context in which a statement is made. Baldwin et al. (1996) demonstrated that infants show evidence of relying on the social criterion of a conversation to establish novel word–novel object relations. According to Baldwin et al., by 18 to 20 months, infants are able to use important pragmatic cues. Specifically, when an adult was present and interacting with infants in a toy play situation, the infants were able to use visual attention (adult's gaze) and motor cues (adult's pointing) to match a novel word with a novel object introduced into the play situation.

Childhood

Children's statements become much more advanced as they continue to develop cognitively and come to master the basic syntactical, pragmatic, phonological, and morphological components of speech. During the third year, children usually develop mastery of grammatical morphemes, for example, the *s* plural, *in* and *on* location prepositions, present progressive *-ing*, past verb tense *-ed*, and possessiveness *'s*. According to Shaffer and Kipp (2010), R. Brown's (1973) study demonstrated that although the three children he observed longitudinally varied in their mastery of grammatical morpheme use the onset of grammatical morpheme use and the absolute time for such mastery, they all learned the 14 morphemes in the same sequence. A cross-sectional study (de Villiers & de Villiers, 1973) with more children corroborated Brown's findings. Brown explained these findings by stating that grammatical morphemes acquired earlier are semantically and syntactically easier than those acquired later, for example, *-ing* is acquired before *-ed*, which is mastered "earlier than the uncontractible forms of the verb *to be* (*is, are, was, were*), all of which are more syntactically complex and specify *three* semantic relations: number (singular or plural), tense (present or past), and action (ongoing process)" (Shaffer & Kipp, 2010, p. 413).

Children then learn to apply these language rules in new situations, such as solving the famous Wug test by inferring that when another Wug or two are added to the formerly single Wug, then Wug → Wug(s) (Berko, 1958).

Shaffer and Kipp (2010) cite research stating that common grammatical errors during this age include overregularization of the regular verb to the irregular verb or noun form (e.g., Clahsen, Hadler, & Weyerts, 2004). Thus, "We went to the store" may become "We goed to the store" when relaying information that the action occurred in the past. Although overregularizations are interesting forms of early childhood speech, they are not modeled in adult speech, nor are children rewarded by others for such speech; they nevertheless occur but are not common. Only about 2.5% to 5% of children's statements are of this type (Maratsos, 2000; Marcus et al., 1992). Marcus et al. (1992) believed that overregularizations occur simply because children "forget" to use the regular noun or verb form and use their newly acquired grammatical rule: *-ed* = past tense.

During this time in language development, children from all language backgrounds learn the rules of transformational grammar specific to their cultures (Shaffer & Kipp, 2010). They use the rules to transform declarative statements " 'The man hit the ball,' passive statements 'The ball was hit by the man,' to produce questions 'Did the man hit the ball?' and negatives 'The man did not hit the ball'" (Schoneberger, 2000, p.63). During this time, children's sentences become more complex and detailed, and their semantic development also improves significantly.

Young children also become more sophisticated at asking questions. Earlier in development, they use a rising intonation at the end of a simple statement to indicate that they are seeking further information in the form of a question. "a doggie," with the "e" sound drifting upward, is a prime example, in this case regarding whether the animal in question is a dog. Question construction then shifts to simple forms that require a yes–no response: "Is that a doggie?" progresses to use of more complex question forms. (Shaffer & Kipp, 2010).

Children are also busy mastering the use of negative statements, which they do in a universal steplike fashion similar to that of question mastery. The initial form of negation involves placing "no" at the beginning of a negation statement, for example, "No hat." L. Bloom (1970) stated that the problem with such statements is that while the intended negation may be perfectly clear to the child, it may be ambiguous to the listener. From here, negation statements become less ambiguous when the child learns to place the negative signifier within the negative statement. The final step in producing adultlike negative statements occurs during this stage as well. For example, 3- to 4-year-olds showed pleasure in playing a game in which they corrected a puppet's incorrect negative statements (de Villiers & de Villiers, 1979).

Children 2 to 5 years of age also show significant progress in the area of semantic development, by understanding and using contrast statements such as "big/little, tall/short, wide/narrow, high/low, in/on, before/after, here/there, and I/you (de Villiers & de Villiers, 1979, 1992)" (Shaffer & Kipp, 2010, p. 415). During this age span, children still make errors in understanding passive sentence forms. Shaffer and Kipp (2010) stated that while 4- to 5-year-olds easily understand active sentences, for example, "The girl hit the boy," they experience significant difficulty understanding the passive form, "The boy was hit by the girl." In most cases of sentences like the latter, preschool children tend to choose a drawing of a boy hitting a girl, because they "assume that the first noun is the agent of the verb and that the second is the object; consequently, they interpret the passive construction as if it were an active sentence" (Shaffer & Kipp, 2010, p. 415). An important related question is why children in this age group make errors in comprehending passive statements. According to de Villiers and de Villiers (1979), this is not because they lack cognitive skills to understand and produce sentences that are clearly passive in nature, for example, "The candy is eaten by the girl" (de Villiers & de Villers, 1979, p. 77), since this statement does not make sense as "The girl was eaten by the candy" (Shaffer & Kipp, 2010, p. 415). The 3-year-olds in the de Villiers's study performed well on understanding such statements. Apparently, the delay in understanding most passive statements is because they are not often used in the English language (Shaffer & Kipp, 2010). According to Shaffer and Kipp, this is supported by the fact that young children in other language cultures in which passive sentence use is more common, for example, Inuktutut and Zulu, understand and produce passive sentences significantly before children from Western cultures do (Allen & Crego, 1996).

Development also progresses in the areas of pragmatic conversational abilities. As early as 3 years of age, preschoolers show evidence that they are at the beginning stages of understanding a variety of language abilities. Shaffer and Kipp (2010) presented an amusing case of a 3-year-old's understanding of *illocutionary intent,* in which the words used may not match exactly with the intended outcome of the statement.

> *Sheila:* Every night I get an ice cream.
> *Babysitter:* That's nice, Sheila.
> *Sheila:* Even when there's a babysitter, I get an ice cream.
> *Babysitter* (to himself): [Backed] into a corner by a 3-year-old's grasp of language as a social tool! (p. 416)

Another pragmatic communication skill acquired by preschoolers between ages 3 and 5 years is their recognition that statements need to be tailored according to the audience for which they are intended. Shatz and Gelman (1973) provided evidence of this in 4-year-olds who used short statements and commands when speaking to a 2-year-old and statements that were more complex in structure when speaking to adults.

During the preschool years, children become very effective communicators, as demonstrated in their use of *referential communication skills*, whereby young children show evidence of requesting clarification of others' ambiguous statements, although they are not as proficient as school-age children in doing so. However, preschoolers are better at detecting the meaning of ambiguous statements in conversations occurring in real-world settings that have more contextual cues, such as "knowledge of a particular speaker's attitudes, preferences, and past behaviors (Ackerman, Szymanski, & Silver, 1990)" (Shaffer

& Kipp, 2010, p. 416). When their own statements are ambiguous, 4-year-olds are more likely than 7-year-olds to blame the listener (Flavell, Miller, & Miller, 1993). It is interesting that 3- to 5-year-olds exhibit greater referential skills when listening to ambiguous statements in real-world settings that possess contextual cues than in controlled laboratory settings lacking such cues. For example, they ask for greater information: "What?" and "Huh?" to partial statements made by a yawning speaker (Shaffer & Kipp, 2010, p. 417). According to Revelle, Wellman, & Karabenick (1985), they also responded with "How can I bring it?" (p.658) when asked by an adult to do an impossible act, i.e., to bring an "'unbringable'" item [that] was present in the room but too heavy for the child to carry (e.g., a real refrigerator)" (p.656). Thus, laboratory-based studies may fail to capture the full richness and degree of preschoolers' referential skills (Shaffer & Kipp, 2010).

School-Age Children and Adolescents

Language development during the middle childhood and adolescent years continues to build on syntactic and semantic skills of previous developmental periods. Specifically, sentences become longer and more complex.

Between the ages of 5 years and adolescence, language learners become much more adept at correcting grammatical and/or syntactical errors that appeared in earlier speech as well as to produce grammatical forms of significantly greater complexity. In fact, for language development, Shaffer and Kipp (2010) cite several studies (e.g., Clark, 1977; Eisele & Lust, 1996) indicating that middle childhood, adolescence, and the early part of adulthood is a time in language acquisition, during which syntactical development is refined.

Semantic development also continues to be perfected during the same time period, especially in the area of vocabulary development. Anglin (1993) noted that the number of comprehended words grows at an amazing rate of some 20 words per day, expanding vocabulary from 10,000 to 40,000 words. While children in middle childhood may not understand or use many words, understanding them is facilitated by "metalinguistic ability, the capacity to think about language" (Bee & Boyd, 2010, p.225). The attainment of formal cognitive operations allows adolescents to comprehend and use words that are uncommon in English language, such as 'liberty' and 'justice' (McGhee-Bidlack, 1991).

Shaffer and Kipp (2010) noted that as school-age children's skills for finding hidden meaning in statements improve, the children become progressively more adept at making inferences when some information may be lacking in a statement (Beal, 1990; Casteel, 1993). The understanding of sarcasm also increases (Dews et al., 1996). These accomplishments are attributed to the development of increased metalinguistic awareness, the "ability to think about language and to comment on its properties (Frost, 2000, Shaoying & Danling, 2005; Whitehurst & Longian, 1998)" (Shaffer & Kipp, 2010, p. 418).

COGNITIVE DEVELOPMENT

In this section, we define cognition, expand on thinking/cognitive processes, and provide some examples of cognitive development. The reader is reminded, however, that thinking/cognitive processes and speech and language skills are inseparable. As in the case of language development, theories of cognition and cognitive development abound. *Cognitive development* is how mental processes such as those referred to in this section occur and change in the individual over time as a result of the child's biological maturation, environmental experiences, and sociocultural interactions. *Cognition* refers to the brain functions of acquiring, processing, evaluating, selecting, and responding to environmental stimuli impinging on the individual's brain through the senses. There are a number of studies suggesting "that young children are quite limited in their knowledge and cognition about cognitive phenomena, or in their *metacognition*, and do relatively little monitoring of their own memory, comprehension, and other cognitive enterprises" (Flavell, 1979, p. 906).

Piaget saw cognitive development as constituting a set of underlying cognitive structures. Piaget stated that intelligence (cognitive processing) is "a form of *equilibrium* toward which all cognitive structures tend (1950, p. 6)" (in Shaffer & Kipp, 2010, p. 250). In a *New Scientist* interview, Norman (2002, in Grossman, 2002, p. 4) referred to cognition as simply the process of "understanding and trying to make sense of the world."

Compared with the other definitions cited above, Norman's definition of cognition is enticing in its simplicity. However, given the multitude of mental processes involved in general cognition and in cognitive development specifically, it may be too simple. For example, as with language development, cognitive development involves numerous theories that attempt to explain the thousands of issues that have been investigated to date. Some theories are broad in scope, attempting to address the whole of cognitive development, whereas others constitute precise perspectives or viewpoints that focus on one or a few issues.

An attempt to address all or even the majority of the issues is well beyond the scope of this chapter. Even if such a task were possible, it would take volumes and years to complete a review and write-up of all the scientific journal articles and books alone (not to mention other sources) on the topics of cognition and cognitive development. For example, in the cognitive area theory of mind, Wellman, Cross, and Watson (2001) found that in 1998 there were at least 178 studies in "the subarea of children's false-belief understanding" (in Flavell, 2004, p. 274). A computer search using the term *theory of mind* listed 399 publications (Flavell, 2004). For *executive function,* a search found more than 2,500 research publications in the 10 years preceding 2006 (Alvarez & Emory, 2006). Therefore, the issues presented in the following sections represent but a sample of the research from some of the more interesting areas of cognitive development.

Executive Function and Cognitive Development

While most researchers would agree that cognitive processes in general, and cognitive development specifically, involve functions such as theory of mind and executive function, which are controlled by different brain structures, they disagree as to which structures and functions are involved and what part(s) of the brain control them (i.e., do executive processes occur exclusively in the frontal lobe?). Alvarez and Emory (2006) stated that many researchers use the terms *frontal functions* and *executive functions* interchangeably to argue that cognitive development is driven by frontal lobe regulation (Duffy & Campbell, 2001; Duke & Kaszniak, 2000; Miyake et al., 2000; Welsh, 2002). Other researchers believe that although the frontal lobe may coordinate executive function activity, other cortical and subcortical areas of the brain are also involved (e.g., Alvarez & Emory, 2006). From their review of lesion and neuroimaging studies, Alvarez and Emory found that exclusive evidence for frontal lobe involvements was inconsistent. Thus, executive functions appear to be controlled cortically and subcortically. Alvarez and Emory concluded,

> It simply may be that the frontal lobes participate to a greater extent than other areas of the brain in functions considered to be "executive." Without input, however, from other cortical and subcortical areas executive functioning would be compromised. Therefore, it may be more worthwhile to conceptualize executive functions as a "macroconstruct" in which multiple executive function subprocesses work in conjunction to solve complex problems and execute complicated decisions (Zelazo et al., 1997). (p. 32)

Heterogeneity Versus Homogeneity and Cognitive Development

Another dispute among cognitive scientists is whether the cognitive developmental process is homogeneous (i.e., stagelike; e.g., Piaget & Inhelder, 1969) or heterogeneous (i.e, nonstagelike; e.g., Fischer, 1980; Flavell, 1981). According to Flavell (1981), a mind that leans heavily toward the homogeneous side "is clearly recognizable as the selfsame cognitive device across all tasks, situations, and conceptual domains" (p. 1), whereas "a very heterogeneous mind is entirely different. The maturity level, complexity, and style of its thinking is enormously variable across occasions and situations" (pp. 1–2).

Flavell (1981) believed that there might be room for a more interactionist approach to the issue of homogeneity and heterogeneity in cognitive development. He suggested that children may operate with greater homogeneity in some areas of cognitive development and more heterogeneity in others. He provided the example of a computer prodigy who, because of her environment and computer scientist father, might possess computer skills surpassing those of many adults. However, in the area of moral reasoning and social inferencing, her skills might be considerably lower. "That is, time spent at the computer terminal is time not spent interacting with and learning about people" (Flavell, 1981, p. 4). Flavell cited Piaget's (1972) example of adults in the formal operations stage of cognitive development.

> Recall that Piaget himself (1972) believed that many adults might be cognitively heterogeneous in the sense that they may display formal-operational thinking mainly in problem areas where their interest, experience, and expertise are greatest in their occupational specialty, for example. But of course, heterogeneity of this sort could also exist during childhood, as in the example just given [referring to the computer science prodigy]. (Flavell, 1981, p. 5)

Thus, according to Flavell (1981), children show evidence of functioning at different levels of heterogeneity in performing different tasks within a stage of cognitive development. Piaget's example shows that this is the same for adults; specifically, not all adults function at the formal-operational level all the time.

Theory of Mind and Cognitive Development

Flavell (2004) listed a number of in-depth reviews on the topic of theory of mind and cognitive development (Baron-Cohen, Tager-Flusberg, & Cohen, 2000; Bartsch & Wellman, 1995; Flavell, 2000; Flavell & Miller, 1998; Mitchell, 1997; Repacholi & Slaughter, 2003; Wellman & Gelman, 1998). Flavell (2000) and Flavell and Miller (1998) attributed the history of theory-of-mind research as mostly grounded in Piaget's work on cognitive development. According to Flavell (2004), the early research concerned claims by Piaget and his supporters' premise "that children begin development by being *cognitively egocentric*. Piaget and his colleagues used egocentrism and other concepts to interpret their developmental studies of a wide variety of social-cognitive topics" (p. 275). Flavell stated that studies initiated in the 1970s centered on the concept of *metacognitive development*. He listed several extensive reviews on this topic (A. L. Brown, Bransford, Ferrara, & Campione, 1983; Flavell, Miller, & Miller, 2002; Kuhn, 1999; Moshman, 1998; Schneider & Bjorklund, 1998). "Metacognition (cognition about cognition—hence the *meta-*) has been defined as any knowledge or cognitive activity that takes as its object, or regulates, any aspect of any cognitive activity (Flavell, Miller, & Miller, 2002)" (in Flavell, 2004, p. 275). Flavell (2004) pointed out that research on metacognition in children continues, but to a significantly lesser extent, while metacognitive research on adults is thriving.

CONCLUSION

In summary, the processes of language and cognitive development are intriguing. There is significant evidence that from the womb through infancy, humans possess the cognitive and prelinguistic processes to recognize previously heard sounds, as with songs heard in utero. As cognitive development progresses, infants show preference for their mother's voice and the language spoken by their mothers. During the period of development of early linguistic skills, children experience advances in cognition that facilitate development of language production and comprehension skills that are perfected during middle childhood and adolescence. Linguistic skills that require the cognitive abilities of abstract thinking and hypothetical deductive reasoning, as well as other sophisticated formal operational skills, may expand into adolescence and young adulthood. As with language development, cognitive development may be explained from a variety of perspectives. Some attempts at explaining cognitive development use a discontinuous stagelike process (e.g., Piaget); others consider cognitive development in a linear fashion (e.g., see the discussion on information-processing perspective in Chapter 2, this volume).

2

COGNITIVE THEORIES AND THEIR PERSPECTIVES ON LANGUAGE

As in Chapter 1, this chapter focuses on language and cognitive development processes and theories in monolinguals. The relationship between language and cognition is complex. Language is related to the inner (cognitive) and outer (sociocultural) world of an individual (Pinker, 2007), making the understanding of language and its development a "matter of intellectual fascination and real-world importance" (p. 2). Spoken language is an external correlate of the individual's cognitive processes, whereas internal language is a cognitive process. Thus, the human cognitive state is undoubtedly influenced by language, which "is adapted to every feature of our experience that is shareable with others, and a large part of the human condition falls into its purview" (Pinker, 2007, p. 427).

Cognitive and language development are therefore intricately intertwined, with increases in a child's cognition likely resulting in corresponding gains in linguistic ability and complexity and vice versa. Pinker (2007), in describing the interactions among language, cognition, and culture, wrote that "the view from language reveals a species with distinctive ways of thinking, feeling, and interacting" (p. 428). Shaffer and Kipp (2010) put it this way, "language acquisition is clearly a holistic process intertwined with the child's cognitive and social development and the child's social and cultural life" (p. 424).

A variety of theoretical models seek to describe the language and cognitive development processes. Over the years, different research camps have proposed and defended their specific views of speech, language, and cognitive development. They have also disagreed on the terminology. Some authors use the terms *theory* or *theories* (Zimmerman & Whitehurst, 1979; Shaffer & Kipp, 2010) to refer to broad well-established attempts to explain the overall language and cognitive development processes. Bohannon and Bonvillian (2008) used *theoretical approaches* for the same purpose. Two major models of language development discussed in this chapter that fall into this category are behaviorism and nativism. Some writers refer to less inclusive models that focus on specific aspects of language and cognitive development (e.g., Vygotsky and information processing) as *viewpoints* or *perspectives* (e.g., Shaffer & Kipp, 2010). Regardless of its label, no single theory, approach, or viewpoint satisfactorily explains language and cognitive development processes.

A major reason for this is the complexity of the processes involved in language and cognition. There seems to be little common ground for collaboration between proponents of the major theories/models, behaviorist/empiricist, and nativist/linguistic. The same often seems true for proponents of newer models. For example, in the case of language development, Akhtar (2004, p. 459) pointed to the opposing views of theorists who support "the Innateness Hypothesis and the theory of Universal Grammar" (e.g., Crain & Thornton, 1998) versus constructivists, who are more concerned with studying how language development evolves from the immature speech of infants and children to adultlike speech (e.g., Tomasello, 2003). Akhtar also noted that nativists singled out linguistic development as the specific focus, "uncontaminated by nonlinguistic influences," whereas "[m]ost constructivists are also committed to studying the relations between language development and other simultaneously developing social and cognitive skills (Clark, 2003)" (Akhtar, 2004, p. 459). However, some researchers, for example, Bohannon and Bonvillian (2008), believe that rather than being at polar extremes on some of their differences, many distinguishing principles between theories are in fact complementary.

Furthermore, some researchers fail to agree on what the important issues in language research should be. Bohannon and Bonvillian (2008) listed a number of factors that distinguish different researchers' attempts to explain language development. For example, researchers are divided about what the goal of language theories should be. On the one hand, researchers such as Derwing (1973) have contended that without understanding the language development process children go through, explanations of adult language cannot be adequate. On the other hand, some researchers (e.g., Gleitman & Wanner, 1982) have contended that theories of language development in children are also flawed unless the ultimate goal is to explain adult language outcomes. Bohannon and Bonvillian (2008) also presented a number of features (other than determining whether language development or adult language outcome is most important) that distinguish among different theories of language development, including structuralism versus functionalism, competence versus performance, and nativism versus empiricism.

Structuralism focuses on evidence of "invariant processes of mechanisms underlying observable data. Chomsky's rules of grammar and Watson's stimulus–response bonds are examples of structures that are used to explain observable behavior" (Bohannon & Bonvillian, 2008, p. 229). *Functionalism* attempts to develop "predictive relationships between environmental or situational variables and language. The aim of a functional account of language is the prediction and control of verbal behavior in different contexts and individuals" (Bohannon & Bonvillian, 2008, p. 229). *Competence* is indicated when children demonstrate knowledge of the "underlying rules that may be deduced from language behavior," whereas *performance* refers to "actual instances of language use" (Bohannon & Bonvillian, 2008, p. 229). *Structuralists* stress the importance of competence, whereas *functionalists* consider performance to be more important (Bohannon & Bonvillian, 2008).

Regarding the relative role that the child's genetic makeup and environmental experiences play in language development and outcome, the basic point of contention among theorists has historically been whether language is mostly an innate or a learned process. Nativists/linguists (e.g., Chomsky) largely argue for biological factors in language development and use computational mathematical logic in their attempts to explain syntactical/grammatical development. Behaviorists/empiricists (e.g., Skinner) strongly support a language development explanation based on empiricism. However, a variety of newer theoretical approaches take a more flexible and interactionist perspective and view language acquisition as possessing important innate and learned attributes as well as cognitive and sociocultural properties. Given all these issues, an important point to keep in mind is that language and cognitive development go hand-in-hand.

THEORIES AND MODELS

Space limitations preclude an exhaustive discussion of language and cognitive acquisition theories and viewpoints in this chapter. The reader is directed to the references here (i.e., Berko Gleason, 2005; Berko Gleason & Bernstein Ratner, 2008; Bohannon & Bonvillian, 2008; Shaffer and Kipp, 2010) that provide excellent descriptions and extended discussions about the strengths and weaknesses of different language and cognitive acquisition perspectives. The theories of language and cognitive development in the following sections are based on discussions covered in depth in these publications.

The nativist/linguistic (Chomsky 1959, 1968) and behaviorist/empiricist (Skinner, 1957) theories constitute major attempts at explaining language development that qualify as theories or theoretical approaches. A third approach, known as the *interactionist* perspective, consists of a variety of theoretical viewpoints and perspectives. Interactionists believe that the biological predisposition to acquire language (nativism) and the environmental learning aspects of language (empiricism) interact with the learner's cognitive abilities and social environment, resulting in language development (e.g., Akhtar, 2004; McKee & McDaniel, 2004; Tomasello, 1995, 2003; Yang, 2004).

We discuss the behaviorist, nativist, and interactionist perspectives next (more detailed coverage can be found in Bohannon and Bonvillian, 2008). We also introduce a more recent evolutionary perspective that views language and cognitive development as resulting from social and cognitive processes that evolved because they provided a survival advantage to humans.

Behaviorist Theory

Proponents of behaviorist (empiricist) theory accept the nativist argument that biological structures are involved in language acquisition. The important distinction is that empiricists believe the child acquires language through the same process embodied in the stimulus–response principles involved in acquisition of all mental processes (Chater & Manning, 2006; Zimmerman & Whitehurst, 1979). Thus, the behaviorists, while recognizing that language is unique to humans, do not consider language acquisition to be special among other processes within the learner's developmental history.

According to behaviorists, the initial language learning mechanism is classical conditioning. Specifically, in the process of interacting with their caregivers, infants associate a word with an outcome. To behaviorists, classical conditioning stimulates the development of receptive speech in the child. However, behaviorists use operant conditioning principles to explain how the child acquires speech (Moerk, 1983; Mowrer, 1960; Osgood, 1953; Staats, 1971). The child produces an overt operant (i.e., a word), which the caregiver reinforces, leading to increased likelihood that the child will repeat the word in similar environmental situations to achieve a desired outcome. Through a system of "rewarding" speech that progressively mirrors that of adults and "punishing" incorrect speech, parents and other teaching agents are said to shape the child's speech so that eventually he or she acquires adult-level speech abilities (Bohannon & Bonvillian, 2008).

Combining multiple words into correct sentences involves the same learning principles. This is guided by a process referred to as *Markov sentence models* (Mowrer, 1960) in which the first word in a sentence and the context in which it is produced stimulate production of the next word and so on, resulting in increasing adultlike statements over time. It is important to note that the child need not hear all words or word combinations to acquire language. "It is only necessary for the child to have associations between pairs of words, between individual words and the environmental context, and between words and possible internal mediating stimuli" (Bohannon & Bonvillian, 2008, p. 233).

The learning process continues into adulthood. However, it is much more rapid during childhood. According to learning theorists, this is due to the process of *imitation*. Children imitate modeled adult speech verbatim or in part immediately after hearing it or after some temporal delay. Success at imitation is rewarded by the adults who model language for the child or personally by the child.

Nativist Theory

Noam Chomsky, the most notable nativist, championed the idea that humans inherit an innate neural structure related to language (i.e., language acquisition device [LAD]). According to Chomsky and his colleagues, the LAD interacts with the child's linguistic environment to produce a set of grammatical rules that allow him or her to learn the grammar of the specific language(s) he or she is exposed to. According to Bohannon and Bonvillian (2008),

> Chomsky (1957) argued that an adequate grammar must be generative or creative in order to account for the myriad of sentences that native speakers of a language can produce and understand. Adult speakers of any language can produce and understand sentences they have never said or heard before, simply by using a single grammatical rule and inserting various lexical items. (p. 237)

Chomsky's theory has evolved over time. His current approach refers to the neural structures involved in language acquisition as the *language faculty*. This faculty is said to be genetically determined and is considered to be similar among humans, with the exception of people with major linguistic or other pathologies (Chomsky & Place, 2000). The initial language faculty is explained by the theory of *universal grammar*. For Chomsky, the language faculty contains a finite set of "switches" controlled by the child's linguistic experiences. The outcome of how the switches are set determines the language(s) the child acquires (Bohannon & Bonvillian, 2008).

Chomsky described the language faculty as consisting of a minimum of two components: a *cognitive system* for information storage and *performance systems* for information access and utilization. The cognitive system is said to interact with the *articulatory–perceptual* and *conceptual–intentional* parts of the performance systems. For example, semantics, syntax, and phonology are considered to be separate subsystems of language acquisition. There is also a "discontinuity between what a speaker wishes to say (intentions or concepts) and the form the utterance eventually takes to convey that meaning (spoken form)" (Bohannon & Bonvillian, 2008, p. 238).

All of Chomsky's systems involve syntactic flexibility to accommodate encoding of communication intentions differently. Bohannon and Bonvillian (2008) gave two good examples, "She hit me" and "I was hit by her," (p.238) in which the same intention is stated in the active and passive forms. The same words can express different meanings, as in Bohannon and Bonvillian's amusing example, "She was killed by the river," which may be interpreted as two different concepts (i.e., "The river killed her" or "Someone killed her near the river") (p.238). Pinker (1984, 1994) stated that one of the major language problems children must master is how to map meaning onto concepts from ambiguous speech of this type that they hear in their linguistic environment. For Chomsky (1980), this problem was so great that it would be impossible for children to acquire speech simply from their environments, which he referred to as the *poverty of stimulus argument*, "because he believed that there was not sufficient useful language-related input available to children in their environments" (Bohannon & Bonvillian, 2008, p. 238)

That language is an innate human process is a basic premise of linguistic theory. However, linguistic theorists differ somewhat as to the meaning of innate behavior. To some, "innateness" puts constraints on a process (i.e., language) that arises from expected experiences. To Chomsky and his supporters, the ability to acquire language (language capacity) is an innate/genetic human ability. An argument in support of this concept is the observation that children learn their native language(s) rather rapidly and that once the grammar for this language(s) is set, the language forms for that specific language(s) are restricted.

Pinker (1987) found it interesting that children learn to speak rather effortlessly despite the ambiguity of language they encounter in their language learning environment, a process referred to as the "learnability problem" (for a more in-depth discussion on universal grammar and learnability, see Pinker, 1987). In sum, nativists are concerned with the innateness and universality of grammar, focusing more on determining linguistic rules as opposed to the development of language per se.

Interactionist Perspective

Many interactionist theorists accept that the complex process of language development can involve basic concepts espoused by the two opposing major theories (i.e., behaviorism and nativism), as well as other processes (e.g., sociocultural influences on the child) that neither theory's proponents considered important. Among the most influential interactionist viewpoints are Bandura's cognitive behaviorism (social learning), Piaget's cognitive development, information processing, and the social interactionist views. Each is discussed next.

Cognitive Behaviorism

Bandura (1971, 1977) viewed environmental processes as important in all learning, including language acquisition. However, Bandura's (1971) approach differs from radical behaviorism (e.g., Skinner) in that Bandura considers internal mental processes to be important contributors to the development of language and cognitive processes. Specifically, Bandura and the radical behaviorists disagreed on the role that internal cognitive processes, such as self-efficacy, play in learning. See Zimmerman and Whitehurst (1979) for an interesting discussion of the radical behaviorist versus the cognitive behavioral view of self-efficacy and learning.

According to Bandura, some nativist researchers contend that the behavioral and cognitive behavioral theorists' assumption that observational learning and imitation play a vital role in language acquisition constitutes a significant difference between the nativist and the behavioral/cognitive and behavioral views of language development. Bandura responded that while supporting the behavioral premise that children acquire language partially through observing and imitating others' speech, he also agreed with the nativist principle that children's language is generative and leads to the production of many statements they have not been directly exposed to. In Bandura's opinion, the nativists contention that his view is behavioral and not nativist in nature, can be attributed to the nativists' mistaken assumption that observational learning and imitation function only for "concrete features of behavior, not for abstract properties" (Bandura, 1971, p. 34). Bandura used his agreement with the nativists that language is generative as evidence that his is an interactionist view of language development that includes both behaviorist and nativist language acquisition components.

Bandura's view of modeling from the perspective of social learning theory is similar to the nativist idea that language acquisition is rule-governed. Bandura (2006) further stated that psycholinguists' distinction between linguistic competence (important to nativists/linguists) and production (important to radical behaviorist and cognitive behaviorists) "corresponds to the distinction made between learning and performance in social learning theory" (p. 35).

Bandura (2006) argued that, rather than being innate, the "basic rules" of grammatical production are learned by interacting with expert language models. "People are innately equipped with information-processing capacities, not with response-productive rules. Rules about grammatical relations between words cannot be learned unless they are exemplified in the verbal behavior of models" (Bandura, 2006, p. 35). In sum, cognitive behaviorism is an inter-actionist model with roots in radical behaviorism, while at the same time, according to Bandura, possessing significant similarities with the nativist model.

Cognitive Development

Piaget's theory is the quintessential example of a cognitive development theory (cf., Vygotsky's, 1978, social interactionist approach, reprinted in Cole, Engeström, & Vasquez, 1997). As an interactionist approach, Piaget's (1954) theory of language development has common elements with the behaviorist and nativist theories (Bohannon & Bonvillian, 2008). Like the nativists, Piaget considered *internal structures* as the driving force in cognitive and lan-guage development. Both Pieaget's and the nativist theories also view the order of development of cognitive structures as invariant and provide this as supporting evidence for their views. The two theories are also in accord that language constitutes a symbolic system in which words represent objects and actions and constitute overt expression of internal intentions. Furthermore, both theories consider that there is a distinction between competence and per-formance and the intentions conveyed in spoken statements (Bohannon & Bonvillian, 2008).

However, there are some basic differences between the two theories. Piaget (1954) contended that language is not a separate cognitive characteris-tic of the child but is one among other cognitive abilities that emerge as a result of cognitive maturation. To Piaget (1954) language development occurs within the constraints of reason. Language development results, as do other cognitive development processes, from changes at lower levels of cognition. In Piaget's view, language development is neither learned nor innate but results from the interaction of the child's existing cognitive structures with his or her current environment, linguistic and general, a process that sees the child as a *construc-tivist* (active participant) of his or her own cognitive development (Jonassen, 1985). Thus, unlike behaviorists or nativists, for Piaget, the child is not merely a passive recipient of innate or environmental experiences (Jonassen, 1985).

While linguists regard linguistic competence as a key indicator of lan-guage ability and basically disregard performance, to Piagetians, performance in the form of linguistic errors provides an important window into the child's current linguistic and cognitive developmental stage (Bohannon & Bonvillian, 2008). In summary, from a Piagetian constructivist perspective, language and cognitive development result from biological brain maturation and environmental experiences that enhance mental structures and mental processes that drive development through progressively mature, qualitatively different stages. Thus, the major driving force behind Piaget's theory is the interaction between biology, environment, and the cognitive processes experienced by the individual.

Information Processing

This type of interactionist model considers linguistic and cognitive acquisition to occur like other mental processes or abilities (e.g., memory, cognition, problem solving [metacognitive abilities]; Bohannon & Bonvillian, 2008). The general model views cognitive activity from the perspective of the brain as an information processor much like a computer.

The brain is considered to possess the cognitive structures (hardware; e.g., neurons, language processing networks) as well as the functional processes (software; e.g., language decoding and encoding abilities) that result in language acquisition. The development of other cognitive processes is seen as consisting of a series of computational steps that start with environmental sensory input (each sense; e.g., auditory is processed separately) that feeds into a sensory memory store where information attended to is selected for further processing. The sensory memory store is said to have a processing duration of less than 1 s (Sperling, 1960), and the information is lost if it is not further attended to and transferred into a short-term memory store that is also limited in processing capacity (five plus or minus two pieces of information [e.g., digits]). According to Neisser (1967), short-term memory store has a life of approximately 17 s, during which the individual can respond to the information attended to. Because the short-term memory can hold information only for a few seconds, the information is either processed as output (response) or organized for transfer into the long-term memory for storage and future reference. Information that is not responded to while in the short-term memory store or transferred to long-term memory deteriorates quickly and is lost.

Long-term memory, in contrast, has unlimited capacity, and the stored information and processing strategies are considered to be long-lasting. Because responses can only be made from short-term memory, one must retrieve stored information from long-term memory to short-term memory to make a response. Some models include executive functions or processes and feedback mechanisms (e.g., metacognitive skills) that make for more efficient information processing (see Shaffer & Kipp, 2010, Figure 8.1, p. 300, for an adapted version of Atkinson & Shiffrin's, 1968, general information-processing model). Figure 2.1 represents an information-processing model specific to bilingualism.

For language production, the information-processing model focuses on language development from the perspective of adult language. Differences in adult and child language abilities are seen as qualitative. What develops is children's ability in language production with maturation (hardware) and environmental (software) improvement.

Output
(Selected Responses)

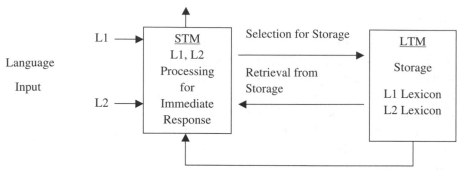

Figure 2.1. Monolingual and bilingual information processing. Note that for the monolingual only L1 input processing and output response occurs. STM = Short Term Memory; LTM = Long Term Memory. L1 referred to in the bilingualism literature as "First Language," "Heritage Language," or "Home Language." L2 referred to in the bilingual literature as "Second Language." Adapted from *The Psychology of Learning and Motivation: Advances in Research and Theory* (Vol. 2; p. 93), by K. W. Spence and J. T. Spence, 1968, Orlando, FL: Academic Press. Copyright 1968 by Academic Press. Adapted with permission. Adapted from *Critical Perspectives on Bilingual Education Research* (p. 59), by R. V. Padilla and A. H. Benavides, 1992, Tempe, AZ: Bilingual Press/Editorial Bilingue. Copyright 1992 by Bilingual Press/ Editorial Bilingue. Adapted with permission. Adapted from *Developmental Psychology: Childhood and Adolescence* (8th ed.; p. 300), by D. Shaffer and K. Kipp, 2010, Belmont, CA: Wadsworth, Cengage Learning. Copyright 2010 by Wadsworth, Cengage Learning. Adapted with permission.

Historically, early information-processing models of language acquisition considered language learning to involve a series of serial mental/cognitive processes. Specifically, communication intentions and simple language production develop before more complex language processes (e.g., understanding of passives and questions). Newer models involve parallel language processing known as *parallel-distributed processors* (PDPs). These PDPs consist of individual neurons or neural networks (activation nodes) that communicate with other neurons or neural networks. These models are known as *connectionist models*. (See Bohannon and Bonvillian [2008, pp. 253–254] for a description of the steps involved in and a reprint of Rummelhart and McClelland's [1987] PDP model.) Note that the PDP model is a more complex monolingual–bilingual processing model (see Figure 2.1, this volume).

According to Bohannon and Bonvillian (2008),

Over the course of development, the patterns that most successfully match adult speech are more likely to occur again (are strengthened), and erroneous, primitive patterns will eventually disappear. This critical matching function takes place when children's responses are matched against the criteria of adult speech the children hear. . . . Children learn speech from the exemplars provided to them. No innate biases or constraints are necessary for them to learn eventually to process language like adults. (p. 255)

Children acquire adultlike language through the presence of cue availability, which they use to determine the likelihood for form–function matches in the languages they hear. Simple form cues that children hear often are learned sooner in the language development process, and more difficult or less used forms are learned later. This may account for why children learn the specific languages that they are exposed to early in their development. Children also learn according to the specific peculiarities of their home language. For example, English speakers learn word order earlier than Italian speakers, because in Italian word order does not predict well the function of a word within a sentence (Bohannon & Bonvillian, 2008).

In summary, information-processing models view the human language learner as acquiring progressively better language skills in a qualitative linear fashion. With maturation and experience, the individual gradually becomes a better language processor, eventually reaching adult-level speech processing ability.

Social Interactionists

The interactionist models described earlier focus on cognitive development. McKee and McDaniel (2004) presented a social interactionist perspective in which biological structures or language architecture (nativism) can undergo change at the same time that language functions (behaviorism) can improve with experience. Social interactionists agree with the nativist view that language involves innate grammatical structures. They also agree with the behaviorist view that environment provides strong input into formation of the structures.

In addition, whereas social interactionists agree with linguists that there is an underlying structure in language and that infants have the ability to convey their intentions to others through their vocalizations, they also agree with behaviorists that through verbal interactions with their infants, caregivers provide meaning and intended message information to children's speech. Social interactionists believe this is the case even in vocal interaction during the prelinguistic phase, with caregivers attempting to derive meaning and intentions from "conversational bouts" with their infants (Golinkoff, 1983). Bohannon and Bonvillian (2008) provided an example of how this might occur: The infant babbles an utterance that is followed by the mother offering different objects to the infant until the infant accepts one. This is repeated every time the infant produces that particular utterance. Eventually, the utterance becomes the accepted label arrived at through sociolinguistic behavior between the infant and the mother for that particular object or action.

Along with vocal exchanges between infants and caregivers, referred to above, some social interactionists (e.g., Zukow-Goldring, 2001) consider gestures, such as pointing to objects in facilitating language development, to be important in communication. For example, the caregiver may point to the infant's bottle and say "baba." Soon the infant learns that uttering "baba" results in the caregiver producing the bottle. The same process leads to applying verbal labels to other objects. Some social interactionists (e.g., Bates & Snyder, 1985) consider pointing to be very important in enhancing early conversational attempts between infants and their caregivers.

> When CDS [child-directed speech] users gesture, their gestures are synchronous with the spoken word, assisting infants in deducing which verbal code corresponds to the referent (Zukow-Goldring, 1996). The importance of gestures is further shown during conversational bouts in which communication breaks down. After failed negotiations of meaning, gesture takes a more central role, directing children's attention to alternative meanings. (Bohannon & Bonvillian, p. 262)

Social interactionists believe that as the child matures and language acquisition progresses, the caregiver adjusts the CDS level and complexity accordingly. The caregiver may also adjust CDS through simplifying and repeating statements when the child appears not to understand. According to Bohannon and Marquis (1977), this process proceeds at a self-pace mode between the child and caregiver. Bohannon and Bonvillian (2008) noted that for social interactionists (e.g., Snow, 1977, 1999), directing focus to (gesturing) and speaking about things within the immediate environment of the child facilitate the language learning process. Caregivers' recasting of the child's early statements for clarification or improvement purposes is also thought to be important in helping the child to gradually approximate adult-like speech (Nelson, 1977, 1981).

A major difference among nativism, behaviorism, and the social interactionist views is what each considers the role of the learner in the language acquisition process to be. Behaviorists consider children to be passive recipients of their linguistic environment. Nativists see children as active participants with their parents and other adults in the construction of their own language development process. Social interactionists see children as forming a dynamic system with those in the environment during the language learning process, a view that regards both language structure and function as important driving forces in language development. To social interactionists, a more complete explanation (than provided by nativists or behaviorists) of language acquisition should include nonlinguistic properties such as turn taking, shared gaze, and attention between speakers, as well as the social context and cultural environment in which conversations occur (Bohannon & Bonvillian, 2008; Ninio & Snow, 1999). For example, Vygotsky (1978), an early interactionist, believed that social speech is instructive when young children engage in such speech (verbal interactions between children and parents or other adults) while involved in cognitive processes, such as problem solving when building a puzzle or when following verbal instructions to construct something from blocks or Legos. According to Vygotsky, social speech facilitates mastery of the cognitive challenges inherent in a task by allowing the child to benefit from interacting with experienced coaches (proficient adult speakers). (See Chapter 7, this volume, for a more detailed discussion of Vygotsky's model within pedagogical settings.) In contrast, the major theories (behaviorism and nativism) focused on maturation of biological structures and learning respectively and did not address sociocultural issues such as social speech.

Social interactionists also consider that certain environmental effects on language learning (i.e., the mother's input through her CDS, earlier known as "motherese" or "parentese") interact with the child's biological mechanisms (i.e., innate language decoding and encoding abilities), and they believe that both are important in language development. According to Field (1982), the infant practices sound production by observing and imitating the actions of the mother's physical language production actions during CDS. Other social interactionists (e.g., Stern, Beebe, Jaffe, & Bennett, 1977) believe that the mother–infant social interactions during their linguistic exchanges help the infant learn pragmatic behaviors, such as verbal turn-taking, necessary for the development of mature speech. (See Chapter 6, this volume, Social Context, Development, and Learning section, for a detailed discussion of how the social interactionist approach can be used to enhance the bilingual child's academic learning experiences.) In summary, social interactionists agree to some degree with both nativists and behaviorists views, but they also believe that sociocultural experiences are important in language development.

Evolutionary Theory

In general, evolutionary theorists would agree that unique human features such as language and cognitive processes evolved because they gave humans enhanced survival fitness. Some proponents believe that such features evolved in a traditional Darwinian natural selection mode (e.g., Corballis, 2009; Pinker & Bloom, 1990), whereas others believe that language is a consequence of the evolution of recursion (e.g., Hauser, Chomsky, & Fitch, 2002). Pinker and Bloom, (1990) refer to *recursion* as "an ability to embed a phrase containing a noun phrase or a clause within another clause, which falls out of pairs of rules as simple as NP → det NPP and PP → PNP" (p. 724).

According to Hauser et al. (2002), there are actually two language systems that have evolved. They argued that all or most of the faculty of language in the broad sense (FLB) is common to all organisms. "FLB includes a sensory-motor system, a conceptual-intentional system, and the computational mechanisms for recursion, providing the capacity to generate an infinite range of expressions from a finite set of elements" (Hauser et al., 2002, p. 1569). Faculty of language in the narrow sense (FLN) is considered unique to humans. Hauser and colleagues concluded that more research needs to be conducted to confirm the FLN hypothesis. In their view, if natural selection was involved in the evolution of the FLN, this system developed to serve systems other than language.

Specifically, the evolved mechanism is the ability for recursion. If this is so, the interesting question becomes less language focused. As Hauser et al. (2002) explained,

> If we find evidence for recursion in animals, but in a noncommunicative domain, then we are more likely to pinpoint the mechanisms underlying this ability and the selective pressures that led to it. This discovery, in turn, would open the door to another suite of puzzles: Why did humans, but no other animals, take the power of recursion to create an open-ended and limitless system of communication? Why does our system of recursion operate over a broader range of elements or inputs (e.g., numbers, words) than other animals? One possibility, consistent with current thinking in the cognitive sciences, is that recursion in animals represents a modular system designed for a particular function (e.g., navigation) and impenetrable with respect to other systems. During evolution, the modular and highly domain-specific system of recursion may have become penetrable and domain-general. This opened the way for humans, perhaps uniquely, to apply the power of recursion to other problems. This change from domain-specific to domain-general may have been guided by particular selective pressures, unique to our evolutionary past, or as a consequence (by-product) of other kinds of neural reorganization. (p. 1578)

Pinker and Jackendoff (2005) disagreed with Hauser et al.'s (2002) claim that the only uniquely human aspect of language is syntactic recursion. They pointed out that this view of the evolution of language is wrong because

> it ignores the many aspects of grammar that are not recursive, such as phonology, morphology, case, agreement, and many properties of words. It is inconsistent with the anatomy and neural control of the human vocal tract. And it is weakened by experiments suggesting that speech perception cannot be reduced to primate audition, that word learning

cannot be reduced to fact learning, and that at least one gene involved in speech and language was evolutionarily selected in the human lineage but is not specific to recursion. (p. 1)

There are several other issues that are of empirical concern for evolutionary researchers. We address them briefly next.

1. *When did the evolution of language occur?* Enard, Przeworski, et al. (2002) stated that the evolution of language depended on development of "fine control of the larynx and mouth (Liebermann, 1984) that are absent in chimpanzees and other great apes" (p. 869). Corballis (2009) suggested that language evolved along with humans' ability to mentally travel forward and backward (Suddendorf & Corballis, 1997, 2007). Corballis (2009) believed that both evolved during the Pleistocene epoch, "when brain size increased dramatically" (p. 553). Pinker and Bloom (1990) postulated that language has been around as long as there have been humans: "All human societies have language. As far as we know, they always did; language was not invented by some groups and spread to others like agriculture or the alphabet" (p. 707). Krause, Croft, and James (2007) assayed the DNA of Neanderthals and found that the selection of two specific amino acids in the *FOXP2* gene in area F5 of the brain is "implicated in the development of speech and language," and in both Neanderthals and modern humans, it predates "the common ancestor (which existed about 300,000–400,000 years ago)" (p. 1908).

Given this finding and the fact that the two amino acid changes differ between humans and chimpanzees, according to this theory, the selection sweeps between the divergence of chimps and humans occurred approximately 6.5 million years ago and 300,000 to 400,000 years ago (Enard, Przeworski, et al., 2002; Krause et al., 2007; Kumar, Filipski, Swarna, Walker, & Hedges, 2005; Patterson, Richter, Gnerre, Lander, & Reich, 2006). "This is in contrast to more recent age estimates of the selective sweep based on extant human diversity data" (Krause et al., 2007, p. 1908). That this gene is involved in language acquisition is supported by observing speech in a family with a point mutation on this gene. "Approximately half of the three-generational KE family have a point mutation in the *FOXP2* gene, and these individuals have pronounced verbal and orofacial dyspraxia (Vargha-Khadem et al., 2005; Zhang, Webb, & Podlaha, 2002) that is transmitted as an autosomal-dominant monogenetic trait (Hofreiter et al., 2001)" (Liégéois et al., 2003, p. 1230).

2. *What did the changes involve?* According to these evolutionary researchers, what occurred was a change in *FOXP2* amino acids that facilitated speech and language in modern humans. This newest DNA and neuroimaging research shows cross-species (animals, apes, and humans) and

intraspecies (human) structural and functional differences that affect language production. According to Enard, Przeworski, et al. (2002),

> Language is a uniquely human trait likely to have been a prerequisite for the development of human culture. The ability to develop articulate speech relies on capabilities, such as fine control of the larynx and mouth [Liebermann, 1984], that are absent in chimpanzees and other great apes. *FOXP2* is the first gene relevant to the human ability to develop language (Lai et al., 2001). A point mutation in *FOXP2* co-segregates with a disorder in a family in which half of the members have severe articulation difficulties accompanied by linguistic and grammatical impairment (Fisher et al., 1998). This gene is disrupted by translocation in an unrelated individual who has a similar disorder. Thus, two functional copies of *FOXP2* seem to be required for acquisition of normal spoken language. (p. 869)

3. *Did language development occur in the traditional Darwinian natural selection mode or as an abrupt change within a relatively short period of evolutionary time?* Many biologists, anthropologists, philosophers, and psychologists support the view that important adaptation in structures (e.g., the larynx and mouth, the human eye) and functions (e.g., speech and language, human vision) developed gradually as a series of small steps resulting from natural selection (e.g., Pinker & Bloom, 1990). According to such scientists, "An important insight, reinforced by Fisher (1930), is that the only way for complex design to evolve is through a sequence of mutations with small effects" (in Pinker & Bloom, 1990, p. 711). Others disagree, believing that language is not a direct result of natural selection but rather is a by-product "of other evolutionary forces such as an increase in overall brain size and constraints of as yet unknown laws of structure and growth (e.g., Chomsky, 1972, 1982a, 1982b, 1988a, 1988b; Gould 1987a; Gould & Piatelli-Palmarini, 1987)" (in Pinker and Bloom, 1990, p. 708). According to Pinker and Bloom (1990), such views are inaccurate because

> they depend on inaccurate assumptions about biology and language or both. Evolutionary theory offers clear criteria for when a trait should be attributed to natural selection: complex design for some function, and the absence of alternative processes capable of explaining such complexity. Human language meets these criteria: Grammar is a complex mechanism tailored to the transmission of propositional structures through a serial interface. Autonomous and arbitrary grammatical phenomena have been offered as counterexamples to the position that language is an adaptation, but this reasoning is unsound: Communication protocols depend on arbitrary conventions that are adaptive as long as they are shared. (p. 707)

Thus, some evolutionary theorists believe that language evolved gradually (through traditional natural selection processes), whereas others believe it occurred in a more abrupt manner. Both camps would agree that speech and language development endowed humans with cognitive abilities that increased survival advantages.

CONCLUSION

In this chapter, we presented numerous theories and viewpoints to explain the various cognitive and language development processes. However, none of these theories by themselves can explain this complex process. Each represents a piece of the language acquisition and cognitive development mosaic. To construct a complete picture, researchers representing different perspectives must collaborate and combine their different approaches into a comprehensive interactionist theory.

3

BILINGUALISM AND COGNITION

The changing demographics with respect to ethnic groups and language in the United States discussed in the Introduction provide a clear view of the evolution of Latinos from an invisible sector of the U.S. population historically subsumed within the "White" category in the census to a prominently visible sector of the U.S. population. To our knowledge, the 1970 census was the first to include the category "Spanish Heritage" (U.S. Census Bureau, 1970, Table 190), in recognition of the significant growth in the Latino population in the United States. As mentioned, the U.S. Census Bureau (2008) projected that people of "Hispanic Origin" (of any race) will constitute approximately 49.7 million by 2010, up from 22.3 million in the 1990 census.

It is imperative, therefore, that U.S. educators, administrators, and policymakers seek research-based knowledge concerning bilingual children, to best serve their needs in the applied classroom setting in order to develop and implement high-quality bilingual education programs that take into account the cognitive processes of the bilingual child. (For an in-depth discussion of important topics on education and policy issues for educating preschool emergent bilingual children, see García & Frede, 2010.) To accomplish this, one of the goals of this chapter is to provide the reader with an improved understanding of the bilingual development process and the relationship between bilingualism and cognition. A second goal is to examine some of the major issues of contention concerning bilingual education and to provide research findings relevant to the issues. By doing this, we hope to inform students, educators, administrators, and policymakers regarding research outcomes, which will accomplish the volume's third goal of contributing to the implementation of research-based programs (see Chapter 7, this volume) to enhance bilingual children's experiences in the classroom and other learning environments.

RELATIONSHIP BETWEEN BILINGUALISM AND COGNITION

In this section, we discuss some of the major issues being debated in the literature. One area of contention is whether, and if so, what conditions lead to individuals experiencing the greatest positive cognitive effects resulting from bilingual mastery. Specifically, what is the relationship between bilingualism and cognitive/intellectual processes? Although a number of early studies (e.g., Darsie, 1926; Haught, 1931; Hill, 1936; Spoerl, 1944) reported a lack of correlation between bilingualism and cognition, most of the studies published in the early part of the 20th century (e.g., Berry, 1922; Feingold, 1924; Garretson, 1928; Giardini & Root, 1923; Goodenough, 1926; Jordan, 1921; Koch & Simmons, 1928; Madsen, 1924; Mann, 1922; Pintner & Keller, 1922; Rigg, 1928) overwhelmingly reported a negative correlation between bilingualism and cognition. Such studies tended to suffer from lack of experimental rigor, and their findings were no doubt influenced by the anti-immigration sociopolitical winds that prevailed during that time in the United States (for an extended discussion of the confounding variables, see Cummins, 1976; Hakuta & Diaz, 1984; Náñez, 2010; Peal & Lambert, 1962).

In fact, Náñez, Padilla, and Lopez-Máez (1992) stated that bilingualism "was credited with the enhancement of intelligence and cognitive flexibility" (p. 50). Specifically, balanced bilinguals (i.e., individuals with high proficiency in two languages) "outperformed monolinguals on both verbal and nonverbal measures of intelligence when variables such as SES [socioeconomic status], language proficiency, sex, and age were controlled" (Náñez et al., 1992, p. 50). Several subsequent studies that also included appropriate methodological control supported Peal and Lambert's (1962) findings (see Bain, 1974; Balkan, 1970; Ben-Zeev, 1972; Gorrell, Bregman, McAllister, & Lipscomb, 1982; Ianco-Worral, 1972; Kessler & Quinn, 1987; Liedtke & Nelson, 1968; Powers & Lopez, 1985). Bialystok (1999) reported that younger (mean age = 4 years 2 months) and older (mean age = 5 years 5 months) bilingual preschoolers outperformed their monolingual counterparts in inhibitory control skills involving a card sort and moving word task (for a detailed description of the tasks, see Bialystok, 1999).

More recent studies have continued to provide support for the positive cognitive benefits of bilingualism throughout development. Preverbal infants raised with two home languages showed greater cognitive control compared with infants from monolingual homes. "These findings show that processing representations from two languages leads to a domain-general enhancement of the cognitive control system well before the onset of speech" (Kovács & Mehler, 2009, p. 6556). Carlson and Meltzoff (2008) compared "native bilinguals, monolinguals (English), and English speakers enrolled in second-language immersion kindergarten" (p. 282). They found that although native bilingual kindergarteners had lower verbal test scores and came from home environments with lower parental education and income,

> after statistically controlling for these factors and age, native bilingual children performed significantly better on the executive function battery than both other groups. Importantly, the relative advantage was significant for tasks that appear to call for managing conflicting attentional demands (Conflict tasks); there was no advantage on impulse-control (Delay tasks). These results advance our understanding of both the generalizability and specificity of the compensatory effects of bilingual experience for children's cognitive development. (Carlson & Meltzoff, 2008, p. 282)

Costa, Hernandez, and Sebastián-Gallés (2008) conducted a study involving young adults (19–32 years old; mean age = 22 years) and found that bilinguals outperformed monolinguals in the attentional network task (Fan et al., 2002). Costa et al. stated, "These results show that bilingualism exerts an influence in the attainment of efficient attentional mechanisms by young adults that are supposed to be at the peak of their attentional capabilities" (p. 59).

BILINGUAL DEVELOPMENT

The process of laying the foundation for becoming bilingual occurs early in development and parallels the process of language and cognitive development in monolinguals (see Chapter 1). To demonstrate that language sensitivity is present in utero, researchers need to show that fetuses respond to language-related stimuli. At least one study (Kisilevsky et al., 2003) has reported that fetuses show a preference (heart rate change) for hearing their mother's voice as opposed to a stranger's tape-recorded voice. Numerous studies have demonstrated behavioral evidence for language sensitivity in infants (see Chapter 1, this volume). Neuroimaging provides a pictorial view of neural language processing in infants. For example, Dehaene-Lambertz, Hertz-Pannier, and Dubois (2006) used several neuroimaging techniques to scan infant brains and found "similarity between functionally immature infants and competent mature adults" (p. 372).

In Chapter 1, we described research that strongly suggests that newborns and prelinguistic infants are universal language responders, attending to sounds inherent in any language. Prenatal and infant responses to language processes demonstrate that fetuses and very young infants are occupied not only with physical development but also with psycholinguistic and cognitive development. With regard to language acquisition, infants in the process of learning one language (monolinguals) and those learning two languages (bilinguals), research shows that infants who will become monolingual focus on processing and learning the sounds and words specific to their language, whereas bilingual and multilingual infants focus on those of the languages they are exposed to. As the language filters begin to close, monolingual infants lose the ability to perceive sounds from other languages, whereas bilingual infants' filters for their different languages remain open.

Along with learning to speak, infants are also developing in the areas of social and cognitive processes (see Chapter 6, this volume). The latest evidence to date shows that language also affects development of social preferences and status (ingroup, outgroup) almost from the start (Kinzler, Dupoux, & Spelke, 2007). Specifically, Kinzler and colleagues found that infants show preferential looking at someone whom they heard speaking their home language previously. As they become older, infants are more likely to accept a toy offered by a native-language speaker, and preschoolers prefer playmates and friends with native-language skills. Also interesting is that infants in the prelanguage phase prefer individuals with their native-language accent. Kinzler et al. (2007) concluded that "early-developing preferences for native-language speakers may serve as a foundation for later-developing preferences and conflicts among social groups" (p. 12577). Another study (Moon, Cooper, & Fifer, 1993) reported that 2-day-olds whose biological mothers were either Spanish or English monolinguals preferred to activate (through nonnutritive sucking) an audio tape of their mother's language, even though the recorded voice was that of a female stranger.

Although these findings can be interpreted as evidence for monolingual (home language) preference early in development, the finding that newborns can process the sounds common to all languages indicates that they come prewired to acquire the multiple languages to which they are exposed. That is, the evidence for a natural predisposition to become simultaneously bilingual (i.e., acquire two languages from the beginning—birth–3 years to five years) is convincing. Parents who expose their children to multiple languages early in the developmental process provide them with a cognitive boost. For example, recent neuroimaging studies indicate that simultaneous bilingualism is associated with functional (Kim, Relkin, Lee, & Hirsch, 1997) and structural (Mechelli et al., 2004) brain plasticity/malleability. Other researchers have found structural changes to a variety of environmental experiences (e.g., see

Draganski et al., 2004; Maguire et al., 2000). Future neuroimaging research should help determine how functional and structural changes of the type found by Kim et al. and Mechelli et al. may benefit bilinguals.

Over the years, empirical findings have presented a strong case for providing infants and children with early multilingual experiences. The bulk of the research shows that early simultaneous bilingual exposure, besides resulting in functional and structural brain changes such as those reported by Kim et al. (1997) and Mechelli et al. (2004), is also correlated with a number of cognitive benefits that may be further enhanced when children are exposed to high-quality early bilingual education (see the discussion of bilingualism issues below).

Regardless of the positive benefits of bilingualism, many parents, educators, and policymakers cling to the popular but misguided belief that very young children are confused by the fact that they are acquiring two languages, whether simultaneously or sequentially, and therefore may experience delays in language acquisition. The literature shows otherwise. Quoting Genesee and Nicoladis (2009, p. 335):

> In spite of less exposure to each language, bilingual children reach a number of important milestones within the same age span as their monolingual peers, such as the onset of canonical babbling (Oller et al., 1997), first words (see Nicoladis & Genesee, 1997), and overall rate of vocabulary growth (Pearson et al., 1997).

(See Genesee and Nicoladis, 2009, for a list of other similarities and differences between monolingual and bilingual language learners.)

According to Shaffer and Kipp (2010),

> by age 3 they (bilingual children) were well aware that the two languages were independent systems and that each was associated with particular contexts in which it was to be spoken (Lanza, 1992; Reich, 1986). By age 4, they displayed normal language proficiency in the language of their community and solid to excellent linguistic skills in the second language, depending on how much they had been exposed to it. Even when preschool children acquired a second language *sequentially* (i.e., after age 3, when they were already conversant in their native language), it often took no more than a year to achieve near-native abilities in second language (Reich, 1986). (p. 421)

Thus, it appears that the ability to acquire multiple languages is innate. However, the process of becoming monolingual begins early, unless the newborn or young child is exposed to multiple languages early as well. While it seems that the best way to achieve bilingualism is through simultaneous exposure to two languages, second and multiple languages can also be acquired sequentially, later in development through exposure or training. Thus, the language development process of bilinguals does not "suffer" in relation to monolinguals, and significant benefits include enhanced cognitive processes and, of course, bilingual status and prestige (Genesee, 2010).

BILINGUALISM AND BILINGUAL EDUCATION

Research shows that by the third generation, parents in the United States, regardless of ethnic background, are largely English monolinguals (Hakuta, 1986, 2007). Parents who are recent immigrants tend to be monolingual in the language of their country of origin, although not exclusively so. For example, the 2000 census data show that most immigrant parents, while stronger in their native language, also speak English to varying degrees. This is attributable to the fact that most of them come to the United States with the expressed goal of learning English in order to prosper in their new land. For example, data from the 2000 census show that in "newcomer families" (i.e., those with at least one parent born in another country) with children ages 0 to 17 years, 58% come from homes with "at least one parent fluent in spoken English" (Hernandez, Denton, & Macartney, 2007, p. 5). (See Hernandez, Macartney, & Denton, 2010, for detailed desegregation of the data regarding bilingual demographics contained in the 2000 U.S. census.)

Immigrant parents' expectation for their children to learn English from the start is also clear. However, some parents consciously limit English or require their children to speak exclusively in their native language at home, with the knowledge that their children will acquire English through interaction with English-speaking peers outside the home environment and upon entering formal education. Such children invariably grow up to be fully proficient bilinguals. According to the U.S. Census Bureau (2000), some 74% of children ages 5 to 17 years from newcomer families are fluent English speakers. The percentage of children with limited English-speaking ability reported in the 2000 census was 26%. Linguistically isolated households "range from a high of 30–33 percent in Arizona, Arkansas, California, Colorado, the district of Columbia, Kansas, Nebraska, Nevada, Oregon, and Texas to a low of 6–9 percent in Maine, Montana, New Hampshire, North Dakota, Vermont, West Virginia, and Wyoming" (Hernandez et al., 2007, p. 6). According to Hernandez et al.,

> children in these families may experience a high degree of isolation from English-speaking society, because not even adolescent children in these households speak English proficiently. These children and families offer both special challenges and opportunities for schools. The challenges are reflected in the need to design policies and programs that will most effectively educate these children in newcomer families and that will engage their parents through outreach in the languages of the families. (p. 6)

(See Chapter 7, this volume, for a discussion of some challenges and opportunities for bilingual students within the U.S. education system.) The problem is how to get these children up-to-par in English proficiency in the shortest time possible so that they can compete academically with their English-speaking classmates. The debate regarding how best to deal with issues of educating bilingual children is ongoing (see García, 2008; see also Part II, this volume). Below we address some of the most notable issues of contention historically debated by supporters and opponents of bilingualism and bilingual education and policy. In Chapter 7, we revisit the topics with a perspective on how they relate to bilingual children in the applied classroom learning environment.

Additive Versus Subtractive Second Language Acquisition

Náñez et al. (1992) reviewed the literature to identify learning conditions that foster enhanced bilingual development, as well as conditions that may hinder it. They found a number of studies indicating that use of an *additive* second language acquisition mode, in which the home language is strongly maintained and improves during the process of second language learning, has positive effects on cognition (e.g., Bhatnagar, 1980; Lambert, 1973; Long & Padilla, 1970), whereas use of a *subtractive* second-language acquisition mode, in which the first language atrophies, leads to negative cognitive outcomes (e.g., Lambert, 1973). More recent studies have continued to support the positive effects finding, when the bilingual programs are additive and of high academic quality (e.g., Barnett, Yarosz, Thomas, Jung, & Blanco, 2007).

Náñez et al. (1992) also reviewed the literature regarding whether the positive effects of bilingualism on cognitive processes are experienced before or after the learner achieves a second language proficiency threshold. They found evidence supporting both sides. Landry (1974), Cummins (1977, 1979, 1981b), and Duncan and De Avila (1979) reported that the positive effects are not experienced until after some threshold in second language acquisition is achieved (this threshold is assumed to vary between individuals). Ricciardelli (1992) considered the relationship between bilingualism and cognition from the threshold theory perspective and noted "that an overall bilingual superiority was found only for those children who had attained a high degree of bilingualism. An overall bilingual superiority was not found for those children who had attained lower degrees of bilingualism" (p. 301). However, Diaz (1985) and Hakuta and Diaz (1984) contended that the cognitive benefits of second language acquisition on the learner begin to appear almost immediately. The discrepancy between the findings may be due to the possibility that children learning a second language may acquire early benefits in language decoding (comprehension), but achieving benefits in language encoding (production) may require a much higher threshold of second-language proficiency. Regardless, all researchers agreed that additive second language acquisition resulting in highly proficient bilinguals gives weight to cognitive thought processes, enhancing cognitive abilities at some time during the second language (L2 in Figure 2.1) acquisition process.

In addition, Náñez et al. (1992) reviewed the literature regarding directional influence between bilingualism and cognition (i.e., does one enhance the other?). Peal and Lambert's (1962) study supported the view that increased bilingual proficiency results in enhanced cognition. Macnamara's (1964) results supported the cognition to bilingualism directional view. Náñez et al. (1992) wrote,

> Macnamara (1964) criticized Peal and Lambert's (1962) original findings because, in his opinion, they confounded bilingualism and intelligence. Given that a positive relationship exists between verbal abilities and psychometric intelligence, Macnamara argued that the more intelligent individuals also were more likely to become bilingual, while the less intelligent remained monolingual. (p. 50)

Lambert and Anisfeld's (1969) convincing rebuttal states in part:

> [Macnamara] suggests that it is more reasonable to argue that the more intelligent children become bilingual than it is to argue that becoming bilingual influences intellectual development. . . . This seems to be a dubious argument. It is difficult to understand how studies purportedly showing that bilingual children are inferior can be used to support the interpretation that the more intelligent become bilingual rather than vice versa. Is it reasonable to argue that children become bilingual because they are inferior intellectually? . . . In fact, our experiences with bilingual communities, bilingual homes, and bilingual youngsters suggests to us that anyone would become bilingual if the motivation of those teaching and learning the two languages were appropriate . . . and if a favourable time period were chosen to introduce the two languages. (p. 126)

Peal and Lambert (1962) and Lambert and Anisfeld's (1969) findings have been corroborated by several studies (e.g., Diaz, 1985; Hakuta & Diaz, 1984; Ricciardelli, 1992). Lambert and his colleagues made a compelling case. It is important to note, however, that the research of both camps (Lambert and Macnamara) as well as many subsequent studies concluded that bilingual acquisition is positively correlated with enhanced cognitive abilities.

English Immersion Versus Two-Way Bilingual Immersion

An ongoing debate in bilingual education involves the effectiveness of the type of bilingual education program. Winsler, Diaz, Espinosa, and Rodríguez (1999) compared receptive language, productive language, and language complexity in Spanish–English bilingual development of Mexican American children from low-income families who attended bilingual preschool or stayed at home. Their study replicated an earlier one (Rodriguez, Díaz, Duran, & Espinosa, 1995). The results with a new group of students were in line with those of the earlier study. Winsler et al. also conducted a 1-year follow-up of Rodriguez et al.'s subjects. The combined findings of the two studies showed that participation in a high-quality, bilingual preschool program led to "significant and parallel gains in Spanish language development and significant and greater increase in English language proficiency over time" (Winsler et al., 1999, p. 349). That is, participation in a bilingual preschool program did not result in loss of proficiency in Spanish.

Barnett, Yarosz, et al. (2007) compared 3- and 4-year-old children's language progress, literacy skills, and math scores. The study used a tight experimental control, including observation of Latino children from a dominant Spanish-speaking home background who attended high-quality preschool programs taught by certified bilingual teachers. Half of the participants were randomly assigned to two-way bilingual immersion (TWI), and the remaining children attended English immersion programs. Over the school year, all of the children made "substantial" gains in English-language skills, vocabulary development, and literacy. Barnett, Yarosz, et al. (2007) and Gormley, Gayer, Phillips, & Dawson (2005) found similar positive results for both types of programs (assuming high-quality program design and teacher training for both). Barnet, Yarosz, et al. (2007) reported that

> the TWI program provided better support for Spanish language receptive vocabulary development without sacrificing gains in English language development. In addition, English-dominant children in the TWI preschool program also made gains in Spanish language and literacy skills without hindering the development of their English language abilities though this last finding is not bolstered by comparison to a control group. (p. 288)

In summary, regarding English immersion versus TWI, research data indicate that starting bilingual children off on the right foot with high-quality, early childhood TWI bilingual education fosters English-language acquisition skills without sacrificing heritage language ability. Readers should note that different writers and researchers refer to the primary language spoken in the emergent bilingual child's home as the home language (HL), heritage language (HL), or first language (L1). In this volume, the words are used interchangeably.

Time-on-Task

Another challenge facing bilingual education is determination of the amount of time children need to spend in bilingual education programs to achieve academic parity with their English-speaking peers. An interesting debate regarding the time-on-task issue took place during the 1990s. Rossell and Baker (1996) used their interpretation of Canadian immersion education to make the case that an immersion model in which all instruction is provided in English would work best for educating second-language learners in the United States. Rossell and Baker's argument was that time-on-task (i.e., the amount of time spent in English instruction) mattered in children's mastery of English. In his critique of Rossell and Baker, Cummins (1999) made a convincing case that of the studies Rossell and Baker interpreted as supportive of structured English immersion over transitional bilingual education (TBE), "90% actually demonstrate the effectiveness of bilingual and even trilingual education" (p. 1). According to Cummins, Rossell and Baker's goal was to advocate for short-term 2-year bilingual education programs based on their claim that after 2 years of monolingual classroom experience in the Canadian program, students approximated grade norms but fell behind grade norms after the bilingual program was introduced. Cummins (1999) countered,

> Rossell and Baker seem oblivious to the fact that at the end of grade one French immersion students are still at very early stages in their acquisition of French. Despite good progress in learning French (particularly receptive skills) during the initial two years of the program, they are still far from native-like in virtually all aspects of proficiency—speaking, listening, reading, and writing. Most grade 1 and 2 French immersion students are still incapable of carrying on even an elementary conversation in French without major errors and insertions of English. (p. 3)

Greene (1997) also criticized Rossell and Baker's (1996) conclusions. He pointed out that their interpretation of "methodologically acceptable" studies was severely flawed. Through his own meta-analysis, Greene concluded that the "use of at least some native language instruction of LEP [limited English proficient] students is more likely to help the average student's achievement, as measured by standardized tests in English, than the use of only English in instruction of those LEP students" (p. 122).

Greene (1997) stated that proponents of California Proposition 227 should not base their support for the proposition on Rossell and Baker's flawed meta-analysis. California Proposition 227 was the English Language for Immigrant Children Statute proposing state law (now enacted) resolving that "all children in California Public Schools shall be taught English as rapidly and effectively as possible" (English Language Education for Immigrant Children, 1998). In his view, there was a limited amount of "high-quality research" on the topic, and what was available did not support Rossell and Baker's argument. Greene (1997) concluded, however, that his meta-analysis results would fall on deaf ears: "Those most afraid of high-quality research are those that depend on ignorance to advance their agendas" (p. 13).

States that implemented federally mandated bilingual education required by the U.S. Supreme Court 1976 decision in *Lau v. Nichols* (1974) were confronted with the challenge of determining how much time children should spend in bilingual education instruction to acquire sufficient English competency to compete academically with their English-speaking peers. One of the issues was whether early-exit or English-immersion programs are better for addressing the time-on-task situation. Two studies, Ramirez, Yuen, and Ramey (1991) and Ramirez, Pasta, Yuen, Billings, and Ramey (1991), reported contrary findings to studies that claimed English-only education is best for young bilinguals (e.g., Porter, 1990). The two studies conducted by Ramirez and his colleagues demonstrated that children in the immersion program failed to exit earlier than those in an early-exit program. Cummins's (1993) review of the Ramirez et al. studies revealed that the late-exit findings clearly "refuted the time-on-task hypothesis" (p. 59). Further, lack of support for time-on-task is provided by the finding that children at one site of the late-exit program, who had greater opportunity to use their Spanish-language skills, exhibited faster growth in English reading than their norming population. Alternatively, children who were "abruptly transitioned into almost all English instruction in the early grades (in a similar fashion to early-exit students) seemed to lose ground in relation to the general population between grades 3 and 6 in mathematics, English language, and reading" (Cummins, 1993, p. 60).

Other countries have explored the time-on-task issue as well. For example, Spanish-Basque programs (Gabiña, Gorostidi, Iruretagoiena, Olaziregi, & Sierra, 1986; Sierra & Olaziregi, 1989) found similar results as J. D. Ramirez and colleagues. Specifically, in a bilingual program in Spain with Basque as the instructional language and Spanish as a subject, children showed superior Basque oral and written scores at Grades 2 and 5. Differences in Spanish-language scores between the two language groups were not significant. In his review of the Basque studies, Cummins (1993) stated that while the goals of the Basque and U.S. programs were different (the Basque programs were additive in nature),

> the findings are remarkably consistent—instruction through the medium of a minority language for a substantial part of the school day entails minimal or no academic disadvantage with respect to achievement in the majority language. Similar findings are reported for minority francophones in Canada (Landry & Allard, 1991). (p. 61)

Studies with Turkish–Dutch bilingual children in the Netherlands have reported similar findings (Verhoeven, 1991).

Hakuta, Goto Butler, and Witt (2000) addressed the question of how long emergent bilingual students require "special services" (e.g., English-as-a-second-language and bilingual education). They noted that even the children in the best districts took 3 to 5 years to achieve oral proficiency and 4 to 7 years to achieve proficiency in academic English. They presented data from two Canadian school districts to support their case. In fact, they proposed that it may take longer than this, given that both the American and Canadian programs included selective sampling.

> The data would suggest that policies that assume rapid acquisition . . . are wildly unrealistic. A much more sensible policy would be one that sets aside the entire spectrum of the elementary grades as the realistic range within which English acquisition is accomplished, and plans balanced curriculum that pays attention not just to English, but to the full array of academic needs of the students. (Hakuta et al., 2000, pp. 13–14)

The most recent research supports Hakuta et al.'s (2000) conclusion. It is becoming increasingly clear that the effects of sustained, high-quality prekindergarten, kindergarten, and elementary school bilingual education programs on a young child's cognitive development are positive in nature (Barnett, Jung, Wong, Cook, & Lamy, 2007; Robin, Frede, & Barnett, 2006). Gormley et al. (2005) also found significant positive effects of prekindergarten participation on "cognitive tests of prereading and reading skills, prewriting and spelling skills, and math reasoning and problem-solving abilities" (p. 880; see Chapter 7, this volume). They also found that half-day and longer all-day programs both had positive effects for three of the groups: Latinos, African Americans, and European Americans (Native Americans in the full-day program did not do better than controls). Thus, it appears that extended high-quality prekindergarten is beneficial for the child's early cognitive development. Robin et al. (2006) reported positive effects of high-quality half-day and full-day preschool attendance in 4-year-old children from low-income families in an urban school district. Children in all-day programs showed significantly higher performance on two of the cognitive subtests, a trend on the expressive vocabulary test, and no difference on the letter word identification subtest. The all-day group also scored significantly higher on the passage comprehension and calculation tests. Robin et al. (2006) concluded, "Although further research is needed to augment this single study of half-day vs. extended-day preschool, the results clearly indicate that duration and intensity matter. Extended-day preschool seems to have dramatic and lasting effects when it is high quality" (p. 19). Thus, spending more time in English-only (time-on-task) education is not as successful as bilingual education in helping young children master English. An added benefit of bilingual education is that children in such programs achieve L2 (English) proficiency without losing L1 proficiency.

Added-Value Bilingual Education

In today's rapidly changing global society, the added value of bilingual education and bilingualism is obvious. Children throughout the world are learning English and other languages for economic as well as sociocultural advantages. Global interest in creating best-practice bilingual education programs for children has been present for some time. Cummins (1993) attributed the increased interest in identifying high-quality bilingual education models to the increased growth in immigration.

In addressing the question of what scientists learned from second-language immersion research in the 3 decades prior to 1998, Cummins (1998) concluded that the potential of immersion bilingual education would be maximized if it is applied with a philosophy that focuses significantly beyond applied linguistics. The truly successful program must allow students opportunity to

> communicate powerfully in the target language if they are going to integrate their language and cognitive development with their growing personal identities. . . . It is in these programs that there is the most potential for truly preparing citizens who can make highly significant contributions to their own and our global societies. For this to happen, however, immersion educators must explicitly locate their pedagogy and educational vision in the realm of global education and ensure that language policies operating in the school are consistent with this philosophy of global education. (Cummins, 1998, p. 45)

(Note that Cummins was referring to immersion and bilingual programs globally.)

Earlier, Tucker (1991) concluded that allowing students to practice the language skills in their regular conversations is the missing component of good immersion bilingual education. Tucker described a truly bilingual program as one based on the successful Canadian additive acquisition model. The ideal program for global bilingual education, according to Tucker, would also include ample instruction in and opportunity for students to practice both languages, which would resolve the "absent peer" dilemma by including approximately equal numbers of L1 and L2 students who would work together to gain literacy skills over time while also developing academic proficiency in both languages. Hakuta and García (1989) reached a similar conclusion

> Bilingualism is too complex to be looked at from the narrow perspective of "linguistic dimension . . . despite the fact that bilingualism is correlated with a number of nonlinguistic parameters. Future research will have to be directed toward a multifaceted vision of bilingualism. (p. 374)

In summary, the added value of bilingual education is considered to accrue in the cognitive, cultural, and socioeconomic areas of the bilingual's life.

Language Transfer

The debate here concerns whether maintaining a strong command of L1 transfers to (facilitates) acquisition of L2. Genesee (2010) cited the following studies regarding "cross-linguistic transfer of specific morpho-syntactic features from one language to another" (p. 62): Dopke (2000), Hulk and van der Linden (1996), Müller (1998), Nicoladis (2002, 2003), Paradis and Navarro (2003), and Yip and Matthews (2000). Barnett, Yarosz, et al. (2007) reported that

> the TWI [two-way immersion] program provided better support for Spanish language receptive vocabulary development without sacrificing gains in English development. In addition, English-dominant children in the TWI preschool program made gains in Spanish language and literacy skills without hindering the development of their English language abilities though this last finding is not bolstered by comparison to a control group. (p. 288)

Another important finding from Barnett, Yarosz, et al.'s (2007) study is that the TWI Spanish-dominant children made significant gains in Spanish vocabulary, whereas the English immersion children fell back relative to the norms for their same-age peers. According to Barnett, Yarosz, et al., this finding provides strong

> evidence that immersion in an English-only preschool setting is accompanied by, though it does not necessarily contribute to, Spanish language loss. The decline in TVIP (Test de Vocabulario en Imagenes Peabody; Dunn et al., 1986) standard gains for Spanish-dominant children in the TWI program indicates that TWI preschool programs can ameliorate this problem with no loss of effectiveness in promoting English language literacy development. (p. 289)

The finding is in line with a number of earlier studies (e.g., Cummins, 1984; Hébert et al., 1976; McLaughlin, 1987) that L1 development contributes to (transfers to) L2 development as well. Hébert et al. (1976) found that children in French–English bilingual education programs in Canada were able to learn L2 without negative impact on L1 (see Cummins, 1980). Cummins (1980) found that "francophone students receiving 80% instruction in French and 20% instruction in English did just as well in English as students receiving 80% instruction in English and 20% in French" (p. 184). Winsler et al. (1999) found that participation in a high-quality, truly bilingual preschool program led to "significant and parallel gains in Spanish language development and significant and greater increase in English-language proficiency over time" (p. 349). Such findings constitute convincing evidence that participation in a bilingual preschool program does not have to result in loss of L1 proficiency.

Other studies, for example, Andreou and Karapetsas (2004), found that proficiency in the native language "can be generalized to a foreign language, revealing a causal connection between native and foreign language learning" (p. 357). Genesee (2004) found that native speakers of a "dominant societal language" (L1; e.g., English) "acquire significantly more advanced levels of functional proficiency in the L2 than students who receive conventional L2 instruction—that is, instruction that focuses primarily on language learning and is restricted to separate, limited periods of time" (p. 6). Further, "students in bilingual programs who speak a dominant societal language usually develop the same levels of proficiency in all aspects of the L1 as comparable students in programs where the L1 is the exclusive medium of instruction" (p. 6). Lindsey, Manis, and Bailey (2003) found that Spanish-speaking ability in a wide range of prereading skills in kindergarten predicted English reading ability in first grade in Spanish–English bilinguals. Miller et al. (2006) observed over 1,500 Spanish–English bilingual children in kindergarten to third-grade and reported that Spanish oral skills predicted Spanish reading scores. The same relationship was found between English oral skills and English reading skills. A significant cross-language transfer effect was also observed, with English oral scores predicting Spanish reading scores and vice versa "beyond the variance accounted for by grade" (Miller et al., 2006, p. 30).

In summary, strong evidence exists that gaining proficiency in one language fosters accompanying gains in a second language, especially if the two languages are related (e.g., English and Spanish vs. English or Spanish and Chinese). The findings presented here strongly suggest that children in the United States should be afforded ample opportunity to experience multiple languages in their home and other environments (e.g., prekindergarten and day-care programs). Globally, many nations already use this practice in an effort to ensure that their children get the positive cognitive and sociocultural benefits associated with early (simultaneous) bilingualism. Their case is bolstered by research findings indicating that speaking multiple languages is not only beneficial for the individual's intellectual development but also for his or her subsequent sociocultural and economic well-being. Bilingualism fosters the development of productive citizens living successfully within a pluralistic global society.

Language Shift and Loss

August and Hakuta (1997) referred to the displacement or replacement of an existing language by another as *language shift*, which they described as "the sociolinguistic phenomenon in which an ethnic group gradually moves its preference and use of language from its original ethnic language to the sociologically dominant language" (p. 40). Language shift occurs intergenerationally and within individuals (i.e., the preference and use of a language shift over a lifetime). The former happens as time since immigration increases across generations. The latter occurs because bilingual individuals gradually show a preference for English use, which usually results in monolingual upbringing of their children (August & Hakuta, 1997; Fishman, 1966; Lopez, 1978, Veltman, 1983).

Through the years, opinion among entrenched Americans has consistently been that L1 maintenance, as a consequence of bilingual education, will result in "the disuniting of America" (Schlesinger, 1991). This attitude has been around for a long time. For example, upon signing the 1924 Immigration Restriction Act, President Calvin Coolidge stated, "America must be kept American" (Tyack, 1974, cited in Yzquierdo McLean, 1995, p. 2). Coolidge was referring to non-Western European immigrants, who also tended to be "bilingual" (i.e., limited- or non-English-speaking). As a result, immigration among Southern and Eastern Europeans was reduced to 2%. Earlier, Benjamin Franklin complained about the large number of German immigrants into Pennsylvania. Crawford (2000, cited in Altarriba & Heredia, 2008, p. 208) quoted Franklin as stating:

> Why should the Palatine Boors be suffered to swarm into our Settlements, and by herding together, establish their Language and Manners, to the Exclusion of ours? Why should Pennsylvania, founded by the English, become a colony of Aliens, who will shortly be so numerous as to Germanize us instead of our Anglifying them, and will never adopt our Language or Customs, any more than they can acquire our Complexion.

Peréa and García Coll (2008) also included this quote and referred to other early cases of scapegoating and discrimination against immigrant bilinguals.

These views have resulted in long-standing public opposition to bilingual education and support for subtractive English-immersion bilingual policy and practice. For example, Krashen (2002) considered that the general public, as well as some prominent politicians, are generally unaware of (or choose to ignore) the presence of the language shift phenomenon. Statements like America needs "the glue of [English] to hold us together" (Bob Dole, in *Los Angeles Times*, October 31, 1995; Shogren, 1995) and "We should replace bilingual education with immersion in English so people learn the common language of the country" (Newt Gingrich, in *The Lantern*, April 2, 2007; Gingrich, 2007) are common among some prominent opponents of bilingual education. Maverick (1997) commented,

> Poor Jesus. We make so many dumb claims about him. There was a woman opposing bilingual education before the State of Texas Textbook Committee. She didn't want any school books in Spanish. "If English was good enough for Jesus," the lady claimed, "it ought to be good enough for Mexicans." (p. 186)

This quote is attributed to Miriam A. "Ma" Ferguson, 1920s Texas governor. The sentiment behind the quote has been around at least as long as the bilingual education debate.

Research shows that rather than threatening the dominance of English in the United States, immigrant languages are in fact the endangered species. For example, Lieberson, Dalto, and Johnston (1975) observed 35 nations with a diverse language "issue." They reported that the amount of minority language loss occurring within one generation in the United States would require some 350 years in other nations. In fact, Veltman (1983, 1988) concluded that were it not for continued immigration, even Spanish would rapidly decline and disappear in the United States.

Although our focus is on bilingual individuals in the United States, the following examples show that language shift occurs globally. Given the global migration explosion, in numerous cases, immigrants are struggling to keep their heritage language (HL) from being subsumed because their children place more value on the more prestigious and socially desirable languages of their host countries. Siren (1991) conducted a comprehensive study in Sweden with parents and children with language origins other than Swedish. Siren observed that a consequence of exposure to the dominant culture and language was a rapid language shift in the children.

Siren (1991) also reported an effect for language use in the child's day care. In minority language day care, a significant number of children retained home language proficiency. This percentage dropped off quickly to about half of the children in day care with some home language use and only one quarter maintaining greater home language fluency in Swedish language day-care programs.

Cummins (1991) reported similar findings from a 2-year study of Portuguese speakers in kindergarten through first grade. A distinct language shift from L1 to L2 (English) occurred even in that short time period. It is clear that language prestige and the accompanying desire by immigrant children to be like their dominant culture peers has a negative linguistic effect (from the point of view of HL maintenance proponents) of decreasing HL use and proficiency, as well as the sociocultural effects of devaluing HL use and shifting toward identification with majority culture values on the part of the children.

Krashen (2002) stated that the most obvious reason for language shift is the lack of or loss of L1 input. This is clearly demonstrated by Siren's (1991) research described previously. More recent research continues to show that there is a predictable increase in language shift with increased exposure to L2 or reduction in L1 use. Studies discussed by Krashen (2002) also support Siren's finding that parental use of the HL correlates highly with HL retention (Kondo, 1998; Hinton, 1998; Portes & Hao, 1998). Living in close proximity to HL speakers also predicts HL retention (Demos, 1988), whereas moving away or not living in the HL community results in HL reduction or loss (Hinton, 1998).

Krashen (2002) cited several psychosocial factors attributed to language shift, including *affective factors*, such as the child's strong desire for assimilation into the dominant culture and active rejection of the HL culture and language, referred to as *ethnic ambivalence* or *ethnic evasion* (Tse, 1998). Alternatively, in cases of *ethnic emergence*, individuals regain interest in their parents' culture and seek to maintain or regain their HL. Krashen also indicated that individuals can develop *language shyness* (another affective factor) if ridiculed by other members of the HL community for lack of HL proficiency. In such cases, the child shies away from HL use and may stop using it altogether.

Cummins (1993) concluded that it is

> clear that language shift takes place at an extremely rapid pace in many minority contexts, and strong institutional support for the L1 is necessary to resist this process. L1 support at the preschool and elementary levels, even to the extent of predominantly L1 instruction throughout the grades, does not seem to impede the acquisition of conversational or academic skills in the majority language. In fact, the trends in the data for minority students who are at risk of school failure point to an inverse relationship between exposure to the majority language and achievement in that language. (p. 65)

Genesee (2010) presented data in support of the idea that L1 maintenance and strengthening supports L2 acquisition through a language transfer effect.

In summary, the fear that English will be replaced by Spanish or some other heritage language has no empirical basis. Rather, immigrants to the United States show a strong intergenerational and intragenerational shift from their heritage language to English.

Cost-Effectiveness

Given federal bilingual education mandates, states must consider which bilingual education programs work best. Civic and educational leaders also face the task of identifying cost-effective programs that produce measurable success in traditional academic subject areas and, in the United States, programs that allow transition to English-language education in the shortest possible time frame. Barnett, Jung et al. (2007) found that

> if offered for the same number of hours, the TWI (two-way immersion) program would not require additional resources. It accomplishes its goals by hiring native Spanish speakers as lead teachers for half of the preschool classrooms than by adding additional staff to existing classrooms. (pp. 289–290)

Reynolds, Temple, Robertson, and Mann (2002) reported a cost–benefit analysis of the Chicago Title I Child–Parent Centers program for 3- to 9-year-olds. They found that providing literacy instruction, intensive parent involvement, well-trained staff, and a single administrative system resulted in a significantly positive cost–benefit ratio. They noted, for example, that "the preschool program provided a return to society of $7.14 per dollar invested by increasing economic well-being and tax revenues, and by reducing public expenditures for remedial education, criminal justice treatment, and crime victims" (Reynolds et al., 2002, p. 267). Reynolds and colleagues also noted that children in the late-exit program who received less overall English instruction compared with the immersion and early-exit students were at near-grade-level compared with children in the general student population. In their discussion of a follow-up study of the Chicago programs, Barnett, Jung et al. (2007) pointed out that the researchers (i.e., Temple & Reynolds, 2007)

> provided a cost–benefit analysis of the Child Parent Centers based on follow-up data through age 21, and they found that benefits far exceeded costs. The estimated benefits are so large, that if one year of participation in these state programs produced even 10% of the estimated benefits of the Chicago program, they would still be likely to pass a cost–benefit test. (p. 26)

Thus, high-quality bilingual education is a cost-effective way of helping bilingual students achieve English-language proficiency. However, the process may take years to accomplish. In view of this finding, citizens, educators, and policymakers need to use this knowledge to advocate for funding and implementation of research-informed, high-quality bilingual education for all American students, pre-K–12.

CONCLUSION

The dramatic increase in ethnic minority and bilingual populations discussed in the Introduction to this volume has spurred controversy regarding issues such as those discussed in this chapter. The chapter has provided a wealth of information suggesting that if bilingual children are to grow up to make a full contribution to the economic well-being of the United States, they must be provided the requisite high-quality educational experiences discussed here. To accomplish this, U.S. researchers must continue to gain greater understanding of the emergent bilingual's linguistic and cognitive processes in order to better inform educators and policymakers concerning how these affect the child's academic achievement in applied learning environments. It is clear that much research remains to be conducted before this goal can be accomplished.

Genesse (2010) recommended that to gain the full cognitive benefits attributable in the literature to proficient bilingualism, all children in the United States, regardless of language spoken at home, should be provided access to bilingual education in preparation for functioning more successfully in today's global society. If this is to be accomplished, citizens, educators, and policymakers in states like Arizona and California must abandon the spirit of Proposition 203—now the English Language Education for Children in Public Schools article of the Arizona Revised Statutes—which states in part: "All children in Arizona public schools schools shall be taught English by being taught in English" (English Language Education for Children, 2000). Based on such a narrow perspective, children in Arizona are thrown into a hostile school environment that requires outdated subtractive English immersion pedagogy. A much more productive approach would be to embrace tolerance and inclusiveness for all ethnic and language groups. Bilingual children should be provided the opportunity to participate in educational programs based on the most current, highest quality, scientific, psychological, cognitive, neuroscience, and education research available (see García, 2008).

Finally, this chapter documented the positive correlation between bilingualism and cognition that has been known for some 50 years. Perhaps it is time that bilingual education opponents acknowledge the overwhelming empirical evidence concerning the positive effects of bilingualism on cognitive and linguistic tasks, as well as the social benefits of bilingualism for the child's sociocultural interactions. Yet, bilingual education opponents continue to cling to their ethnocentric views. Fortunately, many Americans understand that a shift toward acceptance of a broader global perspective and support for linguistic and cultural diversity needs to take place. Some prominent individuals support implementation of research-based educational practices targeted at accomplishing this goal. Although he does not express support for bilingual education directly in his extensive book on U.S. and world economics, former Federal Reserve chair Alan Greenspan (2007) attributed the embattled U.S. economy to the ailing U.S. educational system:

> A dysfunctional U.S. elementary and secondary education system has failed to prepare our students sufficiently rapidly to prevent a shortage of skilled workers and a surfeit of lesser-skilled ones, expanding the pay gap between the two groups. Unless America's education system can raise skill levels as quickly as technology requires, skilled workers will continue to earn greater wage increases, leading to ever more disturbing extremes of income concentration. As I've noted, education reform will take years, and we need to address increasing income inequality now. We can immediately both damp skilled-worker income and enhance the skill level of our workforce by opening our borders to large numbers of immigrants with the vital skills our economy needs. Adaptation is our nature, a fact that leads me to be deeply optimistic about our future. (p. 505)

An obvious consequence of implementation of Greenspan's plan would be a dramatic increase in the numbers of immigrant workers of limited English-speaking ability. There would be a corresponding increase in the need for bilingual education programs to serve their children as well. To continue to be the economic, political, and social world leader, the United States must adopt the best bilingual education programs available. This will help the growing number of emergent bilinguals to successfully become balanced, proficient bilinguals. Bilingual education for all American students will lead to a better educated and enlightened America.

4

INTELLIGENCE AND BILINGUAL ASSESSMENT

The debate concerning ethnic and racial group differences in "intelligence" (defined as one's score on an IQ test) can be traced to the eugenics movement (e.g., see Galton, 1869, 1883). In the late 19th and early 20th centuries, Western Europeans sought to demonstrate their and northern Europeans' superiority over southern and eastern Europeans and native groups from around the world. A major focus was the measurement of intelligence in English-speaking U.S. Army recruits (Whites vs. Blacks) using Yerkes's (1921) U.S. Army Alpha and Beta tests. The army tests were also used to identify IQ differences between Whites and Blacks as well as non-English or limited-English-speaking recruits who were immigrants. Development of the army tests led to researchers applying them to test for intelligence differences between "bilingual" (i.e., non-English-speaking) and English-speaking children and adults. The goal of intellectual and bilingual comparisons in the United States during that time was to exclude or greatly limit the number of immigrants from non-English-speaking racial and ethnic groups and nations.

Before we discuss the measurement of differences in intellectual and cognitive abilities between language groups, we briefly review some of the interesting, albeit sophomoric, early debates that led to today's research on the topic. (Social and behavioral scientists during the late 19th and early

20th centuries occupied much of their time searching for racial and ethnic differences in a variety of physical traits and sensory–perceptual abilities.) We then turn our attention to the debate over intelligence and bilingualism from the early part of the 20th century to the present. We describe some of the psychometric tools and materials used to measure intelligence and bilingual proficiency and balance over time. We conclude the chapter with a caution for researchers engaging in psychometric research with emergent bilinguals.

EVALUATION OF PHYSICAL AND SENSORY–PERCEPTUAL TRAITS

In the late 19th and early 20th centuries, nations in Europe that were recently at war began looking for evidence of superiority of one group over another, a quest that is said to have escalated after the 1870–1871 Franco–Prussian War, with French and German anthropologists leading the way (Brigham, 1923). The passion for group and racial comparisons became widespread, with social scientists, politicians, and the media from different countries focusing their discussion of racial differences on physical characteristics such as skull size, height, brain weight, and skin and hair color. This was accompanied by cartoonish depictions exaggerating physical features and writings lampooning differences in sociocultural customs.

Woodworth (1910) attributed cross-cultural comparisons of physical characteristics and sensory–perceptual abilities to tales brought home by European travelers about native cultures' superior ability in vision and smell, for example. According to Woodworth, "Ranke however, on testing natives of Brazil, a race notable for their superior eyesight found that their ability to discern the position of a letter or similar character at a distance, though good was not remarkable, but fell within the range of European powers" (Woodworth, 1910, p. 175). Similar observations of overlap between group abilities in visual, auditory, olfactory, and tactual abilities were commonly reported by early researchers.

Woodworth (1910) stated that the problem with looking for the average *type* of one group to compare with the same of another group is that often there is more overlap on a trait between than within groups: "The groups overlap to such an extent that the majority of the individuals composing either group might perfectly well belong to the other" (p. 172). He believed the observed differences were small, and therefore group similarities rather than differences should be emphasized. He noted that the evidence for greater group overlap than differences was strong; the considerable within-group variability rendered the differences insignificant and therefore not important.

Early attempts at documenting racial differences were limited to non-scientific comparison of physical as opposed to mental traits. Woodworth (1910) wrote,

> Our inveterate love for types and sharp distinctions is apt to stay with us even after we have become scientific, and vitiate our use of statistics to such an extent that the average becomes a stumbling block rather than aid to knowledge. (p. 172)

Even with great numbers of cases to compare, Woodworth noted that the differences "should become jumbled together, we should never be able to separate the negroes from the whites by aid of brain weight" (p. 172).

EMERGENCE OF PSYCHOLOGY

Woodworth (1910) was perhaps the first to caution that tests standardized on one group should not be applied to other groups because doing so would result in an unfair advantage for the group on which they were standardized. Nevertheless, the emergence of psychology allowed researchers to focus on racial differences in human behavior, such as reaction time (a correlate of mental speed) and IQ tests (proposed correlates of intelligence); such tests were made possible by the scientific method and statistical and psychometric tools that psychologists brought to bear in the search for group/racial/ethnic differences.

Rather than applying statistics to average differences, Woodworth (1910) suggested that statistics be used to measure the distribution of traits, noting that the distribution is a better measure than the average. Woodworth was no fan of documentation of group differences. With great foresight, he cautioned against the misapplication or exaggeration of statistical findings that could lead to a negative impact on one or another group. History reveals that behavioral scientists and education researchers were not aware of Woodworth's warning, did not agree with his thoughts, or simply did not care. Woodworth's admonition fell on the deaf ears of behavioral scientists, whom turned their focus to the search for intellectual differences. (As readers will see later in this chapter, the debate continues to this day.)

EARLY RESEARCH: APPLYING PSYCHOMETRICS TO MEASURE INTELLIGENCE AND BILINGUALISM

The rapid increase in immigration to the United States in the early 20th century led to a socially and politically motivated call from entrenched immigrant groups for immigration reform to restrict the number of newcomers from eastern and southern Europe and from non-English-speaking countries. The earlier debate concerning group differences in physical and sensory–perceptual traits was superseded by a more sinister one, as behavioral scientists and education researchers trained their sights on the search for "intellectual" differences among various ethnic/racial groups arriving on U.S. shores daily.

Studies Focused on Intellectual Differences

Researchers began arming themselves with powerful paper-and-pencil IQ tests to make classifications among racial and ethnic groups based on observed differences on verbal and nonverbal components of the IQ tests. Terman's (1916) newly modified version of the Binet–Simon Intelligence Test (Binet & Simon, 1905, 1908/1911/1916) provided precisely the tool researchers were looking for. A problem that was overlooked or ignored from the beginning, however, was that the original Binet-Simon test was designed to differentiate between "normal" intellectual ability and "mentally delayed" French schoolchildren, not between individuals from different groups with presumably normal intelligence. According to Yzquierdo McLean (1995),

> Binet . . . proclaimed that intelligence was too complex to be measured with a single number (Gould, 1993). Binet and Theodore (1916) argued that intelligence could be augmented by good education and was neither fixed nor an inborn quality. (p. 2)

Between 1904 and 1915, Terman refined and standardized his IQ test for use with Americans. He published *The Measurement of Intelligence: An Explanation of and a Complete Guide for the Use of the Stanford Revision and Extension of the Binet-Simon Intelligence Scale* (Terman, 1916). As Becker (2003) noted, "Although there were other translations of the Binet-Simon available around this time (Binet & Simon, 1916; Kuhlmann, 1912; Melville, 1917; Herring, 1922), Terman's normative studies and his methodical approach are credited with the success of the Stanford-Binet (Minton, 1988)" (p. 2).

Numerous early researchers (e.g., G. L. Brown, 1922; Darsie, 1926; Murdoch, 1920; Pintner & Keller, 1922; Sheldon, 1924; Young, 1922) used the Stanford–Binet. We discuss Katharine Murdoch's and Gilbert L. Brown's studies here as representative of issues addressed by these researchers prior to the passage of the Immigration Restriction Act by the U.S. Congress in 1924, which spurred discriminatory use of IQ tests.

Murdoch (1920) documented intelligence differences among children from four ethnic/cultural groups attending two "rather similar and some-what undesirable localities in New York City." The testing was originally planned to compare "Hebrews and Italians," but later, "Native Americans" (whites) "and negroes" were also tested (all quotes from Murdoch, 1920,

p. 147). Murdoch's goal was to explore ways of helping with the issue of "Americanization." Rather than mixing into the proverbial American cultural melting pot, the groups tended to remain isolated. Murdoch observed "that when Jewish and Italian young people of the same neighborhood attend the same settlement or neighborhood clubs the Italians are almost invariably driven or crowded out by their Jewish neighbors" (p. 147). Murdoch used the Pressey group intelligence test (Pressey & Pressey, 1918) as her measure of intelligence. Her results indicated that Whites and Jews showed almost identical IQ. She also reported that Blacks at ages 9, 10, and 16 "seem to be well up toward equaling or exceeding the native whites and Hebrews."[1]

From her study, Murdoch concluded that the IQ overlap among Jews, Whites, and Blacks was attributable to the lack of reliability inherent in the Pressey test. This did not seem to concern her, however, as she cited Kelley's (1919) statement that lack of reliability results in a constant error showing greater overlap than may be present. "Were the Pressey measure a more perfect instrument we would thus have found a still smaller amount of overlapping of the races" (Murdoch, 1920, p. 149).

Murdoch did not consider language differences or bilingual ability in her study. However, she acknowledged that her findings may have resulted from reduced English proficiency in the Italian group versus the other cultural groups. She did not give this possibility much credence, relying on the verbal assurance from "their school teachers, principal and neighborhood social workers [that the Italians were] laboring under no language difficulty" (p. 150). As we demonstrated in Chapter 3, problems of classification and evaluation of bilingual status plagued many of the early studies that addressed bilingual–monolingual verbal and nonverbal IQ differences. Murdoch also failed to report the socioeconomic status (SES) of the groups, wrongly assuming that children attending the same school have equal SES. Murdoch failed to report whether the Italians were more recent immigrants and therefore less proficient in their English skills. Furthermore, only male subjects were tested. Different results may have been observed if the sample had included girls attending the same schools. Finally, Murdoch failed to inform her readers what the results meant for her original goal of contributing to increased Americanization. Somewhere in the mix, the goal was lost. This may be because the study was a class project for her students in a psychology course and as such lacked scientific rigor.

---

[1]Murdoch's prediction has not come true. Even today, average Black scores on most IQ tests are below those of Whites by approximately 15 to 18 points. Specifically, in their extensive review of *The Bell Curve* (Herrnstein & Murray, 1994), Fischer et al. (1996) stated, "Asians score slightly higher than whites and blacks consistently score about fifteen points below whites" (p. 220). In his review of Jensen's (1998) *The g Factor: The Science of Mental Ability*, Rushton (1998) wrote, "*The g Factor* fully documents that, on average, the American Black population scores below the White population by about 1.2 standard deviations, equivalent to 18 points" (p. 230).

Gilbert Brown (1922) noted group differences in retardation observed between children attending schools in a number of cities in northern Michigan. He conducted a study "to determine whether or not the differences in retardation might be the result of differences in intelligence" (Brown, 1922, p. 324). He used the Stanford Revision of the Binet Scale (p. 324) as his measure of intelligence. Children of immigrant parents from nine European countries were tested. Brown reported "that all the Germanic groups—Norwegian, German, Swede, English, and Austrian—test higher than any of the non-Germanic groups. This agrees with results obtained by the army" (p. 326). Three of the non-Germanic groups—French, Finnish, and Slovak—scored somewhat below the Germanic groups, but the median score of the Italians, 77.5, was significantly below that of the other groups, especially the Germanic group, with 76.56% of the Italians scoring below normal. Brown sought supportive evidence for his findings by citing another study (citation not provided by Brown) that tested 1,700 children of immigrant parents, also conducted in northern Michigan, that ranked the groups "very closely" to his rankings (p. 326). Brown proposed that his finding of between-group intelligence differences "tends to confirm the belief held by many that the best type of immigrant comes from the countries of northern Europe" (p. 326).

Brown arrived at two conclusions. First, lower "intelligence" immigrants, that is, non-Germanic groups and presumably especially Italians, contribute to increases in social ills. "This would be expected since it seems well established that a rather high correlation exists between low intelligence, on the one hand and crime and pauperism" (Brown, 1922, p. 327). Second, he warned that future generations of Americans would likely suffer from lowered intelligence given that lower intelligence groups tend to have larger families than do higher intelligence groups.[2]

Regarding possible effects of language differences between groups, Brown (1922) stated that after 1 to 2 years of schooling in America, most of the children tested "as high" when the test was administered in either language, but he failed to define what constituted "high." He stated, "Of course, there were some exceptions to this general principle, since children vary greatly in their ability to learn language" (Brown, 1922, p. 324). Although Brown basically dismissed it, the issue of English proficiency was likely a significant factor in the observed IQ differences. "Not infrequently we found children who, although

---

[2]Other more recent writers continue to make the claim that less intelligent individuals tend to marry and thus perpetuate genes for low intelligence in their offspring, a condition labeled the *dsygenic prediction* (e.g., see Shockley, 1971c, 1971d). This has not happened, given that intelligence, when defined as a score on an IQ test, has been shown to increase across generations, e.g. Shaffer and Kipp (2010); thus, this debate will continue for the foreseeable future.

they spoke the English language fairly well, tested six to eighteen months higher when their native language was employed" (Brown, 1922, pp. 324–325). This is a significant improvement that Brown failed to address. Parental SES and education level were two other major confounds in Brown's study. "The extremely low intelligence quotients of the Italians may be accounted for in part by the fact that the children tested belonged to two mining locations in which the work pursued by men is unusually slavish" (Brown, 1922, p. 326). According to Brown, some of the employers commented on the low intelligence of the workers. One employer "stated frankly that men of higher intelligence would not remain in the location because of the character of the work" (Brown, 1922, p. 326).

In summary, we discussed Murdoch (1920) and Brown (1922) to provide a sampling of the typical studies of the time that explored racial/ethnic group differences in "intelligence" between recent immigrants and more established earlier immigrant groups. Although not the focus of the studies, it is likely that language differences, SES, and time from immigration among the groups were major confounds in the findings. See Cummins (1976), Hakuta and Diaz (1984), Náñez (2010), and Peal and Lambert (1962) for detailed discussions of the methodological, SES, and other confounds and the inadequate measures of bilingualism that plagued early studies of racial and ethnic differences in IQ and bilingualism.

Research on Intelligence and Bilingualism: Early Studies

When researchers began searching for group intelligence differences, they adopted IQ tests to measure intelligence. The tests were erroneously presumed to be unbiased indices of intellectual abilities and therefore good psychometric tools for documenting group intellectual differences. The goal was to use IQ test results to support passage of sociopolitically driven legislation to curtail or altogether halt immigration from southern and eastern European groups, most of which were non-English- or limited-English-speaking immigrants from nonnative-English-speaking countries.

Over time, a variety of IQ tests have been used. For example, Yerkes (1921) developed a test to distinguish "simpletons" from the "cream of the crop" among U.S. Army recruits (Gould, 1993; Yzquierdo McLean, 1995). The Army Alpha test was used with literate recruits and the Beta test with illiterate recruits. Some of the potential soldiers did not speak English and hence scored zero on the test that was administered in English. Yzquierdo McLean (1995, p. 2) stated, "Consequently, Yerkes categorized many immigrants as 'simpletons' for receiving zeros on the test because they were unable to speak English, could not read, and were unfamiliar with the American culture (Tyack, 1974)." Other researchers followed suit, and this resulted in IQ tests being used widely to document racial and ethnic differences in IQ (intelligence). These researchers simply ignored the fact that the recruits were limited-English or non-English speakers who were administered IQ tests in English. That the researchers knew better (i.e., possessed methodological knowledge) would suggest that they believed in their findings of racial and ethnic differences in IQ (intelligence) or succumbed to sociopolitical pressure to find research evidence for restricting immigration among some racial/ethnic groups. Table 4.1 lists some of the most often used IQ and creativity tests that have historically been used to measure racial and ethnic differences in intelligence.

TABLE 4.1
Commonly Used IQ Tests

Test	Researcher(s) & Publication Year(s)	Test Author(s) & Test Edition	Measures
Part I: Selected early IQ/Intelligence* Studies			
Binet-Stanford Revision	Dickson (1917) Brown (1922) Pintner & Keller (1922) Sheldon (1924) Yeung (1921)	Terman (1916) " " " "	IQ/Intelligence
Pressey Group Intelligence Test	Murdoch (1920) Peterson (1923)	Pressey & Pressey (1918) Pressey & Pressey (1919)	Intelligence and cognitive disability
Army Alpha and Beta	Young (1922)	Yoakam & Yerkes (1920)	Military placement/ verbal and perform- ance tests
Pintner Non-Language Test	Symonds (1924)	Pintner (1919)	Reading/ language impairment
Part II: Selected IQ/Intelligence Studies, 1960s–present			
Stanford-Binet	Peña & Quinn (1997)	Thorndike, Hagen, & Sattler (1986)	IQ/Intelligence
Wechsler Adult Intelligence Scale (WAIS)	Siegel, Minshew, & Goldstein (1996) Campbell & McCord (1999) Villemarette-Pittman, Standford, & Greve (2003) Borghese & Gronau (2005)	Wechsler (1981) " Wechsler (1997) "	IQ/Intelligence

TABLE 4.1
Commonly Used IQ Tests   *(Continued)*

Test	Researcher(s) & Publication Year(s)	Test Author(s) & Test Edition	Measures
Wechsler Intelligence Scale for Children– Revised (WISC-R)	Sandoval (1982) Juan-Espinosa et al. (2000) " Murphy & Dodd (2010)	Wechsler (1974) " TEA SA (1993) Orsini (1993) Wechsler (1991)	IQ/Intelligence
Wechlser Intelligence Preschool & Primary Scale of Intelligence– Revised (WPPSI-R)	diSibio & Whalen (2000) Juan-Espinosa et al. (2000) " "	Wechsler (1989) Wechsler (1974) TEA SA (1993) Orsini & Picone (1996)	IQ/Intelligence
Peabody Picture Vocabulary Test	Villemarette-Pittman, Stanford, & Greve (2003) Caesar & Kohler (2007) LaCroix (2008) Murphy & Dodd (2010)	Dunn & Dunn (1997) " " "	IQ/Intelligence
Raven's Progressive Matrices	Zaidel et al. (1981) Náñez & Padilla (1993;1995) Prabhakaran et al. (1997) Rushton & Cvorovic (2009)	Raven (1965) Raven's Set I (1958); Set II: (1976) Raven (1965), Raven (1976) Raven (1998)	IQ/Intelligence

Note: Part I adapted from "Racial Differences in the Intelligence of School Children," by F. L. Goodenough, 1926, *Journal of Experimental Psychology, 9*, pp. 389–390. In the public domain.
*IQ tests used as measures/indicators of "intelligence".

According to Tyack (1974), Yerkes tested some 1.75 million men in his effort to provide the U.S. Army with an efficient way to screen large numbers of recruits in a short time, thus institutionalizing the use of group IQ tests. The test provided the army with a method to distinguish between recruits to be assigned to the enlisted ranks and those assigned to the officer corps. Soon the tests were being applied in educational settings to distinguish intelligence levels between students. For example, in the field of education, Yerkes was invited by educational institutions to create an adapted version of the army test for evaluating schoolchildren, including those from different language groups. Yzquierdo McLean (1995) wrote,

> Educational placements and entitlements for students have been determined by standardized testing for over 100 years (Tyack 1974). Educational concerns of students from culturally and linguistically diverse (CLD) backgrounds appeared to be unimportant during the turn of the century. During this historically formative period of education in the United States, debates about a national language ensued. As the number of students increased and the limits of public budgets decreased, testing was used to group students for differential instruction based on the relatively meager training of teachers. Intelligence tests were widely used as a measure of educational input to sort pupils so they could be efficiently educated according to their future roles in society (Cremlin, 1961). Testing proved a convenient instrument of social control for superintendents in the late 19th century who sought to use tests as a mean for creating the "one best system" of education (Tyack, 1974). Proponents of IQ tests argued that the use of testing as a tool for tracking students would enhance social justice. (p. 1)

Researchers (e.g., Goodenough, 1926) used the army's findings of IQ differences between native and "foreign-born" White groups and "negroes" (see Brigham, 1923) to buttress their claims of low intelligence among immigrant adults and their children. Goodenough's and many early researchers' negative findings of racial and ethnic differences on IQ tests provided ample fodder to fuel the flame that had been set, fed, and tended to over time by anti-immigration proponents in elected and research positions and among the public.

Specifically, a number of studies conducted in the 1920s just before and soon after passage of the 1924 Immigration Restriction Act (Graham, 1925; Goodenough, 1926; Rigg, 1928; Saer, 1923; Wang, 1926) reported a negative correlation between IQ and bilingualism. Several studies from the 1930s to the 1950s reported similar correlations (Altus, 1953; Darcy, 1946; Pintner, 1932; Thompson, 1952). Typical of researchers' commentaries and conclusions during the early days were Goodenough's (1926) statements such as the following:

> Use of a foreign language in the home is one of the chief factors in producing mental retardation as measured by intelligence tests. A more probable explanation is that those nationality-groups whose average intellectual ability is inferior do not readily learn the new language. (pp. 392–393).
>
> It seems probable, upon the whole, that inferior environment is an effect at least as much as it is a cause of inferior ability, as the latter is indicated by intelligence tests. The person of low intelligence tends to gravitate to those neighborhoods where the economic requirement is minimal; and, once there, he reacts toward his surroundings along the line of least resistance. His children inherit his mental characteristics. (p. 391)

The last part of the statement referred to group differences between Blacks, Jews, Chinese, and Japanese. According to Goodenough (1926), these groups experienced similar or more racial prejudice and slum living conditions, but the latter three groups tended to get out of these living conditions, whereas many Blacks did not. For Goodenough, if the differences were not due to race or prejudice, then they must be due to inherited intellectual inferiority, which parents pass on to their offspring. Goodenough failed to recognize that Blacks and other groups differ in skin color, which is a strong factor in racial, ethnic, and social discrimination. Her simplistic view was shared by a number of researchers of her time. Some well-known researchers were among those who subscribed to such discriminatory stereotypes. (For example, Goodenough became an icon in child development research; Yerkes gained fame for developing group IQ testing methodology and the Yerkes–Dobson law of physiological arousal.) Note, as stated in footnote 2, that this view continues to be prominent among researchers who tout racial and ethnic differences in IQ as irrefutable evidence for "real" intellectual differences (e.g., Jensen, 1975; Nyborg & Jensen, 2000; Rushton, 1998; Rushton & Jensen, 2005; Shockley, 1971c).

Although many of the early studies concluded that bilingual speakers were intellectually inferior to monolingual English speakers, collectively, they suffered numerous methodological weaknesses because the researchers failed to control for important confounding factors. Peal and Lambert's (1962) review of the literature identified a number of such weaknesses. Among other psychometric flaws mentioned earlier, different studies contained a variety of flaws, including lack of control for SES differences among the children's parents, failure to match subjects by age, lack of control for bilingual proficiency, or inadequate measures of bilingual ability (see Peal & Lambert, 1962, for a summary of early studies tainted by these confounds). Literature reviews subsequent to Peal and Lambert (e.g., Cummins, 1976; Diaz, 1985; Hakuta & Diaz, 1984) reported similar confounds to those in Peal and Lambert's list of methodological flaws. In his review, Náñez (2010) noted that "inadequate assessment of bilingual proficiency was common in early studies that tended to utilize bilingual subjects with declining first language (L1) proficiency. Cummins concludes that the studies failed to compare proficient bilinguals with monolinguals" (p. 84). Hakuta and Diaz (1984) reported that the findings of their literature review were in line with the earlier findings of both Peal and Lambert (1962) and Cummins (1976). According to Náñez (2010), Hakuta and Diaz's review

> of the early literature also found lax SES control and lack of adequate definitions of bilingualism. According to them [Hakuta and Diaz], bilingualism was "mostly assumed by foreignness of their parents." Further, "It is difficult to ascertain whether the bilingual subjects of many of the early studies were indeed bilingual or just monolingual of a minority language (p. 321)." (p. 84)

Náñez (2010) discussed three studies identified by Peal and Lambert (1962) as reporting a "lack of correlation between bilingualism and cognition" (p. 84). These studies also contained insufficient methodological control. Specifically, Darsie (1926) failed to control for social class of the subjects' families and for bilingual proficiency. Hill (1936) found no "difference in IQ between monolingual and bilingual Italian-American children." However, "Peal and Lambert (1962) pointed out that by matching mental age, in effect, Hill had controlled for possible language group differences in intelligence test scores" (Náñez, 2010, p. 85). The third study, Spoerl (1944), was also identified by Peal and Lambert (1962) as having adequate bilingualism control and found no group IQ differences. Interestingly, Spoerl included an "academic achievement" measure and found that the bilinguals outperformed the monolinguals on this measure. Perhaps this is the earliest documentation of the positive correlation between bilingualism and cognitive abilities.

Recent Studies

From Peal and Lambert's (1962) pivotal study to the present, research evidence overwhelmingly supports the view that when appropriate methodological control is provided, the relationship between bilingualism and a variety of cognitive factors is strongly positive. However, this has failed to quell opponents, as some researchers continue to support the negative relationship between bilingualism and cognition hypothesis. Marian (2008) cited evidence for both sides:

> If pressed, both sides can provide what appears to be convincing evidence supporting their position. There are, for instance, studies on the impact of bilingualism on cognitive development that point out that bilingualism in children is associated with increased metacognitive skills and superior divergent thinking ability (a type of cognitive flexibility) and with better performance on some perceptual tasks (such as recognizing a perceptual object "embedded" in a visual background) and classification tasks (for reviews, see Bialystok, 2001; Cummins, 1976; Diaz, 1983, 1985). There are also studies that suggest that bilingualism has a negative impact on language development and is associated with delay in lexical acquisition (e.g., Pearson, Fernández, & Oller, 1993; Umbel & Oller, 1995) and a smaller vocabulary than that of monolingual children (Verhallen & Schoonen, 1993; Vermeer, 1992). Both arguments are right in a sense, but . . . let's digress here to provide assurance that, by all accounts, bilingual children catch up with their monolingual counterparts on tests of verbal ability by the time they are in middle school, and well-controlled studies provide no evidence for lower intellectual abilities of bilingual children compared to monolinguals. (p. 25)

See Shaffer and Kipp (2010) for a list of other studies supporting the negative or positive hypotheses.

We favor the positive interaction between bilingualism and cognition hypothesis, because it pays more attention to adequate measurement of bilingualism in recent studies, which improves the power of current studies to detect the true impact of proficient bilingualism on cognitive processes (for reviews, see Cummins, 1976; Hakuta & Diaz, 1984; Náñez, 2010; Peal & Lambert, 1962). We agree with the view that evidence has convincingly tilted in favor of the positive interaction side. In fact, the positive relationship between bilingualism and cognition may be stronger than current evidence suggests. This is because, due to budgetary restrictions, schools cannot provide testing in the multiple heritage languages spoken by emergent bilingual children (Marian, 2008). There are, of course, the related problems of providing equal translations of IQ tests (some concepts do not translate well) and lack of adequate training for bilingual test administrators in the various languages (Marian, 2008). Thus, in many cases, IQ tests are administered in English (L2), in which the child's proficiency may not be as great as in his or her L1 proficiency. "As a result, children may be subject to academic placement below their appropriate level, handicapping their later academic advancement" (Marian, 2008, pp. 25–26). Chapter 5 of this volume addresses placement of bilingual children in lower achievement classrooms based on development of their reading skills.

PSYCHOMETRICS

The field of psychometrics has come a long way in the development and refinement of methodology in the past century. Aspiring bilingualism researchers should refer to Marian (2008) for an in-depth discussion of methodology in designing bilingual experiments and for choosing appropriate psychometric tools.

The search for group differences in intelligence is ongoing, but the focus of the research has split into two camps. One camp continues to focus on the traditional area of racial and ethnic differences in intelligence, as measured by IQ tests. For example, Rushton and Jensen (2005) reported a number of studies that found racial differences in external head size "using simple head size measures" and magnetic resonance imaging (MRI) studies that measured "brain volumes" (p. 253). Larger head size and volume were reported to correlate positively with higher IQ. (To sustain their argument, this camp must assume that an IQ score = intelligence, a premise many other researchers in the field do not accept.) Rushton and Jensen also cited an MRI study by Haier et al. (1995) that examined the "brain efficiency hypothesis." Specifically,

Haier et al. looked at brain volume and glucose uptake. They found evidence "suggesting that more intelligent individuals have more efficient brains because they use less energy in performing a given cognitive task" (Rushton & Jensen, 2005, pp. 253–254). See Rushton and Jensen (2005) for other studies.

The other camp focuses on searching for similarities and differences between monolingual and bilingual cognitive processes. For example, using functional MRI technology, Kim, Relkin, Lee, and Hirsch (1997) reported functional brain differences between early and late bilinguals. Bialystok et al. (2005) found functional differences between bilinguals and monolinguals on a reaction time conflict task. Mechelli et al. (2004) used voxel-based morphometry and recorded structural change (increased gray matter) between simultaneous (early) and sequential (late) bilinguals.

However, both sides still need to show that brain energy efficiency, functional and structural brain changes, and psychomotor activity (measured as reaction time differences) between bilingual and monolingual individuals correlated with performance on particular cognitive task(s) indicate greater overall intelligence.

The IQ Debate

The debate on IQ differences among racial and ethnic groups (based on IQ test scores) has ebbed and flowed since the 1920s. During the 1960s and 1970s, the debate centered on whether the observed racial and ethnic differences in IQ test scores constituted genetic indicators of intelligence differences or were the result of environmental factors. The debate flared with Jensen's (e.g., 1969) and Shockley's (e.g., 1971a, 1971b) proposal that IQ differences between Whites and Blacks have a strong genetic component. Jensen and his supporters made the case that IQ differences between Whites and Blacks are real (e.g., Jensen, 1975; Nyborg & Jensen, 2000; Rushton, 1998; Rushton & Jensen, 2005). They noted that American Blacks average significantly below their White counterparts on the g factor load on a variety of standardized IQ tests (e.g., Rushton & Jensen, 2005; see discussion of g below). Jensen contended, and his followers continue to do so, that the differences are not the outcome of IQ test bias in language, SES, or race and ethnicity.

Jensen and his supporters accepted Spearman's (1927) "hypothesis that variation in the size of the mean W-B [White–Black] difference on various cognitive tests is directly related to variation in the size of the tests' loadings on the g factor" (Nyborg & Jensen, 2000, p. 593). Note, g refers to Spearman's g, a general mental factor, that indicates performance on many cognitive/intellectual factors. Nyborg and Jensen (2000) found "nonsignificant and negligible W-B differences in the factor scores derived from PC2 (spatial + memory) and PC3 (motor dexterity and speed)" (pp. 598–599); however, their results on PC1 (*g* factor test) were similar to those found by 18 previous studies (PC1, PC2, and PC3 refer to principle components 1–3, respectively). Proponents seized upon the findings as gospel.

On the other side of the debate, Light and Smith (e.g., 1969, 1971) argued that Shockley and Jensen were wrong. They created a computer-generated model to show that the IQ differences could be explained on the basis of a 100% environmental contribution model. (For specifics of the debate, see Jensen, 1969; Shockley, 1971a, 1971b vs. Light & Smith, 1969, 1971.)

Recent publications such as Jensen's (1998) *The g Factor: The Science of Mental Ability*, Herrnstein and Murray's (1994) *The Bell Curve*, and Rushton's (1995) *Race, Evolution, and Behavior* have been touted as support for the existence of genetic differences in IQ. However, numerous researchers have continued to critique "Jensenism" (see Rushton, 1998, for the definition of *Jensenism* contained in Webster's Unabridged Dictionary). One influential work of Jensenism opponents is C. S. Fischer et al.'s (1996) critique of *The Bell Curve*. Below we borrow Fischer et al.'s conclusion as representative of the anti-Jensenism camp:

> *The Bell Curve* treatment of racial differences in intelligence is inflammatory and destructive. It is also wrong. Yes, blacks and Latinos consistently score below whites on standardized tests. But notions that this is a "natural" difference, one resulting from genetics, are inadequate. Individual blacks and Latinos confront these tests of school- and school-like knowledge burdened by centuries of disadvantage: family histories rooted in servitude, poverty, and cultural isolation. They also carry heavy disadvantages rooted in conditions today: continuing discrimination, low income, concentration in problem neighborhoods, and inferior schools, to name a few. Like other lower-caste groups around the world, their poor performance in school and school-like situations can be understood as the result of socioeconomic deprivation, segregation, and a stigmatized lower-caste identity. African Americans and Latino Americans score below whites because to be black or Latino in the United States is to be below whites.
>
> But the gap is closing, by the equivalent of several IQ points a generation, as it closed for other groups that moved from the periphery of American society toward its center. If we choose to exaggerate the remaining ethnic differences, to treat them as natural and inevitable, we will slow down the convergence. If we see, instead, that this inequality, like social inequality generally, is under our control, we can choose to close the gap more quickly. Our fate as a multiracial nation is not in our stars, to paraphrase Shakespeare, not in our genes, but in our hands. (pp. 202–203)

Other researchers and philosophers support this view in their writings. For example, see Gould's (1981/1993) influential book, *The Mismeasure of Man*. The revised edition (Gould, 1996) is subtitled *The Definitive Refutation of the Argument of* The Bell Curve. Also see Jacoby, Russell and Glauberman's (1995) *The Bell Curve Debate* and Kincheloe, Steinberg, and Gresson's (1996) *Measured Lies:* The Bell Curve *Examined.* For a summary of these publications, see Jacobs (1999).

Thus, the debate continues on what IQ measures, with both sides claiming victory. On the one hand, Rushton's (1998) statement may be considered representative of the stand taken by supporters of Jensenism:

> In recent years, the equalitarian dogma has run into some bad karma. In the wake of the success of the *Bell Curve* (Herrnstein and Murray, 1994), and other recent books about race (including my own) to provide race-realists answers to the question of differential group achievement, there has been an intense effort to get the "race genie" back in the bottle, to get the previously tabooed toothpaste back in the tube. By firmly establishing the psychometric, neurophysiological, behavior genetic, and comparative evidence for the existence and importance of Spearman's g, Jensen's *The g Factor* makes it near certain that such efforts will end up shredded by Occam's razor. (p. 232)

On the other hand, "equalitarians" counter that the narrow components of g should not be used to doom low-IQ individuals to classification for economic, social, or intellectual failure. They argue that attempts to measure intelligence should include broad measures such as those used in multiple intelligence tests (e.g., H. Gardner, 1999). C. S. Fischer et al.'s (1996) comments may be considered representative of equalitarian researchers and philosophers' views:

> We are impelled to write this book by the publication in late 1994 of *The Bell Curve*. That immensely well publicized book was then the latest statement of a philosophy that gained extensive credence in the 1990s: The widening inequalities among Americans that developed in the last quarter-century are inevitable. Because of human nature, because of the nature of the market, because of the nature of modern society, Americans will necessarily divide more and more by social class and race. We reject this philosophy. Besides being morally complacent, it is a doctrine without scientific foundation. Research has shown that "nature" determines neither the level of inequality in America nor which Americans in particular will be privileged or disprivileged; social conditions and national policies do. Inequality is in that sense designed. (p. xi)

BILINGUAL PSYCHOMETRICS

Researchers continue to explore the relationship between bilingualism and a variety of cognitive abilities, with a specific focus on comparisons between bilinguals/multilinguals and monolinguals. Their goal is to study the benefits, or lack thereof, of speaking multiple languages. Supporters of bilingual education use findings of positive interactions between bilingualism and cognitive abilities to advocate for best-practice-driven bilingual education, whereas opponents continue to search for research-based counterevidence, with the expressed goal of advocating for English-immersion (English-only) education for bilingual children. Although this debate is old and tired, the consequences are often not trivial. Minority, emerging bilingual, immigrant, and low-income children continue to be assigned to remedial, less-efficient educational settings, and college and university students from these groups continue to be significantly excluded from the best higher education institutions, and these facts serve as unequivocal evidence that lower scores on standardized tests still plague the U.S. educational system.

Table 4.2 in no way constitutes an exhaustive list of the psychometric tools used to assess bilingual proficiency and balance. It is provided for heuristic purposes for readers to sample the variety of tests that have been used in the conduct of bilingualism research.

Although important strides have been made in the development of appropriate tests and testing procedures for culturally and linguistically diverse students (Clifford et al., 2005; Paredes Scribner, 2002; Rhodes, Ochoa, & Ortiz, 2005), more research and development are still needed. Tests are still limited in terms of their overall number as well as the domains and skills they cover (Espinosa & López, 2006). Moreover, several tests developed for specific language minority groups are merely translations of original English versions, which tend to be based on European American cultural values. Their view of competence, in many cases, is simply not applicable to other groups with different backgrounds. As such, the content and construct validity of an English measure may not be the same when translated into Spanish. Furthermore, tests with appropriate psychometric properties should contain enough items to assess an identified skill and be standardized with representative samples of Latino and other language minority children from diverse national origins, language backgrounds, and socioeconomic conditions (Espinosa, 2010a).

The National Association for the Education of Young Children (2005) adopted a series of recommendations on the screening and assessment of young emergent bilingual students. These are particularly useful for those working with young Latino children.

The first recommendation is that assessments be guided by specific purposes with appropriate applications to meet the needs of the child. Assessments and screenings should be used to offer better services and to develop more informed interventions. This would encourage accountability systems to include bilingual students and to provide meaningful measures that improve learning outcomes, allowing useful accommodations where appropriate (Abedi, Hofstetter, & Lord, 2004).

TABLE 4.2
Commonly Used Language and Bilingualism Tests

Test	Researcher(s) & Publication Years(s)	Test Author(s) & Test Edition	Language(s)	Measures
Language Assessment Scale (LAS)	Gersten (1985)	Duncan & DeAvila (1977)	Spanish/ English	Language proficiency and language dominance
	Pray (2005)	Duncan & DeAvila (1990)	"	
Language Assessment Scale Oral (LAS-O)	Náñez & Padilla (1995)	Duncan & DeAvila (1969)	Spanish/ English	
Bilingual Verbal Ability Test (BVAT)	Borghese & Gronau (2005)	Munoz-Sandoval, Cummins, Alvarado, & Ruef (1998)	Spanish/ English	Bilingual verbal ability
	LaCroix (2008)	"		
Bilingual Syntax Measure (BSM)	Menke (2010)	Burt, Dulay, & Hernandez-Chavez (1978)	Spanish/ English	Language proficiency/ English as Second Language (ESL) placement
Clinical Evaluation of Language Fundamentals-Revised (CELF-R)	Ballantyne, Spilkin, & Trauner (2007)	Semel et al. (1997)	Spanish/ English	Language and com-munication disorders
	Murphy & Dodd (2010)	Semel et al. (2006)	"	
Clinical Evaluation of Language Fundamentals (CELF-3)	Ballantyne, Spilkin, & Trauner (2007)	Semel et al. (1995)	Spanish/ English	

Second, instruments used to assess young bilingual students should align with the specific cultural and linguistic characteristics of the child being assessed. This means that the cultural and linguistic content and context of the tests should be congruent with the child's background.

Third, the main purpose of assessment should be to improve children's learning and development. For this to occur, multiple methods, measures, and informants should be incorporated in an assessment of the child's ongoing performance, given the curricular content and instructional approaches used in class.

Fourth, formal standardized assessments should be used with a clear understanding of the intent and limitations of the assessment. Formal assessments may be appropriate to identify disabilities, evaluate programs (for accountability purposes), and monitor and improve individual learning. However, test developers, evaluators, and decision makers should be aware of the limitations and biases introduced by many of these tests (e.g., sampling and norming, test equivalence, test administration, test content).

Fifth, those conducting assessments should have cultural and linguistic competence, knowledge of the child being assessed, and specific assessment-related knowledge and skills. It is important to remember that assessments are more likely to be reliable when carried out by teams of professionals who are bicultural, bilingual, and knowledgeable about first- and second-language acquisition.

Last, families of young emergent bilingual students should play critical roles in the assessment process. Parents (or legal guardians) should be queried as sources of data and should be involved in the interpretation of comprehensive assessments. In addition, parents (or legal guardians) should always be aware of the reasons for the assessment, the procedures involved, and the significance of the outcomes. Their voices should be sought out and influence program placement and other intervention strategies (Lazarin, 2005).

It is also important that conceptual and empirical work on student assessment move beyond the individual level. Most of the discussions in the assessment literature focus on processes and outcomes within the individual, assessing language, cognitive development, academic learning, and so forth. With this knowledge base, teachers and schools are expected to adjust aspects of the environment to improve learning. While it has become clear that processes outside the individual—including within the classroom (e.g., teacher–student interactions, peer–peer interactions), the home (e.g., frequency of words spoken, amount of books), and within the school (e.g., language instruction policies)—affect learning, the assessment field lacks conceptual frameworks and the measures necessary to move research forward to systematically improve student learning. Preliminary research on the role of context in learning suggests that variations in environmental factors can increase student engagement and participation (Christenson, 2004; Goldenberg, Rueda, & August, 2006), which, in turn, can lead to increased learning; that is, the influence of contextual contingencies on learning outcomes is mediated by children's motivation to learn (Rueda, 2007; Rueda, MacGillivray, Monzó & Arzubiaga, 2001; Rueda & Yaden, 2006). Conceptual frameworks should account for the multilevel nature of contexts associated with language development and use, including the nesting of individuals within classrooms and families, class-rooms within schools, and schools within school districts, communities, and institutions. Moreover, the role of culture and the feasibility of cultural congruence across within- and out-of-school contexts will be important to this work. Meaningful empirical work in this area will require the convergence of research methods (e.g., multilevel statistics and the mixing of qualitative approaches with quasi-experimental designs) and social science disciplines (e.g., cognitive psychology, educational anthropology, sociology of education).

CONCLUSION

With regard to bilingual intelligence testing, we echo C. S. Fischer et al.'s (1996) comments and reinforce the call for fairness in testing. If IQ tests are used to evaluate bilingual children's intellectual abilities, the extensive methodological problems reported in this chapter, dating back to Peal and Lambert (1962), must be addressed before one can assume that IQ tests are fair indicators of bilingual and monolingual intelligence similarities or differences. If IQ tests are to be used with bilingual children, researchers must take into account bilingual balance and proficiency and ensure that the tests tap multiple intelligence indicators.

Psychometricians also need to exercise great caution and restraint regarding their interpretation of how environmental factors affect cognitive outcomes. For example, Espinosa (2010a) stated that while there is a growing number of psychometric tools (especially in Spanish) designed to gauge cognitive similarities and differences between monolinguals and emergent bilinguals, and while those in use are continually being refined, the new research findings gained from such tools should be integrated with information on sociocultural and socioeconomic factors, to gain greater insight into the emergent bilingual child's cognitive abilities. Researchers need to investigate the interaction between these factors and how the investigation affects the emergent bilingual's linguistic and cognitive development. Thus, according to bilingual education experts like Espinosa, research has a long way to go in informing our understanding of the myriad environmental factors (not to mention genetic factors) that interact to determine emergent bilingual children's language and cognitive/intellectual development processes and outcomes.

Genesee (2010) contended that educators' and policymakers' lack of understanding of what constitutes "normal" bilingual development may lead them to the erroneous conclusion that some bilingual characteristics constitute delay or lag (and thus cognitive deficits) in linguistic achievement relative to monolinguals. For example, while emergent bilinguals may possess fewer words in L1 or L2 compared with monolinguals, this in fact constitutes normal bilingual linguistic development and is not a cognitive deficit. Genesee indicated that a better comparison would be to combine the number of words in the bilingual's two languages:

> A lack of understanding of what can be expected of young dual language learners may lead evaluation or educational specialists to interpret a bilingual child's language performance as symptomatic of delay or even impairment when, in fact, it is typical of dual language learning. (p. 60)

Thus, cognitive abilities in bilinguals are the results of the interaction of genetic–environmental factors that is much too complex to be measured by current psychometric tools such as IQ tests. Because of the many ethnic, cultural, and SES factors that form an intricate interaction with genetic factors to influence the emergent bilingual's cognitive and intellectual abilities, psychometricians should conduct their work with great caution, cultural sensitivity, and responsibility as they investigate bilingual psychometrics.

What does the future hold for measurement of intelligence and bilingualism? And where do we go from here to advance knowledge concerning the relationship between intellectual/cognitive processes and bilingualism? Researchers interested in exploring the bilingual–cognition relationship at the functional and structural levels of the brain can use neuroimaging, including the various brain-imaging technologies available (see Náñez, 2010). According to Náñez (2010), "Neuroimaging methodology shows significant promise for gaining increased understanding concerning *where* (brain areas), *what* (specific neurons or neural networks) are involved, and *how* (functional and structural changes) bilingual processing occurs" (p. 89).

Recent neuroimaging studies have begun to reveal real- or near-real-time images of the monolingual and bilingual brain at work. For example, Bialystok et al. (2005) used magnetoencephalography recordings to measure problem-solving differences between bilinguals and monolinguals on the Simon task, a measure of a subject's reaction time to congruent and incongruent trials presented on a computer monitor. Kim et al. (1997) discovered differences in Broca's area but not Wernicke's area function between simultaneous bilinguals and later bilinguals. Mechelli et al. (2004) observed differences in gray matter (involved in cognitive power) between the brains of early and later bilinguals. See Náñez (2010) for a detailed discussion of these studies (Bialystok et al, 2005, Kim et al., 1997, and Mechelli et al., 2004).

These studies are among the first to begin transforming the research agenda concerning the relationship between bilingualism and cognition beyond the traditional genetic–environmental debate. Neuroimaging promises to inform basic and applied research on the function of children's brains and how the brain responds to different environmental experiences, such as learning multiple languages and exposure to enriched educational experiences (e.g., sustained high-quality early bilingual education). If a picture is worth a thousand words, perhaps the images of differences in brain function and structure resulting from exercising the language centers of the brain will finally convince educators, administrators, and policymakers to support high-quality, sustained bilingual education for all of America's children.

II

EDUCATION

Demographic data presented in the chapters in Part I demonstrate that bilingual children in the United States are exposed, at various levels, to more than one language in the home, and that the home environment is one likely to be characterized by aspects of the immigrant experience as well as other educational risk factors, such as poverty, diminished parental education background, and so on. These circumstances are important given that home language practices–different from language use—are highly relevant to early literacy outcomes (Goldenberg, Rueda, & August, 2006; Nord, Lennon, Liu, & Chandler, 1999; Tabors, 1997; Tabors & Snow, 2002). Moreover, given that higher order cognitive and literacy skills tend to transfer from the native language to the second language (August, Calderón, & Carlo, 2002; Genesee, 2003; Genesee, Geva, Dressler, Kamil, 2006; Goldenberg, Rezaei, & Fletcher, 2005; see Chapters 3 and 7, this volume), it is critical that educators adequately assess, develop, and leverage the child's non-English native language skills. This means tailoring instruction, curricular content, and schooling practices in general to meet the child's particular language development circumstances—based on individual, school, and family factors—as well as the social and cultural contexts to take full advantage of the child's home resources and parental support (García, 2005; Genesee et al., 2006; Goldenberg, Gallimore, Reese, & Garnier, 2001; Goldenberg et al., 2006; Reese, Garnier, Gallimore, & Goldenberg, 2000; Scheffner Hammer & Miccio, 2004; Shannon, 1995). In this section, we discuss the present status of bilingual student academic achievement levels, including early literacy skills, and discuss how theories, practices, and policies play a part in these outcomes. We comb the literature to highlight which programs work and, more specifically, the features and strategies of the most effective programs used to leverage young bilingual children's strengths to produce the most favorable outcomes. We include in our discussion potential directions that can best serve the early educational needs of bilingual children in the United States.

5

EDUCATION CIRCUMSTANCES

The overall population of children speaking a non-English native language in the United States rose from 6% in 1979 to 14% in 1999 (National Clearinghouse for English Language Acquisition, 2006), with the K–12 population of these children estimated to be more than 14 million (August & Shanahan, 2006). The representation of bilingual children in U.S. schools has its highest concentration in early education. The bilingual share of students from prekindergarten to Grade 5 rose from 4.7% to 7.4% from 1980 to 2000, whereas the bilingual share of students in Grades 6 to 12 rose from 3.1% to 5.5% during the same time period (Capps et al., 2005). Young bilinguals (ages 0–8 years), therefore, have been the fastest growing student population in the United States over the past few decades (Hernandez, Denton, & Macartney, 2008).

EARLY ACHIEVEMENT

One cannot fully understand the academic performance patterns of bilingual students as a whole without taking into consideration their social and economic characteristics in comparison with native English speakers

(Jensen, 2008a). Although a great deal of socioeconomic variation exists among children from bilingual families, they are more likely than native English-speaking children, on average, to live in poverty and to have parents with limited formal education (García & Cuellar, 2006). In addition, bilingual students are more likely to be members of an ethnic or racial minority (Capps et al., 2005). Each of these factors—low income, low parent education, and ethnic or racial minority status—decreases group achievement averages across academic areas, leading to the relatively low performance of bilingual students.

Currently, bilingual students lag behind their monolingual same-age and same-grade peers at all proficiency levels of reading and mathematics (by at least a half of a standard deviation) at the beginning and throughout K–12 schooling (Braswell, Daane, & Grigg, 2003; García, Jensen, Miller, & Huerta, 2005; García & Miller, 2008; National Center for Education Statistics, 2003; Reardon & Galindo, 2006a). Educational achievement patterns of virtually all racial and ethnic groups are established during the early years of school and change little thereafter. Although some of the difference between racial and ethnic groups is accounted for by socioeconomic differences among groups (on average, bilingual students have lower socioeconomic status [SES] than monolingual White and Asian American students), much of it is not (Reardon & Galindo, 2006a). Using data from the Early Childhood Longitudinal Study, Kindergarten Cohort (ECLS-K; National Center for Education Statistics, 2001), Reardon and Galindo (2006b) found that bilingual children scored 0.3 to 0.5 of a standard deviation lower in mathematics and reading than their monolingual White peers within all five SES quintiles (SES in ECLS-K is a composite of household income and parents' level of education and occupation). Hence, race/ethnicity had a substantial effect on early achievement over and above SES. In a separate analysis of ECLS-K data, Reardon (2003) noted that these achievement differences by SES and race/ethnicity from kindergarten through first grade were attributable to processes within, between, and out of schools. That is, practices in the home (including the use of a non-English language in the home) and the school bear meaningful influences on the racial/ethnic and SES achievement gaps in early education (García, Jensen, & Cuéllar, 2006).

Reardon and Galindo (2006b) also found that reading and mathematics achievement patterns from kindergarten through third grade varied by home language environments. Emergent bilingual Latino children living in homes in which primarily Spanish or only Spanish was spoken lagged further behind monolingual White children in reading and mathematics than did Latino children who lived in homes in which primarily English or English only was spoken. García (1983) documented the low literacy levels of children from Spanish-speaking homes more than 2 decades ago. The impact of language background on achievement outcomes should not be surprising, given the relationship between SES and achievement and the positive correlation between low SES and non-English language use in homes of young Spanish-speaking children in the United States (Collier, 1987). Nonetheless, it does highlight the academic risk faced by young bilinguals who come from homes in which little or no English is spoken, which has been documented as early as the preschool years (National Center for Education Statistics, 1995).

Not all young bilinguals are equally at risk for academic underachievement and reading difficulties. In their analyses of group differences in mathematics and reading outcomes from kindergarten through third grade, Reardon and Galindo (2006b) found that Latino bilingual children from Mexican, Central American, and Puerto Rican ethnic backgrounds scored lower than those from South American and Cuban backgrounds, and first- and second-generation children from Mexican backgrounds scored lower than those from third or more generation Mexican American children. In addition, achievement differences between Whites and Latinos were found within SES quintiles, suggesting that the difference is due to more than just poverty. Indeed, early risk is attributable to a combination of factors. A report by the National Center for Education Statistics (1995; NCES) on the prevalence of selected accomplishments and difficulties in a national sample of children ages 3 to 5 years found that small motor skills and signs of emerging literacy skills varied by several family characteristics. The NCES report specifically identified five family risk factors to be associated with fewer accomplishments and more difficulties: (a) The mother has less than a high school education; (b) the family is below the official poverty line; (c) the mother speaks a language other than English as her main language; (d) the mother was unmarried at the time of the child's birth; and (e) only one parent is present in the home. The report highlighted that greater risk was associated with a higher number of prevalent risk factors.

> In general, the more risk factors the child is subject to, the lower the number of accomplishments and the higher the number of difficulties he or she is likely to have exhibited. Compared to children from families with no risk factors, twice as many 4-year-olds from families with three or more risk factors have short attention spans (37 percent versus 17 percent) and nearly double the number are said to be very restless (41 percent versus 22 percent). Three times as many speak in a way that is not understandable to strangers (14 percent versus 5 percent) or stutter or stammer (16 percent versus 5 percent). Almost five times as many are in less than very good health (23 percent versus 5 percent). Four-year-olds from families with three or more risk factors have nearly one-and-a-half *fewer* literacy accomplishments (an average of 2.5 out of five) than those from families with no risk factors (who have an average of 3.9 accomplishments). (pp. vi–vii)

The more risk factors the child is subject to, the lower the probability the child will do well in school in terms of learning and attainment in the standard educational environment. Because bilingual children, on average, exhibit three of the five above-mentioned risk factors at higher rates than native English speakers, they are generally at greater risk for academic under-achievement (Hernandez et al., 2008). Using the U.S. Census Bureau (2000) data, Capps et al. (2005) found that 68% of emergent bilingual students in pre-K through fifth grade lived in low-income families, compared with 36% of English-proficient monolingual children. The percentages changed to 60% and 32%, respectively, for sixth- to 12th-grade students. Moreover, 48% of bilingual children in pre-K through fifth grade and 35% of bilinguals in the higher grades had a parent with less than a high school education, compared with 11% and 9% of English-proficient children in the same grades (Capps et al., 2005).

However, this view of educational risk typically overshadows the relative strengths that students bring to schools (García & Jensen, 2007a). Children of immigrants, for example, are more likely than children in native families to live with two parents and with siblings who may serve as an asset to their educational success (Hernandez et al., 2008). Particularly for students with origins in Mexico, Central America, the Dominican Republic, Haiti, Indochina, and Afghanistan, bilinguals are also more likely than their native English-speaking monolingual peers to have a grandparent or other relative in the home, which can buffer expenses such as child care. Additional analyses of census data show that parents of bilingual students have a relatively stronger work ethic than U.S.-born parents (Hernandez et al., 2008).

RACIAL/ETHNIC/BILINGUAL READING READINESS AND READING ACHIEVEMENT PATTERNS

The data presented in this section describe reading achievement patterns at the various school levels, beginning at the start of kindergarten. Among the key findings are that (a) on average, African American and Latino children, particularly bilingual Latino students, lag well behind monolingual Whites and Asians on measures of reading readiness at the start of kindergarten; (b) among Latino children who speak some English at the start of kindergarten, the reading gaps with monolingual Whites and Asians close somewhat over the K–5 years, although in absolute terms the gaps remain substantial; and (c) low-SES Latino children who speak little or no English at the start of kindergarten are reading at very low levels on average at the end of the fifth grade.

Elementary School Readiness and Achievement Patterns

One of the best current sources of information on the reading readiness and early reading achievement of American youngsters is the ECLS-K of 1998–1999 (National Center for Education Statistics, 2001), which followed a large national sample of children who enrolled in kindergarten for the first time in fall 1998. Reading proficiency data are now available from the start of kindergarten through the end of the fifth grade (see Table 5.1).

Table 5.1 shows that the overall English reading readiness patterns of African American and Latino children at the start of kindergarten were well below those of non-Latino White and Asian American children. The data indicate that Black and Latino children were further behind Asian American and White children at the start of kindergarten. For example, 20% of African

TABLE 5.1

Percentages of Hispanic, White, Black, and Asian American Students Scoring at or Above Levels 1, 2, 3, and 4 in Reading at the Start of Kindergarten Overall and by SES Quintile

Group	Level 1	Level 2	Level 3	Level 4
70% of Hispanics English proficient, fall K	54	20	10	2
First (lowest) SES quintile	37	8	3	0
Second SES quintile	54	17	8	1
Third SES quintile	54	20	11	3
Fourth SES quintile	72	33	17	2
Fifth (highest) SES quintile	73	41	25	5
All third-generation Whites	73	34	20	4
First (lowest) SES quintile	48	13	5	0
Second SES quintile	60	20	10	1
Third SES quintile	69	29	16	3
Fourth SES quintile	80	38	21	3
Fifth (highest) SES	86	50	33	8
All third-generation Blacks	56	20	10	1
First (lowest) SES quintile	43	9	3	0
Second SES quintile	52	12	5	1
Third SES quintile	63	26	13	1
Fourth SES quintile	79	43	26	4
Fifth (highest) SES quintile	84	31	20	3
All Asian Americans[a]	75	42	27	8

Note. SES = socioeconomic status; Level 1 = recognizing letters and sounds; Level 2 = understanding beginning sound of words; Level 3 = understanding ending sounds of words; Level 4 = comprehending what is read. Reprinted from *A Reading-Focused Early Childhood Education Research and Strategy Development Agenda for African Americans and Hispanics at All Social Class Levels Who Are English Speakers or English Language Learners* (p. 13), by L. S. Miller and E. E. Garcia, 2008, Tempe, AZ: Arizona State University. Copyright 2008 by Arizona State University. Reprinted with permission.
[a]The sample of Asian American children in the Early Childhood Longitudinal Study, Kindergarten Cohort was too small to break down by SES quintile.

American and Latino children understood beginning sounds of words (Level 2) at the start of kindergarten, compared with 42% of the Asian American and 34% of the White children.

It is important to note, however, that these data exclude about 30% of the Latino children and 19% of the Asian children in the ECLS-K sample because they did not have strong enough oral English skills to be given the English reading assessment that was used in the study at that time. That is to say, these Latino and Asian children were English-language learners with little or no knowledge of English when they entered kindergarten.

The data in Table 5.1 also show that in addition to having markedly lower overall reading scores at the start of kindergarten than Asian American and White children, Latino and African American children also lagged somewhat behind White children in most SES quintiles (i.e., there were within-class gaps). For example, 13% of White children in the first (lowest) SES quintile scored at Level 2 (understanding beginning sounds of words), compared with 9% of the African American children and 8% of the Latino children. In the fifth (highest) SES quintile, 33% of the White, 25% of the Latino, and 20% of the African American children scored at Level 3 (understanding ending sounds of words). Over the five SES quintiles, the within-class reading readiness gaps between Latinos and Whites were one eighth to two fifths of a standard deviation, whereas the within-class gaps between Blacks and Whites were somewhat smaller (Reardon & Galindo, 2006b).

The data in Table 5.2 show that the reading situation had changed considerably by the end of the fifth grade. Importantly, the 70% of the Latino children who had been assessed in English at the start of kindergarten demonstrated stronger reading skills than the African American youngsters at the end of the fifth grade, even though the Latino children continued to lag well behind the White and Asian American children. For instance, among the 70% of Latino children, 41% were proficient at evaluating and interpreting beyond text (Level 8), compared with 31% of the Black, 52% of the White, and 54% of the Asian American children.

It is unclear why the gap between Latino and White children grew smaller while the gap between Black and White children grew larger over the K–5 period. It is known that much of the improvement for the 70% of Latino children who had been assessed in English at the start of kindergarten was among students who had low reading readiness scores on the English assessment, that many of these children were from immigrant families, and that most of the gains relative to the White children took place during kindergarten and first grade (Reardon & Galindo, 2006b). An important aspect of the growth in the gaps is that they were centered on reading comprehension skills (e.g., evaluating and interpreting beyond text) rather than technical reading skills (e.g., understanding ending sounds of words). Reading compre-

TABLE 5.2
Percentages of Hispanic, White, Black, and Asian American Students
Scoring at or Above Levels 6, 7, 8, and 9 in Reading at the End of
Fifth Grade Overall and by SES Quintile

Group	Level 6	Level 7	Level 8	Level 9
30% of Hispanics not English proficient, Fall K	72	41	23	1
70% of Hispanics English proficient, Fall K	86	69	41	5
First (lowest) SES quintile	77	51	29	1
Second SES quintile	89	74	44	6
Third SES quintile	86	66	38	2
Fourth SES quintile	92	81	51	9
Fifth (highest) SES quintile	95	87	59	13
All third-generation Whites	91	79	52	10
First (lowest) SES quintile	73	51	30	3
Second SES quintile	86	68	40	4
Third SES quintile	91	77	48	7
Fourth SES quintile	94	86	55	9
Fifth (highest) SES quintile	96	91	64	20
All third-generation Blacks	78	53	31	2
First (lowest) SES quintile	70	39	23	2
Second SES quintile	76	52	30	2
Third SES quintile	83	59	33	2
Fourth SES quintile	88	72	44	7
Highest SES quintile	85	66	39	4
81% of Asian Americans English proficient, Fall K[a]	93	84	54	10

Note. SES = socioeconomic status; Level 6 = evaluating text; Level 7 = interpreting text; Level 8 = evaluating and interpreting beyond text; Level 9 = evaluating and interpreting text relevant to previous texts. Reprinted from *A Reading-Focused Early Childhood Education Research and Strategy Development Agenda for African Americans and Hispanics at All Social Class Levels Who Are English Speakers or English Language Learners* (p. 14), by L. S. Miller and E. E. Garcia, 2008, Tempe, AZ: Arizona State University. Copyright 2008 by Arizona State University. Reprinted with permission.
[a]The sample of Asian American children in the Early Childhood Longitudinal Study, Kindergarten Cohort was too small to break down by SES quintile.

hension in the fourth grade and beyond is heavily dependent on students' vocabularies and experiences with the use of words. Similarly, other data sets show large gaps at the start of kindergarten on vocabulary–word meaning dimensions (S. E. Duncan & Magnuson, 2005; Rock & Stenner, 2005).

Table 5.2 also includes fifth-grade reading data for the 30% of Latino children who did not know enough oral English at the start of kindergarten to be assessed at that point. This group of Latino children had about the same English reading proficiency pattern at the end of the fifth grade as the lowest SES quintile African American youngsters. (Most of the Latino emergent bilinguals also were from the lowest SES quintile; Reardon & Galindo, 2006b.) For example, Table 5.3 shows that 23% of the Latino emergent bilinguals demonstrated Level 8 reading proficiency, the same percentage as the

TABLE 5.3
Percentages of Fourth Graders in U.S. Public Schools Scoring at or Above Basic, Proficient, and Advanced Levels on the 2007 National Assessment of Educational Progress Reading Assessment, by Race/Ethnicity, Eligibility for Free or Reduced Lunch, and Language Status

Racial/ethnic group	Eligible for free or reduced lunch						Not eligible for free or reduced lunch					
	Emergent bilingual			Not emergent bilingual			Emergent bilingual			Not emergent bilingual		
	≥ Basic	≥ Proficient	Advanced	≥ Basic	≥ Proficient	Advanced	≥ Basic	≥ Proficient	Advanced	≥ Basic	≥ Proficient	Advanced
White	35.2	9.5	2.0	62.6	24.5	3.7	50.9	19.4	4.5	82.7	47.9	12.8
Black	35.4	12.1	1.4	40.2	10.2	1.0	48.0	12.3	0.7	62.2	24.6	4.0
Hispanic	25.1	4.8	0.3	57.0	18.6	2.6	32.5	7.7	1.0	71.1	32.6	6.2
Asian/Pacific Islander	42.5	12.6	1.7	71.5	35.9	8.2	60.9	24.7	4.4	87.3	57.5	20.7
Native American	17.7	2.9	0.1	47.3	16.3	2.9	NA	NA	NA	65.5	29.4	7.1

Note. Reprinted from A Reading-Focused Early Childhood Education Research and Strategy Development Agenda for African Americans and Hispanics at All Social Class Levels Who Are English Speakers or English Language Learners (p. 16), by L. S. Miller and E. E. Garcia, 2008, Tempe, AZ: Arizona State University. Copyright 2008 by Arizona State University. Reprinted with permission.

Black children in the lowest SES quintile. Thus, at the end of the fifth grade, both of these segments were doing less well in reading not only than the low-SES White children but also than the low-SES Latino children who were among the 70% of Latino children who had sufficiently strong oral English skills at the start of kindergarten to be assessed in it.

Reading Readiness and Reading Achievement Trends

There are no nationally representative standardized test trend data on reading readiness at the start of kindergarten or on reading achievement during the primary grades that focus specifically on bilingual students. The earliest point in the education system for which there are recent national trend data on reading achievement is the fourth grade, and those data are best understood with regard to bilingual students by assessing Latino student results. National Assessment of Educational Progress (NAEP) fourth-grade reading assessment data are available for 1992 to 2007. During that 15-year interval, the Black–White reading score gap was reduced modestly, whereas the Latino–White gap remained about the same size. Furthermore, the Black–White and Latino–White reading score gaps on the NAEP reading assessment for eighth graders were about the same in 2007 as they had been in 1992. There also were no changes among 12th graders (Lee, Grigg, & Dion, 2007; Lee, Grigg, & Donahue, 2007).

Although NAEP reading score gaps between Latinos and Whites have changed little since the early 1990s, the high level of Latino immigration during that period may be masking progress on an intergenerational basis. Many Latino newcomers to the United States are adults with little formal education, which is an important educational risk factor for their children, whether the latter are themselves immigrants (first generation) or U.S.-born (second generation). Third-generation Latino children (those with two U.S.-born parents) may fare better, because these youngsters' parents tend to have completed more years of schooling than their parents did. (Educational attainment data on this point are presented in the next section.)

ECLS-K data support this conclusion for the largest segment of Latino children, Mexican Americans. In the ECLS-K sample, third-generation Mexican American children had a somewhat higher level of reading readiness (in English) at the start of kindergarten and higher reading achievement at the end of the fifth grade than first- and second-generation Mexican American children. Table 5.4 presents data for beginning kindergartners, and Table 5.5 presents data for the end of the fifth grade.

The data in Table 5.4 probably underestimate the readiness and achievement differences between third-generation and first- and second-generation Mexican American children because the data exclude the Mexican Americans

TABLE 5.4

Percentages of Children Scoring at or Above Levels 1, 2, 3, and 4 in
Reading at the Start of Kindergarten: Third-Generation Whites and
First-, Second-, and Third-Generation Mexican Americans

Group	Level 1	Level 2	Level 3	Level 4
Third-generation Whites	73	34	20	4
Third-generation Mexican Americans	60	23	12	2
Second-generation Mexican Americans	43	14	8	2
First-generation Mexican Americans	42	14	6	0

Note. Level 1 = recognizing letters and sounds; Level 2 = understanding beginning sound of words; Level 3 = understanding ending sounds of words; Level 4 = comprehending what is read. Reprinted from *A Reading-Focused Early Childhood Education Research and Strategy Development Agenda for African Americans and Hispanics at All Social Class Levels Who Are English Speakers or English Language Learners* (p. 21), by L. S. Miller and E. E. Garcia, 2008, Tempe, AZ: Arizona State University. Copyright 2008 by Arizona State University. Reprinted with permission.

in the 30% of Latinos who had little or no knowledge of English at the start of kindergarten. That group was heavily first- and second-generation in its composition (Reardon & Galindo, 2006b).

The better outcomes for third-generation Mexican American children are related to the fact that they had a stronger family SES distribution than the first- and second-generation Mexican American children. For instance, more of the third-generation children were from families in the top two SES quintiles. Still, as Tables 5.4 and 5.5 show, third-generation Mexican American children lagged well behind third-generation White children in reading skills at the start of kindergarten and at the end of fifth grade. Consistent with these patterns, a smaller percentage of third-generation Mexican Americans than third-generation Whites were from families in the top two SES quintiles (Reardon & Galindo, 2006b).

TABLE 5.5

Percentages of Children Scoring at or Above Levels 6, 7, 8, and 9 in
Reading at the Start of Fifth Grade: Third-Generation Whites and
First-, Second-, and Third-Generation Mexican Americans

Group	Level 6	Level 7	Level 8	Level 9
Third-generation Whites	91	79	52	10
Third-generation Mexican Americans	89	72	43	5
Second-generation Mexican Americans	83	61	38	6
First-generation Mexican Americans	83	61	32	1

Note. Level 6 = evaluating text; Level 7 = interpreting text; Level 8 = evaluating and interpreting beyond text; Level 9 = evaluating and interpreting text relevant to previous texts. Reprinted from *A Reading-Focused Early Childhood Education Research and Strategy Development Agenda for African Americans and Hispanics at All Social Class Levels Who Are English Speakers or English Language Learners* (p. 21), by L. S. Miller and E. E. Garcia, 2008, Tempe, AZ: Arizona State University. Copyright 2008 by Arizona State University. Reprinted with permission.

Intergenerational Educational Advancement and Human Capital Accumulation Among Individuals, Families, and Racial/Ethnic/Linguistic Groups

The data showing different educational attainment patterns over a long period of time are important for understanding racial and ethnic group differences in children's reading readiness and reading achievement because human capital derived from formal schooling is invested in children both by the schools they attend and by their parents (and other adults and peers in their homes and communities). On average, families that have several generations of extensive access to formal schooling have much more intergenerational accumulated human capital to invest in their children than families that have had limited access to formal schooling over time (Miller, 1995).

This is most obvious in situations in which one group of parents includes many who are second- and third-generation college graduates and another group of parents includes many who have only completed grade school and whose parents and grandparents also had very limited formal schooling. However, substantial human capital differences can exist even when parents in each group have college degrees and the grandparents have had a fair amount of formal schooling as well. Differences in human capital in that case could occur when the quality of the schooling was much higher for one group in one or both generations, even though attainment levels were similar.

Differences in the amount and quality of formal schooling over time among groups in the United States can help shed light not only on the reading readiness and achievement differences between children from high- and low-SES families but also on the within-class differences in racial and ethnic achievement described in the data presented in previous sections of this chapter. For example, because Latino bilingual children have historically had much less access to formal education directly related to their language than monolingual English-speaking White children, and the schools, colleges, and universities that Latino bilingual children attended were generally much less well resourced, it would be surprising if there were not still differences in the amount of human capital possessed by young White and Latino college graduates. The lower college grade point averages (GPAs) of "minorities," relative to Whites, that have been documented over the past few decades are consistent with this long history of differences in educational opportunity (Bowen & Bok, 1998). As a result, college-educated Latino parents who have bilingual backgrounds in the United States evidently have less human capital, on average, to invest in their children than college-educated White parents.

One would expect this situation to continue even among students who attend the same colleges and universities, including selective ones. For instance, the lower K–12 achievement of Blacks and Latinos than Whites at each SES level over the past 4 decades has meant that the African Americans and Latinos enrolling at selective institutions have been significantly less well prepared academically for higher education, on average, than their White counterparts since the late 1960s, when selective institutions first began enrolling much larger numbers of minority students. This has contributed to the persistent pattern of lower GPAs for Blacks and Latinos than Whites at those institutions (Bowen & Bok, 1998; Cole & Barber, 2003). Thus, each year for the past two generations, African American and Latino bachelor's degree recipients at selective institutions have graduated, on average, with less human capital than their White counterparts (as measured by GPA). In fact, extensive research has shown that African Americans have actually had lower grades, on average, in college—including at selective institutions—than their high school grades and college admissions test scores would have predicted. This has also been the case for Latinos, albeit to a lesser degree (Bowen & Bok, 1998; Klitgaard, 1985; Ramist, Lewis, & McCamley-Jenkins, 1994).

CONCLUSION

This chapter has attempted to impart a more comprehensive understanding of the specific and comparative educational circumstances of bilingual students in U.S. schools. Achievement gaps are the norm, yet they are better understood as a result of various factors, one of which relates to the language attributes of these students. However, as the last section of this chapter points out, the quality of the schooling available to these students can be an important attribute of their academic success. We explore those sets of schooling factors in the chapters that follow.

6

THEORETICAL CONCEPTUALIZATIONS: BILINGUALISM AND SCHOOLING

People's social lives, often considered by most to be the products of culture and language, are instead regarded by sociocultural theorists as the major ingredients of cognition. Sociocultural theorists see social experience as inseparable from thought: Moment by moment, people construct reality. That process of construction and the understanding it generates depend on people's previous understandings and previous social experiences.

SOCIAL CONTEXT, DEVELOPMENT, AND LEARNING

During the past decade or so, many educational theorists have become interested in the social contexts of children as a critical variable related to overall learning and development (Nasir & Hand, 2006; Rogoff, 2003). This empirical interest is tied conceptually to sociocultural theory, which brings together the disciplines of psychology, semiotics, education, sociology, and anthropology. This conceptualization draws on work done earlier in the 20th century by the Russian theorists L. S. Vygotsky and Mikhail Bakhtin (Cole & Cole, 2001) and relates development and learning to such theoreticians and philosophers of education as William James, John Dewey, C. S. Pierce, and Jean Piaget (García, 2002). The aim of this chapter is to find a unified way of understanding the issues of language, cognition, culture, human development, and teaching and learning.

Sociocultural theorists posit that the psychology of the individual learner is deeply shaped by social interaction. In essence, both children and those with whom they interact are engaged in the process of constructing knowledge primarily through social activity. Therefore, knowledge is created between individuals primarily through social interaction. Higher order mental processes, the tendency to look at things in certain ways, and values are produced by shared activity and dialogue (Rogoff, 1990). In a broader sense, these social interactions are highly determined by culture and directly affect language, cognitive, and social development as well as the acquisition of any new knowledge and behavior—a phenomenon we call *learning*.

The focus of sociocultural theory is especially important for understanding the development and early education of bilingual children, partly because this population brings to the formal schooling process a language and culture with distinct social contexts that deviate in many cases from the norm in the United States. Educators of culturally diverse students, including young Latino children learning English as a second language, often find this theoretical framework helpful because it conceives of learning as an interaction between individual learners and an embedding context. That embedding context may be as immediate as the social environment of the classroom or as indirect as the traditions and institutions that constitute the history of education. Both these contexts and many other factors come into play whenever teachers and students interact. Important contexts for teaching and learning include (a) close detailed instruction of individual learners; (b) concern for the social organization of classrooms; and (c) a consideration of the cultural and linguistic attributes of teachers, students, and peers. We can follow these interconnected contexts to gain a better understanding of the relationship between language, culture, and cognition.

It is useful, therefore, to conceive of the co-occurring linguistic, cognitive, and social character of a child's development as inherently interrelated (García, 2005). As children develop their ability to use language, they absorb a greater understanding of social situations and improve their thinking skills. This in turn allows them to learn how to control their own actions and thoughts. It is through a culturally bound and socially mediated process of language development that children construct mental frameworks (or schema) for perceiving the world around them. If language is a tool of thought, it follows that as children develop more complex thinking skills, the mental representations through which language and culture embody the child's world play a significant role. This perspective is especially important for young children negotiating two or more languages (Scheffner-Hammer, Miccio, & Rodriguez, 2004).

Empirical analyses indicate that young Latino bilingual children in the United States use cognitive and linguistic strategies to negotiate complex elements of social environments. Language use and social interactive strategies adopted by children in such studies have been found to vary by the linguistic ability of the addressee(s) (Fantini, 1985; García, 1983; García & Carrasco, 1981; Poplack, 1980; Reyes, 1998), topic of discussion (Heath, 1983, 1986; Zentella, 1997), level of familiarity with addressee(s) (Dolson, 1985; García, 1983; García & Carrasco, 1981), the child's shared history with the addressee(s) (Genishi, 1981; Zentella, 1997), and the child's attitudinal features (Ramirez, 1985). This research evidence supports the notion that a young bilingual child's language use and preference cannot be conceived solely in linguistic or cognitive terms; they are contextually dependent and predicated on attributes of cultural relevance.

If, as Vygotsky (in Cole & Cole, 2001) proposed, a child's cognitive schema for operating in the world is culturally bound, what are the effects of trying to learn in an environment where the culture of the classroom differs from the culture of the home? (See Chapter 2, this volume, for a discussion of Vygotsky's interactionist model.) Do young Latino children exposed to Spanish in the home face the challenge of accommodating their existing schema or constructing new schemas once they enter formal schooling? Indeed, when the educational focus is on transitioning culturally and linguistically diverse students to a mainstream culture rather than building on what they already know, students may be forced to change to meet the needs of the classroom. Duquette (1991) concluded,

> Children need to be understood and to express themselves (in the same positive light experienced by other children) in their own first language, home context and culture. Their minority background brings out the limitations not of the children but of the professionals who are asked to respond to those needs. (p. 194)

Unfortunately, educational policy and practice discussions about the education of bilingual students are often overly simplistic and focus only on the language difference of this population (Garcia, 2005; Jensen, 2008a; Rolstad, Mahoney, & Glass, 2005; Tharp & Gallimore, 1989). They tend to neglect the complex interweaving of students' cultural, linguistic, and cognitive development. In their study of the possible effects of language on cognitive development, Hakuta, Ferdman, and Diaz (1987) recognized the importance of acknowledging these three important strands in children's development and addressing them in schools. They concluded that most of the variance in cognitive growth directly relates to the way in which society affects and manipulates cognitive capacities. Therefore, cultural and contextual sensitivity theories that examine the social and cultural aspects of cognitive development will best serve diverse students.

RESEARCH ON SOCIOCULTURAL CONTEXT AND LITERACY

Language and cognitive development are critical to the maturity of literacy skills. Although scholars and researchers agree that social and cultural features also play important roles in the literacy development of young children, they use different paradigms and methodologies to investigate the role of sociocultural contexts on literacy development and attainment. Some use qualitative and ethnographic methods, whereas others restrict themselves to quantitative and purely deductive models. Because sociocultural constructs (e.g., discourse patterns, attitudinal features, routines, and so forth) are complex and interact with cognitive and linguistic properties in subtle yet meaningful ways, research necessitates dynamic designs and multiple methods to account for ways in which contextual factors influence literacy learning (Ercikan & Roth, 2006; Smith, 2006). To date, this type of research is limited; most research has either followed quantitative a priori models or used only qualitative designs.

In a synthesis of empirical studies commissioned by the National Literacy Panel on Language-Minority Children and Youth, Goldenberg, Rueda, and August (2006) presented a report on the influences of social and cultural contexts on minority children and youths' literacy development and attainment of language. Goldenberg and colleagues defined social and cultural influences broadly as factors that contribute to the contexts in which children and youths live and go to school, including their beliefs, attitudes, behaviors, routine practices, social and political relations, and physical resources connected with groups of people who share some characteristic (e.g., socioeconomic status [SES], educational status, race or ethnicity, national origin, linguistic group). Moreover, Goldenberg et al. evaluated studies using six operational definitions and domains of social and cultural contexts: immigration, home–school discourse differences, characteristics of students and teachers, the influence of parents and families, educational policy, and language status or prestige. The studies they reviewed reported data on (a) factors in one or more sociocultural domains and (b) student outcomes, including cognitive, affective, and/or behavioral, presumably affected by one or more of these factors. Outcomes could be gauged in the child's first language, second language, or both. Here we focus our attention specifically on studies that evaluated young Latinos, the largest emergent bilingual group in the United States.

Only a few studies have assessed the influence of immigration circumstances on literacy outcomes. These did not provide convincing evidence to suggest that Latino immigration, on its own, influences literacy achievement (Arzubiaga, Rueda, & Monzó, 2002; Goldenberg, 1987; Monzó & Rueda, 2001; Rueda, MacGillivray, Monzó, & Arzubiaga, 2001). Although there is clear evidence that immigration as a variable is associated with Mexican-origin students' academic achievement in the early grades (Reardon & Galindo, 2006a), the effects of immigration (via generation status and circumstances associated with immigration) on literacy achievement seem to be mediated by various out-of-school processes. Moreover, "literacy outcomes are more likely to relate to home (and school) language and literacy learning opportunities, irrespective of immigration status" (Goldenberg et al., 2006, p. 255).

Differences in home–school discourse and interaction patterns were found between some language-minority groups (Au & Mason, 1981; Rueda, August, & Goldenberg, 2006), but "the consequences of these differences for students' literacy attainment and the effects of attempts to address or accommodate these differences in the classroom are not clear" (Goldenberg et al., 2006, pp. 255–256). The few studies that claimed an association between literacy-related student outcomes and different discourse and interaction patterns between home and school for Latino youngsters (Huerta-Macías & Quintero, 1992; Kucer & Silva, 1999; L. C. Wilkinson, Milosky, & Genishi, 1986) contained certain methodological flaws. Problems in design, data collection, and analysis prevented clear interpretations. Goldenberg et al. (2006), therefore, concluded that

> the most we can say given the available research is that bridging home–school difference in interaction can enhance students' engagement and level of participation in classroom instruction. This outcome is certainly not trivial, but it is not the same as enhancing student achievement or other types of learning outcomes—effects the existing data cannot confirm. (p. 256)

Related research on social and cultural characteristics of Latino students and their teachers, however, lends some support to the notion that the cultural relevance of materials and testing procedures plays a role in literacy outcomes (G. E. García, 1991; Jiménez, 1997; Reyes, 2001). G. E. García (1991), for example, offered compelling evidence that the lack of relevant background knowledge impeded Latino bilingual students on reading comprehension tests. In this study, García used qualitative and quantitative methodologies to identify sociocultural factors that influenced the English reading test performance of 104 fifth- and sixth-grade students from two elementary schools of similar SES (low to low-middle) in the same school district. Fifty-one of the children were identified as bilingual (Spanish–English) Latinos, and 53 were identified as monolingual (English-speaking) White. Latino students' reading test scores in this study were found to underestimate their reading potential. García concluded that test performance was affected by the students' limited prior knowledge of certain test topics, unfamiliarity with vocabulary terms in test questions and answer choices, and their tendency to interpret the test literally when determining answers. Indeed, post hoc interviews revealed that Latino students tended to be more literal in their reading and did not use vocabulary that they had to draw correct inferences. Furthermore, for the topic on which the Latino students had greater background knowledge (i.e., the word *piñata*), scores between bilingual Latinos and monolingual Whites were equivalent. Although these data on comprehension outcomes and the general notion that teacher and student characteristics influence literacy development are compelling, further research is needed, particularly for younger children.

The body of research on the influence of parents and families on literacy outcomes is stronger. That is, more research has been conducted on this issue and suggests three major findings. First, parents of language-minority students, in general, value literacy development for their children, yet for various reasons school personnel underestimate and do not take full advantage of home resources and parents' interest, motivation, and involvement (Brooker, 2002; Goldenberg, 1987; Goldenberg & Gallimore, 1991; Goldenberg et al., 2006; Harry & Klingner, 2006; Scheffner Hammer & Miccio, 2004; Scheffner Hammer, Miccio, & Wagstaff, 2003; Shannon, 1995). Second, measures of parent and family literacy practices often predict literacy attainment of their children, but findings in this regard are not consistent across the board (Arzubiaga et al., 2002; Durán & Weffer, 1992; Goldenberg, Gallimore, Reese, & Garnier, 2001; Goldenberg, Reese, & Gallimore, 1992; Pucci & Ulanoff, 1998; Reese, Garnier, Gallimore, & Goldenberg, 2000). Third, sociocultural studies suggest that the relationship between language use in the home and literacy outcomes of language-minority students (in the school) is not clear (Buriel & Cardoza, 1988; Dolson, 1985; Hancock, 2002; Hansen, 1989; Monzó & Rueda, 2001). It is unclear whether the use of Spanish or English in the home is preferable in terms of optimizing bilingual Latino students' literacy development. Again, this result appears to be associated with methodological problems and inconsistencies across studies. Most of the studies control for obvious confounds, such as parent education, but fail to do so for other critical factors, such as quality of instruction in school, parents' Spanish and English abilities, quality and quantity of language in the home, and parents' attitudes regarding home language practices. As we discuss later in the chapter, studies in linguistics have considered in greater detail literacy and language development for Latino bilingual and emerging bilingual students. In general, these demonstrate that word- and text-level skills cross-transfer between languages. Moreover, the language system used in the home is not as important as the quantity of language used in the home and the quality of linguistic interactions. Literacy development appears to be associated with home literacy practices and parent educational attainment, whereby parents with less formal education, on average, read less to their children and engage their children in less frequent conversation (López, Barrueco, & Miles, 2006; Raikes et al., 2006; Risley & Hart, 2006).

The small body of research connecting policies at the district, state, and federal levels to literacy outcomes of emergent bilingual Latinos does not allow us to draw firm conclusions. Practitioners often vary in their interpretation of legislation regarding language use in schools (i.e., Proposition 227 in California and Proposition 203 in Arizona, both discussed in earlier chapters), and, therefore, language practices in schools and by teachers themselves vary as well (Shannon, 1995). Goldenberg et al. (2006) found that three factors influenced the implementation of state law prohibiting bilingual education (in California): the local school context, teachers' personal ideologies, and pedagogical reactions to the new policy.

Finally, research has evaluated the influence of language status or prestige on literacy achievement of speakers of that language. These studies demonstrate that Spanish is generally perceived as a low-status language, which can affect teachers' assessment of student competence and thus result in low expectations and low-level instructional practices (Buriel & Cardoza, 1988; Carreira, 2000; Goldenberg et al., 2006; Shannon, 1995).

Research that uses mixed and complex methodologies is needed to better understand the particular ways in which domains and levels of social and cultural contexts influence the literacy development of young Latino bilinguals. These studies will need to account for differences across levels of parent education; SES; ethnicity; immigration status; beliefs and attitudes of parents, teachers, and students; discourse features at school, at home, and in the community; instructional features in the classroom; parent involvement strategies; educational policy; language status/prestige; and so on. This work will require linking well-designed experiments with high-quality ethnographic research to verify findings, provide relative frequency of events or occurrences, examine competing explanations, and make generalizations based on available data. The combination of qualitative and quantitative methods will have a much greater probability of shedding light on complex topics than either one does individually (Green, Camilli, & Elmore, 2006; Smith, 2006; Weisner, 2005).

This section is summarized as follows:

- Sociocultural theory—bringing together the disciplines of psychology, semiotics, education, sociology, and anthropology—is a unified way of understanding issues of language, cognition, culture, human development, and teaching and learning.

- This approach posits that children's linguistic, cognitive, and social characters are fundamentally interrelated. A child's basic cognitive framework is shaped by his or her native language, early linguistic experiences, and cultural context.
- Young Latino children from Spanish-speaking homes are often compelled to adjust their cognitive and linguistic representations to negotiate the social exchanges within the school environment.
- The extant literature suggests that bridging home–school differences in interaction and discourse patterns can enhance students' engagement and level of participation in classroom instruction.
- Home linguistic interactions (which vary by SES indicators, e.g., parent education) and teacher practices, perspectives, and expectations influence literacy attainment. Teachers who recognize and take full advantage of children's home resources (e.g., children's home language and cultural practices) and parental supports are more likely to witness optimal educational outcomes for their students.
- More research is needed to better understand ways in which social and cultural contexts influence literacy development and attainment of young Latinos managing two languages. Future research should combine well-designed experiments with quality ethnographic research. These studies will need to account for differences across levels of parent education; SES; ethnicity; immigration status; beliefs and attitudes of parents, teachers, and students; discourse features at school, home, and in the community; instructional features in the classroom; parent involvement strategies; educational policy; language status/prestige; and so on.

DEVELOPMENT OF LANGUAGE PROPERTIES OF BILINGUALS RELEVANT TO EDUCATION

The intersection of the two languages of bilinguals during language development is a critical feature of this population. Our understanding of bilingual development and the specific development of English as a second language in the schooling environments for U.S. bilinguals continues to expand. The accumulating body of evidence indicates that young children can attain proficiency in more than one language at early ages (Baker, 2000; Genesee, Lindholm-Leary, Saunders, & Christian, 2005). The process by which this occurs is quite complex, and linguistic properties between languages intersect in intricate ways.

As documented earlier, a clear majority of young bilinguals live in homes in which Spanish is spoken, with fluctuating amounts of English. It is therefore important to note that most young bilinguals are influenced by two languages, and a growing number of them are positioned to be bilingual. In this section, we draw from research that spans the past 3 decades to assess the development and interchange of linguistic properties between languages (i.e., English and Spanish). Focusing mostly on native Spanish-speaking children who learn English as a second language, these studies evaluate the developmental structure (phonology, morphology, and syntax) of language and show that bilingual development is complex and varies between children as a function of their environment. Moreover, linguistic properties between language systems influence one another, suggesting that bilingualism cannot be viewed simply as "the arithmetic sum of two languages" (García, 2005, pp. 21–38; see Chapter 3, this volume).

Theories of Second Language Acquisition

Several theories have been presented over the past few decades to explain how young children learn a second language and the ways in which linguistic properties between the first and second language interact. These theories have diverged on the influences native language development has on the acquisition and proficiency in the second language. The target language theory guided much of the early work in second language acquisition with children. It posited that second language acquisition could largely be explained by reference to features of the target language being learned (Dulay & Burt, 1974). That is, linguistic errors made by emergent bilinguals would strongly resemble those made by native English speakers during the developmental learning process. Under this theory, linguistic challenges associated with learning a second language were inherent in the language itself and do not necessarily relate to the child's first, or native, language. The target language theory, therefore, was not cross-linguistic in nature. It did not account for the interaction of linguistic development between the native and second languages.

Developed by researchers and theorists working on second language acquisition in adults, *interlanguage* theories did, however, acknowledge the role of linguistic attributes between the first and second languages in the development of the second language (Nemser, 1971; Selinker, 1972). This view suggested that the abstract system of rules of the target language created by second-language learners was best described as an interlanguage, which had a unique organizational scheme. Ways in which language is organized would directly relate to the first and second languages (Towell & Hawkins, 1994). The interlanguage, however, could not be empirically identified and thus remains a conceptual construct.

Cognitive theoretical approaches suggested that underlying cognitive abilities could explain the relationships between first and second language acquisition (Geva & Ryan, 1993). This perspective posited that the successful interplay between languages used to acquire proficiency in a second language was attributed to the individual's particular underlying cognitive abilities. More specifically, working memory, phonological short-term memory, phonological awareness, and phonological recoding were predictive of second language acquisition and functioning (Genesee, Geva, Dressler, & Kamil, 2006). These abilities were thought to be inherent, composing part of one's general cognitive capacity. Correlations between cognitive abilities and second language proficiency, however, were weak.

Transfer theories are currently the most common frameworks used to explain second language acquisition and the relationships between linguistic properties of the first and second languages. They assert that language skills from the first language transfer to the second. Two theoretical orientations attempt to explain this process: contrastive analysis hypothesis (and interdependence hypothesis (Cummins, 1981a, 2000). The contrastive analysis hypothesis postulates that errors (i.e., interference) in second-language production occur when grammatical differences between the two languages are present. When the first and second languages have similar grammatical structures, the child will learn the second language in a relatively easy and rapid manner (Genesee, 2003). Conversely, learning a second language that has a dissimilar grammatical format to the first will be slower and more difficult.

The interdependence hypothesis postulates that the acquisition and development of the first and second languages are interdependent (Cummins, 1981b, 2000). In other words, development of the first language can influence— by facilitating or inhibiting—development in the second. However, under this theoretical orientation, not all aspects of second language development are affected by the first language. Cummins (2000) explained that language that is contextually embedded (e.g., casual, culturally laden social communication) and cognitively undemanding (i.e., automatic and overlearned interaction) does not lend itself well to transfer. Namely, language skills involved in day-to-day interpersonal communication are not developmentally interdependent. In contrast, language that is contextually reduced and cognitively demanding is developmentally interdependent; that is, transfer is much more likely to occur. This means that higher order cognitive skills, such as academic language, are more developmentally interdependent and amenable to transfer between languages. Indeed, Cummins (2000) stated that "academic proficiency transfers across languages such that students who have developed literacy in their first language will tend to make stronger progress in acquiring literacy in their second language" (p. 173). Known as the *threshold hypothesis*, transfer of academic language is posited to occur after the individual attains sufficient competence in the second language.

Of course, as related to the teaching and learning of a second language, some have called on these theories to suggest practices consistent with the presuppositions of the components of one or more of the theories mentioned above (Krashen, 1997). In terms of theories used to explain the relationship of linguistic properties between first and second languages, a broad range of variables have been found to moderate substantially cross-linguistic processes (Genesee et al., 2006). Moderators include such factors as proficiency level in both the first and the second language, the quality and quantity of first language use in the home, socioeconomic status, generational status, instructional approaches, and individual factors such as personality (Genesee et al., 2006).

Considering the Data

The studies reviewed in this section support the idea that the linguistic skills of young emergent bilingual Latino children tend to transfer. Indeed, current research and scholarly discussions of first and second language relationships emphasize the transfer theory, which tends to be the most powerful and most frequently cited frameworks (Genesee et al., 2006). However, the transfer theory does not account for all associations among linguistic attributes for young emergent bilingual Latinos. That is, common underlying abilities, typological differences between languages, unique features of the target language, and well-developed oral and literacy skills in the first language all contribute to second language learning to some extent (Genesee et al., 2006). Moreover, there is insufficient large-sample research available of children ages 3 and 4 years to suggest that the process of cross-linguistic transfer functions in the same way as it does for older children.

In an early study of bilingual development in young children, Padilla and Liebman (1975) reported a longitudinal linguistic analysis of Spanish–English acquisition in two 3-year-olds. By analyzing several dependent linguistic variables (phonological, morphological, and syntactic characteristics) over time, the authors observed gains in both languages, although several English forms were evident whereas similar Spanish forms were not. They also reported the differentiation of linguistic systems at phonological, lexical, and syntactic levels. They concluded that

> the appropriate use of both languages in mixed utterances was evident; that is, correct word order was preserved. For example, there were no occurrences of "raining esta" or "a es baby," note there was evidence for such utterances as "esta raining" and "es a baby." There was also an

absence of the redundancy of unnecessary words, which might tend to confuse meaning. (Padilla & Liebman, 1975, p. 51)

García (1983) reported developmental data related to the acquisition of Spanish and English by Chicano preschoolers (3–4 years old) and the acquisition of English by a group of matched English-only speakers. The results of García's study can be summarized as follows: (a) Acquisition of both Spanish and English was evident at complex morphological levels for Spanish–English 4-year-olds; (b) for the bilingual children, English was more advanced based on the quantity and quality of obtained morphological instances of language productions; and (c) there was no quantitative or qualitative difference between Spanish–English bilingual children and matched English-only controls on English language morphological productions.

Huerta (1977) conducted a longitudinal analysis of a Spanish–English 2-year-old child. She reported that similar identifiable stages appeared in which one language forged ahead of the other. Moreover, she reported the significant occurrence of mixed-language utterances that made use of both Spanish and English vocabulary and Spanish and English morphology. In all such cases, these mixed linguistic utterances were well formed and communicative.

Wong Fillmore (1976) spent a year observing five Spanish-speaking children acquiring English. The first thing the children did was to figure out what was being said by observing the relationship between certain expressions and the situational context. The children inferred the meaning of certain words, which they began to use as "formulaic expressions" (these expressions were acquired and used as analyzed wholes). The formulaic expressions became the raw material used by the children to figure out the structure of the language. Wong Fillmore provided two examples of how children use first-language acquisition strategies to begin to analyze these expressions: (a) Children notice how parts of expressions used by others vary in accordance with changes in the speech situation in which they occur, and (b) children notice which parts of the formulaic expressions are like other utterances in the speech of others. As the children figured out which formulas in their speech could be varied, they were able to "free" the constituents they contained and use them in productive speech.

Code Switching

Code switching is a common phenomenon observed in bilingual populations of young Latino children. It is a term used in linguistics to refer to the alternation between two (or more) language in a single conversation or utterance. In an early study of this phenomenon, Fantini (1985) noticed that one of his children, Mario, was able to switch easily between two languages according to characteristics of the addressee. Mario spoke Spanish if he knew that a person was a Spanish-dominant speaker, or English if he knew a person was an English-dominant speaker. There was an exception that Fantini noticed when both his children became close and felt comfortable with an English-speaking person. They tended to switch to Spanish, which was the language they related to intimately and comfortably with loved ones. Young bilinguals also have a tendency to switch languages when talking about a specific topic (Zentella, 1997). They tend to switch to the more comfortable language; for some this might be the first language, but this is not necessarily so for everyone, since some bilinguals become dominant in the second language.

Studies of children's code switching have reported the frequent use of one-word switches (Genishi, 1981; McClure 1981; Reyes, 1998; Zentella, 1997). One explanation for the occurrence of code switching among children is that they lack the vocabulary in one language, so they switch to the other language. There are, however, cases in which children do seem to have the equivalents in both languages. Reyes (1998) observed cases in which children code switched for one word in utterance, but later on during the same conversation, the same child was observed using the same word in the other language. It might be a more accurate explanation to say that code switching is used mainly to express a word that is not immediately accessible in the other language. Moreover, code switching seems to be a way in which young learners of a second language begin playing with language, exploring the use of their two languages by imitating the sounds of new words learned in their second language (Arias & Lakshmanan, 2003). This way, children start gaining confidence and practicing their skills in the second language.

The evidence to date concerning the development of code switching behavior in young bilingual children consistently shows that both knowledge of the grammatical capabilities and sensitivity to the norms of code choice upheld by their flexible use of grammar are major factors determining language choice. Grosjean (1982), Fantini (1985), and McClure (1981) stressed the importance of the child's social role. If a child is taking care of younger siblings, she or he will tend to switch to the language with which the youngest child feels most comfortable. In addition, older children tend to use code switching as a clarification device when other children do not seem to understand. Similarly, García (1983) observed that mothers used mixed utterances in Spanish and English when speaking to their young children "as a teaching aide" to clarify from one language to the other.

The listener's level of fluency is another important factor in language choice (McClure 1981; Poplack, 1980). Fantini (1985) noticed that as early as age 4, his children could determine in their interactions the ability of their audience to understand mixed language utterances. Reyes (1998) also observed this phenomenon among immigrant children who were Spanish–English speakers.

When children were paired with a friend, older children (10-year-olds) seemed to monitor their partner's level of understanding and tended to accommodate by code switching to the language in which the other child was most proficient. Moreover, the relative fluency of the speaker is a determining factor for code switching. It is when children have competence in both languages that code-switching is used as a verbal or communicative strategy and as markers of group membership (Zentella, 1997).

Zentella (1997) reported that Puerto Rican children in New York switched freely among speakers of *el barrio* (the community where the children lived). However, children did show respect for those who they knew were monolinguals or dominant in one of the languages, thereby accommodating and addressing them in their respective languages. For these children, a complete separation of languages seems almost impossible. This was not because they could not linguistically achieve language separation but because continuous mixing of their two languages was the norm in their everyday communication. These children see code switching as an acceptable and natural conversational strategy. Therefore, code switching is more of a complex communicative skill than a linguistic deficiency.

The fact that children use two languages seems to make them more aware of the available possibilities for multiple language use with community members who speak their two languages than with those who do not. This awareness to understand and use two languages is referred to as the child's *metalinguistic* awareness (Bialystok, 2001; Jensen, 2008b). With time, children achieve and maintain a level of fluency in each language skill that in general reflects the need for that skill in a particular language (Grosjean, 1982).

CONCLUSION

The findings in this chapter show that children can competently acquire two or more languages, and the acquisition of two languages can be parallel but need not be. That is, the qualitative character of one language may lag behind, surge ahead, or develop equally with the other language. The relationship of linguistic properties between languages is complex. Transfer theory is the most widely accepted theory used to explain the linguistic and literacy development of young bilingual Latino children in the United States. However, a broad range of variables moderate cross-linguistic processes. These include individual factors, such as personality, as well as contextual factors, such as language practices in the home and instructional practices in the school. Code switching is a common occurrence among bilingual children. Children who acquire two languages are likely to mix those languages in regular, systematic ways that assist in the enhancement of meaning. Language choice of bilingual Latino children depends on characteristics of and the particular relationship with the addressee(s) as well as attitudinal features of the child. The quality of literacy skill development in the second language is associated with the developmental quality of parallel skills in the native language. Oral skills (i.e., the integration of vocabulary, grammar, and semantics driven by contextual circumstances; Saunders & O'Brien, 2006) in the second language do not appear to transfer in the same way but are greatly influenced by second language exposure and language use in the home.

7

BEST PRACTICES AND
SUCCESSFUL STRATEGIES

There are many possible program options for bilingual students and children learning English as a second language. These are variously referred to as *transitional bilingual education, maintenance bilingual education, 90–10 bilingual education, 50–50 bilingual education, developmental bilingual education, dual-language education, two-way immersion, English as a second language, English immersion, sheltered English, structured English, submersion,* and so forth. These programs differ in the way in which they use the native language and English during instruction (Ovando, Collier, & Combs, 2006). They also differ in theoretical rationale, language goals, cultural goals, academic goals, student characteristics, ages served, entry grades, length of student participation, participation of mainstream teachers, teacher qualifications, and instructional materials (Genesee, 1999). The extent to which a program is successful depends on local conditions, choices, and innovations. Chapter 3 (this volume) contains a discussion of topics and issues debated by educators, policymakers, and researchers related to evaluation and implementation of best-practice-informed bilingual education programs. In this chapter, we evaluate those issues with regard to serving the bilingual child in applied learning environments, such as the classroom.

Because each community is different (e.g., sociodemographic conditions) and local and state policies demand assorted objectives from their schools and teachers, no single program works best in every situation. In the selection of a program, one of the most fundamental decisions that should be considered is whether bilingual proficiency will be an objective. Given the cognitive and economic advantages of bilingual proficiency in a world that is becoming increasingly globalized, promoting bilingualism is an intuitive goal (García & Jensen, 2006). If we expect our future workers, civil servants, and academics to compete in a global, multilingual world, it makes sense that we would prepare them with the skills to do so. Bilingualism, therefore, represents a social and academic skill that ought to be infused into all areas of curriculum with students learning in both English and at least one other language, if not more, throughout their academic careers.

A second feature that should be considered when selecting a program designed for bilinguals is the optimization of individual achievement and literacy development. Academic performance continues to be the driving force behind educational policy reform and practice in the United States. And programs developed for bilinguals should strive to reduce achievement gaps. In addition, it is important that programs support the development of the whole child, simultaneously sustaining cognitive, social, emotional, and psychological development. A holistic approach is especially important during the early years (i.e., pre-K–3) of schooling (Zigler, Gilliam, & Jones, 2006).

Third, on the basis of the analyses provided in the previous chapters, attention to the cognitive intersections of bilingualism and instruction becomes a critical component. With specific regard to developing educational interventions for bilinguals, the cognitive attributes associated with bilingual development are essential as instruction is designed and implemented. In summary, contrary to early evidence that bilingualism could be deleterious to learning, we know that it can be quite advantageous in various domains, specifically to formally constructed education environments; bilingualism confers a number of cognitive benefits that can translate directly into instruction.

Bilinguals are more able to control their attention while engaged in nonverbal and linguistics tasks (this is discussed more extensively in Chapter 3). In doing so, they are more capable of attending, or controlling their attention, to selective aspects of their environment, an inherent task in using two languages to communicate effectively. From an instruction design perspective, using two languages for instructions should not be detrimental to bilingual students. In addition, access to working memory seems to be enhanced for bilinguals. Bilingual students' ability to inhibit one language while using the other increases the efficiency of working memory; thus, rigorous implementation of an instructional curriculum that draws on working memory can be quite beneficial for these students.

Bilinguals also show advanced abilities to problem solve. This is particularly the case in executive control functions such as planning, rule acquisition, abstract thinking, and cognitive flexibility. Because bilinguals must choose between two languages, along with all the complexities related to the use of those languages, these executive functions are enhanced. Instructionally, then, the use of project learning, thematic instruction, or cooperative learning may very well be beneficial for bilinguals. Similarly, bilinguals have been identified with advantageous learning characteristics related to creativity, divergent thinking, and symbolic reasoning. Communicating in two languages often requires switching between those languages and the cognitive structures that underlie them. This may be related to the symbolic reasoning advantages for bilinguals. Instructionally, the use of various symbolic systems in mathematics, science, and other content areas could be emphasized so as to leverage these advantages.

Finally, there is the cognitive *meta*—knowing about—advantages of bilingualism. The most common meta-attribute is related to awareness of cognitive operations, that is, the awareness of one's own learning strategies, particularly related to self-regulation of the learning process. Processing of learning vocabulary, syntax, phonology, and morphology in more than one language seems to provide bilinguals a particularly enhanced set of insights into learning strategies that they are using. Instructionally, bilingual students may benefit more from strategies that examine the processing of learning, utilizing reflections, examining, and articulating of learning processes that they may be engaged in at all levels of the curriculum. And, of course, the meta that is specific to linguistic repertoires can make one realize that words are arbitrary and languages are rule governed (although the rules may be different) and can be related in rule-governed ways to one another, such as adding an "o" to some English words to make them Spanish words. The clearest example of using metalinguistic awareness in instruction with bilinguals is in the instructional acknowledgement related to cognates in some languages. Cognates are words in two languages that share the same ancestral origin. For example, the word *science* in English has the same Latin roots and becomes *sciencias* in Spanish. Cognates in Spanish and English are prolific in math, science, music, and the arts. Having bilingual students use this metalinguistic skill is a must in effective instruction.

LANGUAGE, SCHOOLING, AND THE EVIDENCE

The knowledge base reviewed in previous chapters is directly related to understanding instructional programs, teaching strategies, and educational policies that seek to provide optimal literacy and academic outcomes for bilingual students. The demographic data, for example, demonstrate that young bilingual children in the United States are exposed, at some level, to a heritage language in approximately three in four homes (López, Barrueco, & Miles, 2006) and that the home environment is likely to be characterized by aspects of the immigrant experience. This set of circumstances is important given that home language practices—different from language use—are highly relevant to early literacy outcomes (Goldenberg, Rueda, & August, 2006; Nord, Lennon, Liu, & Chandler, 1999; Tabors, 1997; Tabors & Snow, 2002). Moreover, given that higher order cognitive and literacy skills tend to transfer from the native to the second language (August, Calderón, & Carlo, 2002; Genesee, 2003; Genesee, Geva, Dressler, & Kamil, 2006; Goldenberg, Rezaei, & Fletcher, 2005), it is critical that educators adequately assess, develop, and leverage the child's non-English native language skills. This means tailoring instruction, curricular content, and schooling practices in general to meet the child's particular language development circumstances— based on individual, school, and family factors—as well as the social and cultural contexts to take full advantage of the child's home resources and parental support (Genesee et al., 2006; Goldenberg, Gallimore, Reese, & Garnier, 2001; Goldenberg et al., 2006; Reese, Garnier, Gallimore, & Goldenberg, 2000; Scheffner Hammer & Miccio, 2004; Shannon, 1995). In this section, we discuss the present status of young Latinos children's academic achievement levels, including early literacy skills, and discuss how policies and practices play a part in these outcomes. We comb the literature to highlight the features and strategies of the most effective programs used to build on young Latino children's strengths to produce the most favorable outcomes, with a particular emphasis on preschool participation.

Present Circumstances

As discussed in the Early Achievement section of Chapter 5 (this volume), Latino children continue to lag behind their White and Asian American peers on reading and math abilities during the K–12 years. Because Latino children, on average, exhibit more risk factors than do White children, they are generally at greater risk for academic underachievement (Hernandez, 2006). It is important to note that risk is not due solely to non-English proficiency but to a number of sociodemographic conditions that correlate with speaking Spanish in the home. In an analysis of Early Childhood Longitudinal Study, Kindergarten Cohort (ECLS-K) data, which drew from a nationally representative sample of children beginning kindergarten in 1998, Jensen (2007) compared Spanish-speaking kindergarteners with their peers in general education on a number of outcomes, including socioeconomic status (SES), parent education, and mathematics achievement (i.e., numeracy, shape/size recognition, and ordinality). He found that Spanish-speaking kindergartners, on average, scored four fifths of a standard deviation lower than the general body of kindergartners in mathematics. Moreover, Spanish-speaking kindergartners fared an entire standard deviation below their peers in SES and maternal education. Nearly half of the kindergarteners from Spanish-speaking homes, for example, had mothers who had not completed high school. The low scores of young Latino children compared with White and Asian children during the early years of schooling (Reardon & Galindo, 2007) are associated with a combination of family risk factors, including Spanish home language use, low income, and low educational attainment of their parents.

Home Language Practices

The risk factors, including parent education, family income, and home language (National Center for Education Statistics, 1995), affect academic and literacy development because they tend to correlate with early conversational practices and word learning in the home. In an often-cited research program, Hart and Risley (1995, 1999; Risley & Hart, 2006) conducted a rigorous qualitative, longitudinal project in which they followed 42 families for nearly 2.5 years, observing their everyday lives and interactions. Children were followed from 7 months of age until they were 36 months old. Of the families, 13 were upper SES, 10 were middle SES, 13 were lower SES, and six were on welfare. Although none of the families included in the study were of Latino origins (the sample consisted entirely of African Americans and Whites), this work has fundamental implications for the importance of early language development, the cyclical effects of socioeconomic conditions on language development, and the importance of the amount of early exposure to language.

In their longitudinal study, Hart and Risley found the everyday talk between parents and their infants and toddlers to be very meaningful. In their analysis of over 1,200 hr of audio recordings and field notes, Hart and Risley found that the amount of family talk accounted for children's vocabulary growth and expressive language and related strongly to intellectual outcomes at ages 3 and 9 years. Furthermore, the amount of family talk was characteristic of social class. Welfare parents were taciturn, working-class parents varied greatly, and parents with advanced professional degrees were uniformly talkative. The difference between taciturn and talkative parents was found in the amount of "extra" talk rendered. That is, the amount of talk parents provided per hour to govern their child—what Hart and Risley called "business" talk—did not vary much between households. How they differed was in the extra talk, which consisted of conversational chit-chat, ongoing commentary, and gossip that were inherently loaded with varied vocabulary, complex ideas, subtle guidance, and positive reinforcement—all ingredients considered important to intellectual and psychological development. Toddlers raised in households in which extra talk was plentiful continued to develop complex cognitive skills through language exploration and experimentation. The language development of toddlers raised in households in which very little extra talk was available stalled once their utterances matched their parents' frequency of talking.

Children from economically advantaged homes, therefore, were provided more opportunities to learn through informal conversational exchanges than children in poverty-level and working-class homes. Again, this was not because of the difference in quality of linguistic exchanges but in the frequency, that is, the quantity of linguistic exchanges.

Socioeconomic conditions also have been associated with the amount of mother–child book-reading during early childhood. This finding is significant because parental book-reading is reliably linked to language and school readiness outcomes (Bus, van IJzendoorn, & Pellgrini, 1995; DeBaryshe, 1995; Sénéchal & Cornell, 1993; Sénéchal, LeFevre, Hudson, & Lawson, 1996; Snow & Goldfield, 1983). And research has found that book-reading during children's first 3 years of life is associated with vocabulary development and comprehension at 14 months of age, vocabulary and cognitive development at 24 months of age, and children's language and cognition at 36 months (Raikes et al., 2006). Raikes et al. (2006) documented book-reading frequency and variation in a large sample ($N = 2,581$) of low-income mothers and children in the context of an Early Head Start program. Critical links were made between reported maternal book-reading, children's language and cognitive development, and mother and child characteristics. Raikes et al. found that book-reading frequency was positively associated with language, vocabulary, and comprehension at 14 months and related to cognitive measures, with increased vocabulary and cognitive development at 24 months and with cognitive scores at 36 months. For Spanish-speaking children, only daily reading at 36 months was significantly associated with language and cognitive outcomes. Moreover, book-reading tendencies at 14 months predicted book-reading at 24 and 36 months of age.

Raikes et al. (2006) thus argued that maternal book-reading plays an influential role on language and cognitive development during the dynamic early childhood years (14–36 months). Moreover, they found considerable variation within low-income families. Spanish-speaking mothers, for example, read less frequently to their children than English-speaking mothers. In addition, Spanish-speaking Latino families had far fewer books in the home than did other families in the sample. It is not clear from Raikes et al.'s study how the cultural mechanisms and the availability of books in non-English languages (e.g., Spanish) influenced maternal book-reading patterns in Latino homes. Other bodies of research have suggested that Latino families tend to *tell* stories to their children rather than *read* them (Portes & Hoa, 2002). Nonetheless, given the above-mentioned links between maternal book-reading and cognitive and linguistic outcomes, it is important to consider the impact of home literacy practices on early learning. In Raikes et al.'s study, variations in low-income families were found to predict differences in language and cognitive outcomes as early as 14 months of age.

In an analysis of developmental protective and risk factors in a nationally representative sample of children born in 2001 (i.e., ECLS-K data), López, Barrueco, and Miles (2006) found differences in parenting practices between SES and racial/ethnic groups. Among other important findings related to the early health and development of Latino infants and the homes in which they were reared, López et al. found important differences in parent–child interactions. Namely, they found differences in parent–child linguistic engagement—assessing how often parents engage with their infants (at 9 months) by reading, telling stories, or singing songs—and parenting practices, as measured by the Nursing Child Assessment Teaching Scale (NCATS) used to assess the parent–child teaching interactions for early precursors of cognitive and social skills. For the linguistic engagement construct, López et al. compared means of self-reported ratings across racial and ethnic groups and found that Latino parents read, told stories, and sang songs to their infants less frequently than did White and multiracial parents (all comparisons were statistically significant). In addition, Latino mothers scored statistically lower than White, multiracial, and Asian mothers on the NCATS, suggesting that Latino mothers, in general, were less responsive to their infants' distress and less likely to foster socioemotional and cognitive growth. López et al. observed that group differences remained even after controlling for SES: Latino mothers scored significantly lower than White and Asian mothers. It should be noted that some concern has been raised about the cultural sensitivity of the NCATS (Gross, Conrad, Fogg, Willis, & Garvey, 1993). Moreover, further research should continue to investigate how linguistic and educational practices in the home influence early literacy outcomes, as well as ways in which cultural practices of meaning-making interact with this development.

Duration of English Acquisition

An important aspect for the bilingual development of young children is the time required to attain English proficiency Chapter 3 (this volume) presented the discussion of this issue between bilingual education supporters and opponents. Here we present evidence for research-informed best-practice information regarding the duration of bilingual education that best serves the needs of emergent and balanced proficient bilinguals.

Second-language proficiency refers generally to two types: oral and academic. *Oral proficiency* usually precedes academic proficiency and refers to the development of conversational vocabulary, grammar, and listening comprehension. *Academic proficiency* refers to various skills, including word reading, spelling, reading fluency, reading comprehension, and writing. Under the U.S. Supreme Court's interpretation of the Civil Rights Act in *Lau v. Nichols* (1974), local school districts and states have an obligation to provide linguistically appropriate services to emergent bilingual students, yet policymakers often debate over how much time students need to attain English proficiency and, therefore, how long they should receive services. Indeed, estimates suggest that academic English proficiency takes bilingual students anywhere from 3 to 10 years to develop (Collier, 1989, 1995; Cummins, 1981b; Mitchell, Destino, & Karam, 1997).

Reporting on data from 5,585 emergent bilinguals from four different school districts (two from the San Francisco Bay area and two from Canada) to address the question of duration, Hakuta, Goto Butler, and Witt (2000) analyzed various forms of English proficiency as a function of length of exposure to English. Using standardized tests to determine both oral proficiency (i.e., the Idea Proficiency Test, the Language Assessment Scales, the Bilingual Syntax Measure) and academic proficiency (i.e., the SAT-9 [Stanford Achievement Test Series] and CTBS [Comprehensive Tests of Basic Skills]), this study plotted English proficiency as a function of length of residence, which was calculated by subtracting age at the time of immigration from present age. Hakuta et al. (2000) found that "even in districts that are considered the most successful in teaching English to emergent bilingual students, oral proficiency takes 3 to 5 years to develop, and academic English proficiency can take 4 to 7 years" (p. 13). It is important to note that Hakuta and colleagues found that socioeconomic factors tended to slow the rate of English acquisition. Moreover, studies on the duration of English acquisition have been conducted mostly with school-age children. Comparable evidence for preschool-age children, to our knowledge, does not exist. Yet it has been posited that the emergent bilinguals who are exposed to English at any earlier age acquire it quicker (Hakuta et al., 2000).

Rather than stipulating time limits for emergent bilinguals to attain English skills, those involved in education policy and practices should continue to identify and leverage children's abilities and provide empirically sound instructional and curricular practices to help children succeed academically, understanding that the development of satisfactory English skills requires a number of years. Historically, school districts and states have approached the language development and education of emergent bilinguals in very different ways. These approaches are typically not influenced by rigorous research but by politics and ideology (Jensen, 2008a).

ASSESSMENT

Children's cognitive and linguistic abilities and performance are generally obtained from measurements of specific skills, typically through standardized testing. Several concerns and issues (including litigations) have come to bear over the past few decades in relation to test development and assessment practices for culturally and linguistically diverse students. There are ongoing efforts to develop appropriate measures and procedures that take into account children's cultural and linguistic backgrounds so as to not penalize those who fall outside the cultural mainstream in the United States. The goal of these tests and procedures, in general, is to create culturally and linguistically relevant scores that accurately portray the abilities and concurrent performance levels for a diverse body of children. See Chapter 4 (this volume) for a more detailed discussion of assessment of linguistic and intellectual/cognitive skills in psychometric assessment of bilinguals.

Enhancing Reading and Developing Literacy

In Chapter 3 (this volume), we discussed the language transfer phenomenon among emergent and bilingual children. Here we discuss language transfer from the perspective of enhancing bilingual children's reading and literacy development to provide the reader with the extant data concerning what works. The development of reading in young children has become a key goal for education in the United States (August & Shanahan, 2006). Primary language instruction has been an important focus of literacy/reading researchers, especially those studying Latino children. Instead of assessing the influence of language use (i.e., whether Spanish or English is primarily spoken in the home) on literacy outcomes, linguistics researchers have evaluated ways in which literacy outcomes between English and Spanish are related. They have considered the extent to which oral, word-level, text-level, and comprehension skills in both languages correlate, assessing cross-linguistic literacy skills.

August, Calderón, and Carlo (2002), for example, followed a cohort of 287 bilingual students from the end of second grade through the end of fourth grade in Boston, Massachusetts; El Paso, Texas; and Chicago, Illinois. They examined how performance on indicators of Spanish reading at the end of second grade predicted parallel indicators of English reading at the end of third and fourth grades. More specifically, they examined transfer from Spanish to English in the areas of phonological awareness, letter identification, word reading, word knowledge, and comprehension over a 3-year period. In each analysis, August et al. controlled for general ability, oral English proficiency, performance in English on the reading measure of interest at the beginning of the study, and the number of years of formal instruction in English reading.

Three findings from August et al.'s (2002) longitudinal study are worth noting. First, they found that Spanish phonemic awareness, Spanish letter identification, and Spanish word reading were all reliable predictors of performance on parallel tasks in English at the end of the third and fourth grades. Second, with regard to passage comprehension, a positive relationship was found between Spanish passage comprehension at the end of second grade and English passage comprehension at the end of fourth grade. In other words, bilingual students who had the highest Spanish passage comprehension scores at the end of second grade had the highest English passage comprehension scores at the end of fourth grade. Third, the authors found that the effect of Spanish letter identification and Spanish word reading on English letter identification and English word reading emerged only for students who had received formal instruction in Spanish reading. That is, successful transfer was at least partly due to whether Spanish was integrated in classroom instruction. In short, findings from August et al.'s study indicate that there was a transfer effect from Spanish to English for phonemic segmentation skills for all Spanish-speaking students and for letter identification and word reading skills for those Spanish-speaking students who received initial instruction in their native language.

A study by Goldenberg, Rezaei and Fletcher (2005) supported the idea that knowledge and skills developed in one language can be transferable to another. Goldenberg et al. analyzed oral language literacy development among bilingual children during the 2001–2002 school year. Their analysis involved 14 schools and their surrounding communities in Texas and California and included 904 students in Grades K–2 in different types of instructional programs for English learners. The sample comprised children from urban, suburban, and rural communities in southern California, central Texas, and along the Texas–Mexico border. Analyses were conducted to determine the relationship between home language use, grade, and the program language. Among other findings, analyses supported the transfer hypothesis (i.e., common underlying proficiency) on measures of basic reading and passage comprehension. Goldenberg et al. found, however, that oral language skills did not correlate (or transfer) across languages. They showed that variation in oral language skills was more strongly accounted for by home experiences. Family members in this sample conversed predominantly in Spanish in the home.

A cross-sectional study by Kohnert and Bates (2002) evaluated developmental changes in lexical comprehension and cognitive processing in early sequential bilinguals, for whom Spanish was the native language and English was the second language. A total of 100 participants—20 in each of the five age groups (age in years: 5–7, 8–10, 11–13, 14–16, and adults)—were evaluated in both Spanish and English to explore the effects of age, years of experience, and basic-level cognitive processing on lexical comprehension. Gains in lexical comprehension were found in all age groups, in both languages. These gains, however, were greater in English. Participants in the youngest age group were relatively balanced in their cross-linguistic performance. By middle childhood, however, performance was better in English. These findings show a clear shift from Spanish to English.

Lesaux and Geva (2006) provided a comprehensive literature review on the literacy development of language-minority students in the United States. They noted that literacy skills for language-minority children and youths, on average, take longer to develop and lag behind those of their English monolingual peers. Children learning English as a second language, therefore, often find themselves more likely to be categorized as having a specific learning disability in reading (Artiles, Rueda, Salazar, & Higareda, 2002). Moreover, the process underlying literacy skills in a second language follows the same general pattern for monolinguals. In a loosely linear fashion, oral and phonological processing skills (including phonemic awareness and rapid naming skills) precede word-level skills and text-level skills, such as reading comprehension and writing abilities. As expected, variations in student characteristics (e.g., working memory, attention), student background (e.g., parent education, SES), and the quality of language and literacy development in Spanish (i.e., native language) influence the rate and quality of literacy acquisition (Lesaux & Geva, 2006; Lesaux, Koda, Siegel, & Shanahan, 2006).

Several studies have incorporated correlation-based models to understand how aspects of linguistic development (e.g., oral proficiency and phonological processing) relate to and predict literacy outcomes (e.g., word-level skills, text-level skills, reading comprehension) for young Latinos learning English as a second language. Four major findings have emerged from this research. First, aspects of native-language oral proficiency (i.e., Spanish phonological awareness skills) predict word-level skills in English (Durgunoglu, Nagy, & Hancin-Bhatt, 1993; Geva & Genesee, 2006; Quiroga, Lemos-Britton, Mostafapour, Abbott, & Berninger, 2002). To date, two studies have shown that the Spanish phonological awareness skills of native Spanish-speaking children accounted significantly for variations in word reading and pseudoword decoding in English (Durgunoglu, Nagy, & Hancin-Bhatt, 1993; Quiroga et al., 2002). This might not be surprising given the strong correlation between phonological awareness skills across languages, which suggests that phonological awareness is a common underlying proficiency (Geva & Genesee, 2006). Atwill, Blanchard, Gorin, and Burnstein (2006) provided evidence that phonological awareness skills of Spanish-speaking kindergartners indeed correlate with the same skills in English, but only for those who attain oral proficiency (measured in this study by receptive vocabulary scores) in Spanish, their native language. As mentioned earlier, other aspects of Spanish oral proficiency (e.g., morphology, syntax, and semantics) have not generally been found to predict word-level English skills.

Second, in terms of bilingual (Spanish–English) literacy outcomes, data support the notion of linguistic transfer. Dressler and Kamil (2006) conducted a thorough research review of the intersection between first- and second-language literacy of emergent bilingual children and youths—a synthesis of the cross-linguistic influences of literacy knowledge, processes, and strategies. Although more research is needed in this area, extant data suggest that word reading skills (Durgunoglu, Nagy, & Hancin-Bhatt, 1993), vocabulary (G. E. García, 1991; Jiménez, García, & Pearson, 1996; Nagy, García, Durgunoglu, & Hancin-Bhatt, 1993), and reading comprehension (Goldman, Reyes, & Varnhagen, 1984; Nagy, McClure, & Mir, 1997; Reese, Garnier, Gallimore, & Goldenberg, 2000; Royer & Carlo, 1991) transfer between languages. For transfer of vocabulary skills, it should be noted that cognate rather than complex vocabulary skills transfer between Spanish and English. Moreover, Nagy et al. (1997) observed that this transfer can be negative, as when meaning is erroneously assigned to words on the basis of the first language's syntax or when meanings between languages are not differentiated.

Third, second-language (i.e., English) oral proficiency, such as vocabulary and grammatical skills, explains only a modest proportion of the unique variance of students' word-level reading scores. Phonological skills and working memory in English are more robust predictors and explain more proportional variance of accurate word reading in English than does oral proficiency (Durgunoglu, Nagy, & Hancin-Bhatt, 1993; Geva, 2006; Geva, Yaghoub-Zadeh, & Schuster, 2000; Gottardo, 2002; Quiroga et al., 2002).

Fourth, oral English-language proficiency is strongly related to text-level skills, including English reading comprehension and writing. Studies of young emergent bilingual Latino children have consistently found that oral language proficiency in English and English reading comprehension are positively correlated (Carlisle, Beeman, Davis, & Spharim, 1999; Carlisle, Beeman, & Shah, 1996; Geva, 2006; Goldstein, Harris, & Klein, 1993; Jiménez, García, & Pearson, 1996; Peregoy, 1989; Peregoy & Boyle, 1991; Pérez, 1981; Royer & Carlo, 1991). In addition, it appears from the small body of research on the topic that English writing skills, which involve the integration of several literacy and higher order cognitive skills, are also predicted by students' oral English proficiency (Davis, Carlisle, & Beeman, 1999; Lanauze & Snow, 1989).

Comparing Programs

In Chapter 3, we considered the debate among educators and policymakers regarding program type in the development of early education programs in general. Here we evaluate the literature regarding what type of program best serves the academic needs in language and literacy skills specific to emergent bilingual children in the educational setting. The effectiveness of programs targeted at young emergent bilinguals is widely contested. Debates regarding program types that best develop the academic skills of children whose native language is not English continue among practitioners, academics, and policymakers. The fundamental issue underlying the debate has been whether bilingual or English-only approaches are more effective in boosting and sustaining the academic achievement of emergent bilinguals. Early research surrounding this issue was inconclusive. Some researchers, such as Baker and de Kanter (1981) and Baker and Pelavin (1984), have asserted that the research evidence did not support the effectiveness of bilingual instruction and that bilingual education simply does not work. Others, such as Willig (1985), have refuted this argument and provided evidence to support the efficacy of bilingual programs. Here we present the most recent empirical evidence, including original studies, syntheses, and meta-analyses, that assesses this question at the national level. (See Chapter 3 for a discussion of the related issue of time-on-task.)

Greene (1998) was one of the first to conduct a systematic meta-analysis of the effectiveness of bilingual education in the United States. He included 11 of 75 original studies in his meta-analysis, and each of the 11 studies met minimal standards for quality (i.e., randomization) of research design. They included standardized test scores from 2,719 students—1,562 of whom were enrolled in bilingual programs—in 13 states. The average student in bilingual programs was tested in third grade, after 2 years of bilingual instruction. Greene found that, overall, bilingual programs produced 0.21 of a standard deviation improvement on reading tests and 0.12 of a standard deviation improvement on math tests measured in English. The gain in all test scores measured in Spanish was 0.74 of a standard deviation. Greene noted that although these data showed the general academic benefits of bilingual programs, a few critical programmatic concerns remained unclear. Namely, this study did not ascertain the ideal length of time students should be in bilingual programs, the ideal amount of native language used for instruction, and the age groups in which these techniques were most appropriate. These concerns are especially important for young Latino children.

More recently, Slavin and Cheung (2005) published a best-evidence synthesis (Slavin, 1986) reviewing experimental studies that compared bilingual and English-only reading programs for emergent bilinguals. The authors used a systematic literature search, quantification of outcomes as effect sizes, and extensive discussion of individual studies ($N = 17$) that met inclusion criteria. Thirteen of the 17 studies focused on elementary school reading for Spanish-dominant students. Of these, nine favored bilingual approaches on English reading measures and four found no significant difference, producing a median effect size of 0.45 in favor of bilingual approaches. Weighted by sample size, an effect size of 0.33 was calculated, in favor of programs with bilingual approaches. Slavin and Cheung concluded that the available body of empirical research is limited; more high-quality studies should be conducted to ascertain the effectiveness of reading programs for emergent bilinguals. They recommended that such studies should incorporate longitudinal, randomized designs to produce satisfying answers to questions surrounding program effectiveness for emergent bilinguals.

Rolstad, Mahoney, and Glass (2005) presented another meta-analysis, including 17 studies conducted since 1985 on the effectiveness of bilingual approaches compared with English-only approaches. Unlike the earlier-mentioned studies, Rolstad et al. decided to include as many studies as possible in their analysis instead of excluding on the basis of a priori criteria. They computed the effect size of program effectiveness by calculating mean outcome differences between new treatment and traditional treatment groups, and then dividing by the standard deviation of the traditional treatment group (Glass, McGaw, & Smith, 1981). Using this method, Rolstad et al. found that bilingual approaches were consistently better than English-only approaches. With bilingual status controlled for, analysis yielded a positive effect for bilingual programs at 0.23 of a standard deviation.

Unlike the above-mentioned reviews, August, Calderón, Carlo, and Nuttall (2006) focused their follow-up study of program effectiveness on a particular linguistic group: fifth-grade bilingual students ($N = 113$). Moreover, the authors evaluated the effectiveness of the language of instruction on broad reading outcomes (combining word reading and passage comprehension) for three groups: (a) Spanish-speaking students instructed in Spanish only, (b) Spanish-speaking students instructed in English, and (c) Spanish-speaking students instructed first in Spanish and then transitioned into English-only instruction in third or fourth grade. All of the students in the study were in one of the three programs from the time they began school and were exposed to the same intervention with parallel versions in English and Spanish. Implementation data were collected across classrooms and sites to ensure integrity of implementation.

Measures for August et al.'s (2006) study included the Computer-Based Academic Assessment System (CAAS) and two subsets of the Woodcock Language Proficiency Battery, including letter–word identification and passage comprehension. All assessments were conducted in Spanish and English. Using an analysis of covariance and controlling for the mothers' level of education and students' initial performance (during second grade), August et al. found meaningful between-groups differences on students' broad reading scores in English and Spanish. For the English reading scores, those in the Spanish-only group scored significantly lower than those in the bilingual and

English-only groups. No significant difference was found between the bilingual and English-only groups. For the Spanish reading scores, significant differences were found among all three groups. Moreover, the bilingual group scored significantly higher than the English-only group, and the Spanish-only group scored significantly higher than the bilingual group. These findings suggest that sound instruction in Spanish followed by sound instruction in English benefits Spanish-speaking children. On measures of broad reading in English, the bilingual group performed as well as their English-only peers and better than their English-only peers on measures of broad reading in Spanish. Without English instruction, students in the Spanish-only group did not perform as well as the others in English. Similarly, without Spanish instruction, students in the English-only group did not perform as well as the others in Spanish. These data support the notion that bilingual instruction is beneficial in that students acquire bilingual literacy skills and are not disadvantaged with regard to the acquisition of literacy in English.

Finally, Borman, Hewes, Reilly, and Alvarado (2006) conducted a meta-analysis on the achievement effects of the nationally disseminated and externally developed school improvement programs known as *whole-school* or *comprehensive* reforms implemented in schools that serve predominantly Latino students. They compared the specific achievement effects of the 12 most widely implemented models of comprehensive school reform (CSR) for Latinos. They found that the effects of CSR for schools serving mostly Latino students were somewhat limited but that the current body of evidence suggests that CSR programs that show particular promise for Latino students include appreciation of cultural practices that are directly relevant to language.

When weighing the importance of including the child's native language in classroom instruction, researchers must consider key characteristics of the child, classroom, and staff (García, 2005). At the level of the child, it is important to consider his or her native language and exposure to and acquisition of English. It is also important to assess the general linguistic development of students within the same classroom. There should also be an assessment of staff characteristics. Given the needs of the class and the individuals within the classroom, what staff and resources are necessary to implement the desired instruction? For young emergent bilingual students, programs that include meaningful integration of students' native language become critical as these children develop fundamental literacy skills.

Meta-analyses and best-evidence studies have concluded that the academic benefits of bilingual over English-only programs demonstrate, on average, an academic performance benefit of 0.2 to 0.3 standard deviations for young Latino emergent bilinguals over and above English-only programs. This is enough to close about one fifth to one third of the overall Latino–White achievement gap in reading in the early elementary school years.

DUAL-LANGUAGE PROGRAMS

Dual-language (DL) programs, also known as *two-way immersion*, are relatively new in the United States. Unique among program alternatives, the goals of DL programs are to provide high-quality instruction for students who come to school speaking primarily a language other than English and to provide instruction in a second language for English-speaking students. We discussed the debate over two-way immersion and other bilingual programs versus English immersion in Chapter 3. Here we undertake an extended discussion of the effectiveness of DL programs for educating emergent bilingual and bilingual children. Schools offering DL programs thus teach children language through content, with teachers adapting their instruction to ensure children's comprehension and using content lessons to convey vocabulary and language structure. Striving for half language-minority students and half native-English-speaking students in each classroom, DL programs also aim to teach cross-cultural awareness. Programs vary in the amount of time they devote to each language, which grade levels and populations they serve, and how much structure they impose for the division of language and curriculum. The Center for Applied Linguistics (2005) compiled research-based strategies and practices associated with DL program development and implementation. Titled *Guiding Principles for Dual-Language Education*, the report lists seven dimensions to help with planning and ongoing implementation of DL programs: (a) assessment and accountability, (b) curriculum, (c) instruction, (d) staff quality and professional development, (e) program structure, (f) family and community, and (g) support and resources.

There are two widely adopted models of language division in DL programs: the 50-50 and the 90-10 models. In the 50-50 model, instruction is given half the day in English and half the day in a non-English native language (i.e., the target language) throughout the grades. In the 90-10 model, children spend 90% of their kindergarten school days in the non-English minority language, and this percentage gradually decreases to 50% by fourth or fifth grade.

The installation of DL programs is based on a strong theoretical rationale and supported by empirical research findings concerning both first- and second language acquisition (Genesee, 1999). This rationale grows out of sociocultural theory, which maintains that learning occurs through naturalistic social interaction (Vygotsky, 1978). That is, the integration of native English speakers and speakers of other languages facilitates second language acquisition because it promotes natural, substantive interaction among speakers of different languages.

Currently in the United States, there are more than 400 DL programs, and the number is growing rapidly (Center for Applied Linguistics, 2004).

Although the vast majority offer instruction in Spanish and English, there are also DL programs that target Korean, Cantonese, Arabic, French, Japanese, Navajo, Portuguese, and Russian (García, 2005; Howard, Sugarman, & Christian, 2003). Typically, these programs have three major goals: (a) to help children to learn English and find success in U.S. schools; (b) to help these children become competent in their own language without sacrificing their own success in school; and (c) to promote linguistic and ethnic equity among the children, encouraging them to bridge the gaps between cultures and languages. These goals are naturally interdependent and relate to the individual student at differing levels, depending on his or her particular sociolinguistic and sociocultural background. For example, native English-speaking children benefit by coming to understand that another language and culture hold equal importance to their own. Spanish-speaking Latino children enrolled in a DL program are given equal school status due to their knowledge of their home language rather than being penalized and segregated because of it.

Research evidence suggests that DL programs can be an excellent model for academic achievement for both language-minority and language-majority children. Studies have shown that DL programs promote English-language learning as well or better than other special programs designed for language-minority children. For example, 100% of Spanish-dominant children in the Key School, a 50-50 DL school in Arlington County, Virginia, demonstrated oral English fluency by third grade, as shown by the Language Assessment Scales–Oral English Proficiency measure and classroom observations (Christian, 1997). English writing samples collected from native Spanish speakers in fifth and sixth grade were indistinguishable from those of native English speakers, and all were of high quality (Christian, 1997). In a separate study of four DL schools following the 90-10 program model in California, Lindholm (1999) found that by fifth grade most students were clearly fluent in English and made gains in English reading at most school sites (although they did not attain grade-level performance in reading).

DL immersion programs appear to encourage achievement in academic subjects in both English and the minority languages. In an early study comparing DL students with a control population, Christian (1994) found that third graders from the Amigos Dual Immersion Program in Cambridge, Massachusetts, outperformed a Spanish-speaking cohort in a more conventional bilingual education program in reading and mathematics in both Spanish and English using English-plus-Spanish approaches. In fact, students in this program performed consistently at grade-level norms for children their age, which included children who spoke only English. The DL program provided children with the tools they needed to perform well in school assessments in English, even though the majority of their school time had been spent in Spanish instruction. This was further shown in another study conducted several years later at the Amigos school (Cazabon, Lambert, & Hall, 1999). Here, children from fourth through eighth grade were shown to perform consistently as well and often significantly better than control populations on standardized tests in both English and Spanish.

In another longitudinal study, Cobb, Vega, and Kronauge (2005) analyzed the effects of a DL elementary school program on academic achievement at the end of elementary school and at the end of the first year of junior high school. Achievements scores were obtained from standardized measures in reading, writing, and mathematics from native English speakers ($n = 83$) and native Spanish speakers ($n = 83$) from DL programs and matched controls, using an ex post facto quasi-experimental design. All students had been continuously enrolled in their schools (experimental or control) for a minimum of 4 years before initial data collection. Participants were tracked from third grade through middle school and measured on their reading, writing, and mathematics achievement in sixth and seventh grades. Cobb et al. analyzed mean differences between groups using a series of analyses of variance. They found that English and Spanish native speakers in DL programs scored as well or better than their peers in control groups. The greatest effect for native English speakers was in reading, whereas native Spanish speakers appeared to benefit more in writing and mathematics. Because of the small sample size in this study, however, it is difficult to assess the generalizability of the results.

As part of a 7-year study of two-way immersion, researchers at the Center for Applied Linguistics collected data on the language development and academic achievement of 344 students in 11 Spanish–English DL programs across the United States that incorporated English-plus-Spanish strategies (Sugarman & Howard, 2001). Half of the students in the study were native Spanish speakers, and half were native English speakers. All had been enrolled in the program since kindergarten or first grade.

English and Spanish narrative writing samples were collected at three intervals (October, February, and May) during the 3 years of the study (1997–1998, 1998–1999, and 1999–2000), when the students were in third, fourth, and fifth grade, respectively. English and Spanish oral proficiency assessments and English cloze reading assessments were administered in third and fifth grades, and a Spanish cloze reading assessment was administered in third grade only. In cloze reading exercises, the reader has to supply words that have been intentionally deleted from a passage.

Results for the writing assessment included the scores of native Spanish speakers compared with the scores of native English speakers on the English and Spanish assessments across the 3 years. Sugarman and Howard (2001) found that average scores for both groups increased significantly in both languages of instruction over 3 years. On average, native English speakers scored 0.4 to 0.6 points higher than native Spanish speakers on the English writing assessment, whereas native Spanish speakers scored 0.1 to 0.4 points higher than native English speakers on the Spanish writing assessment. Although the native English speakers nearly closed the Spanish writing gap to 0.1 points by fifth grade, the gap between the two language groups in English writing remained fairly constant over the 3 years. In English writing, for the three components of the writing sample, both native English speakers and native Spanish speakers performed highest in grammar, followed by mechanics, then composition. In short, for writing, gains in both languages were observed for both native English and native Spanish speakers in each of the languages of instruction.

For reading, both native Spanish and native English speakers showed growth in the English cloze assessment from third grade to fifth grade, each reaching grade-level performance at fifth grade with no significant differences in English reading ability apparent between the groups on this measure. With regard to oral language, both groups also showed growth. On the English oral language assessment, native Spanish speakers had an average score of 4.4 and native English speakers had an average score of 4.8 in third grade, but the average score of both native English speakers and native Spanish speakers in fifth grade was a nearly perfect, 4.9 out of 5.0. The average scores for native Spanish speakers on the Spanish oral assessment were 4.6 in third grade and 4.8 in fifth grade, and for native English speakers, the average score rose from 3.6 in third grade to 4.1 in fifth grade.

These comprehensive longitudinal data for DL students showed that both native English speakers and native Spanish speakers in the study showed progress in their language and literacy skills from the beginning of third grade through the end of fifth grade. In addition, native Spanish speakers demonstrated more balanced language and literacy skills in the two languages, whereas native English speakers demonstrated clear dominance in English, yet the DL program produced academic functioning for both groups of students over the period studied.

As a follow-up to the longitudinal study by Sugarman and Howard (2001), Howard, Sugarman, and Christian (2003) summarized the research literature on DL programs, synthesizing key findings across studies and highlighting areas in need of further research. Specifically, they looked at studies analyzing achievement patterns of DL participants, language and literacy outcomes, the cultural context and social impact of DL programs, the integration of language-minority and language-majority students, language status issues, students' attitudes, teacher experiences, and parents' attitudes and involvement. In terms of academic achievement and language and literacy development, Howard et al. found that both native Spanish speakers and native English speakers in DL programs performed as well or better than their peers in other types of programs, both on English standardized achievement tests and Spanish standardized achievement tests. Within DL programs, they found that native speakers tended to perform better than second language learners, such that native English speakers scored higher on English achievement tests and native Spanish speakers scored higher on Spanish achievement tests. Moreover, balanced bilingual children, on average, outperformed other students. The authors mentioned, however, that many of the studies reviewed did not control sufficiently for student background, general quality of the school environment, and fidelity of program implementation. Nevertheless, the consistency of the findings across studies (of varying degrees in methodological rigor) suggests credibility.

Language and literacy outcomes from Howard et al. (2003) were similar. Native speakers tended to perform better than second language speakers in both oral and written language proficiency. Language-minority students, on the whole, demonstrated more bilingual dominance than their native English-speaking peers; their performance on language and literacy measures across language was more similar to that of the native English speakers. These data also supported the notion of linguistic transfer of literacy and higher order cognitive skills.

Positive effects of DL programs have also been found for Latinos during the earliest years of schooling. Figueroa (2005) conducted a study with 24 emergent bilingual kindergarteners (10 girls, 14 boys) in a DL program looking at associations between the development of prereading knowledge in the child's native language and the development of English skills. Figueroa examined means and standard deviations from tests of phonological reasoning and oral fluency during the fall of kindergarten, winter of kindergarten, and spring of kindergarten. She found that participants made significant gains in Spanish and English for every subtest of phonological awareness, in both languages, and at each of the three waves of data collection. Moreover, all participants met or exceeded district requirements. Although the sampling methods in this study do not allow for robust generalizations to the larger population of young Latino emergent bilinguals, the results support what we know about the relationships between first- and second language acquisition: Meaningful use and development of the primary language in the early years facilitate prereading skills in a second language. This is because higher order cognitive skills tend to transfer between language, and during the early years, acquisition of fundamental language and cognitive skills is very important (Genesee et al., 2006).

In an experimental study, Barnett, Yarosz, Thomas, Jung, and Blanco (2007) compared the effects of a DL and a monolingual English immersion (EI) preschool program on children's learning. Children in the study ($N = 150$) were from both English and Spanish home language backgrounds; 85 children were randomly assigned to the DL program, and 65 were randomly assigned to the

EI program in the same school district. The two programs were compared on measures of children's growth in language, emergent literacy, and mathematics. Compared with those in the EI group, children in the DL program produced large and significant gains in Spanish vocabulary. In addition, all children (including native Spanish speakers and native English speakers) in the DL program made greater phonological awareness gains in English, yet no group differences were found on measures of English language and literacy development. The results of this study, therefore, suggest that early DL programs can support native-language development without sacrificing gains in English-language development. Moreover, English-native children in the DL program also made gains in Spanish language and literacy without hindering development in their native language. Additional analyses would be needed to determine the longitudinal impact of preschool DL programs on literacy development and academic outcomes throughout the elementary years.

Thus, the present knowledge base demonstrates that DL programs lead to positive achievement outcomes for both language-minority and language-majority students, especially for young children developing fundamental language and literacy skills. Research supports the idea that higher order cognitive and literacy skills transfer between languages, that developing native language skills can improve second language skills, and that the DL program model corresponds well with these findings. Yet, the question remains: What specific programmatic features predict variation in quality among sites offering DL programs? To answer this question, Christian, Genesee, Lindholm-Leary, and Howard (2004) conducted an in-depth examination of DL programs. Specifically, they evaluated the variation in educational attainment among school sites, the characteristics of effective classroom instruction, and the skills and knowledge required of professionals to work in DL programs. They followed 484 students in 11 DL programs across the United States for 3 years, from third through fifth grade (this is the same sample mentioned earlier). Christian et al. looked specifically at features and practices of the DL programs that contributed to levels of English language proficiency for Spanish-speaking emergent bilinguals. Specifically, their study considered student outcome differences across DL program types (i.e., 90-10 vs. 50-50), relative performance of at-risk students in three schools, and teacher characteristics and strategies deemed critical to effective program implementation.

First, Christian et al. (2004) compared the performance of students in the 90-10 DL programs with that of students in the 50-50 programs. For oral English proficiency, native Spanish speakers from both programs made progress over time, from the beginning of third grade through the end of fifth grade. The rate of growth did not appear to be different, and both groups had high levels of oral English proficiency at the end of fifth grade, suggesting no difference between program models for oral English proficiency. For English reading and English narrative writing ability, however, slight differences were found between program types. Namely, at the third grade, students in the 50-50 program had slightly higher mean scores than 90-10 students. However, by the end of fifth grade there were no significant differences, which indicates that native Spanish speakers in the 90-10 group had higher growth over this 3-year period. Thus, although the development of reading and writing ability in English may have been influenced by the program, attainment at fifth grade was not.

Second, Christian et al. (2004) compared mathematics, reading, and writing achievements across three sites to determine whether DL programs were effective for students at risk of academic difficulty (including low-income students, emergent bilinguals, and/or racial/ethnic minorities). Analyses showed that these students, who often present special learning needs, were able to make substantial gains and function well. Moreover, analyses showed that DL programs were capable of supporting strong academic performance of at-risk students, suggesting that students should not be excluded from DL programs on the basis of their at-risk status.

Finally, Christian et al. (2004) analyzed particular teacher characteristics and strategies deemed important to effective implementation of DL programs. More specifically, they conducted classroom observations and focus groups with veteran teachers to investigate school- and classroom-level practices found to support language and literacy development in DL programs. Analyses of their data provided a list of key teaching strategies and teacher characteristics. They found that successful teachers "prioritize balanced literacy, cooperative and student-centered learning, focus on strategies that can be used across the content areas and language, thematic units, integrating language and content, and using sheltered instruction strategies" (Christian et al., 2004, p. 6). Moreover, successful teachers prioritize the development of thinking, reading, and writing skills, emphasizing that these skills are not language specific per se. The authors continued,

> Thematic instruction reinforces concepts in multiple contexts. Lessons are not repeated in both program languages, but the same language and literacy skills can be reinforced through the various activities that are done in difference content areas. This type of teaching requires a great deal of coordination and joint planning time for the teachers involved. Teachers plan lessons with language and content goals in mind and reinforce reading and writing skills taught during language arts by applying them to content areas. (Christian et al., 2004, p. 7)

Teachers who were able to implement these successful strategies, in general, shared the following characteristics: (a) fluency in both languages of instruction to model high language performance; (b) awareness of second language acquisition patterns to identify students' needs and tailor lessons to meet those needs; (c) mastery of instructional strategies (i.e., cooperative learning, sheltered instruction, differentiated instruction, and strategic teaching); and (d) strong organizational and communication skills.

Although research has revealed much about best practices in programs that promote English-plus-Spanish strategies, further research is needed to assess the effectiveness of such strategies within diverse segments of the Latino child population. Analyses are needed by SES, parent educational attainment, immigrant status (first, second, and third-plus generation), and school and classroom variants, including teacher characteristics and competencies (Espinosa, 2010a; Espinosa, 2010b; Garcia & Jensen, 2007a; Garcia & Jensen, 2007b).

PREKINDERGARTEN

Across the United States, policymakers at all levels of government are making substantial investments and commitments to prekindergarten programs (for children ages 3 and 4 years). The provision of high-quality educational access for young children in the country is motivated by research in child development and in economics. In terms of development, neuropsychological research shows that the brains of very young children are extremely malleable during the early years of life (Náñez, 2010; Ramey & Ramey, 1998; Shonkoff & Phillips, 2000). Indeed, a key characteristic of early childhood (0–3 years old) is remarkably rapid brain development. In many ways, these early years provide the foundation for the brain's lifelong capacity for growth and change. A strong neurological groundwork is established in early childhood through rich experiences that allow the brain to develop to the point of being able to process, encode, and interact with the environment (Goncz & Kodzepeljic, 1991). High-quality early education programs are able to provide the necessary scaffolding and facilitate this development (Wong Fillmore, 1991).

With regard to financial investment in early education programs, economists Heckman and Masterov (2004) found that "enriched prekindergarten programs available to disadvantaged children on a voluntary basis . . . have [a] strong track record of promoting achievement for disadvantaged children, improving their labor market outcomes and reducing involvement in crime" (p. 17). Moreover, educational policies that stress financial investment in early educational development are much cheaper than those that seek to remedy early educational deficits at the middle school and high school levels. Simply stated, the later in life the attempts are made to repair early deficits, the costlier remediation becomes (Ramey & Ramey, 1998; Reynolds, 2003; Reynolds & Temple, 2005). (See Chapter 3, this volume, for a more detailed review.)

Given the size and rapid growth of the Latino population and their comparatively low achievement levels, young Latino children are situated particularly well to benefit from high-quality prekindergarten programs (García & González, 2006). However, although enrollments among Latino children are increasing, they are less likely than their White, Asian, and African American peers to attend any sort of preschool program (García, Jensen, Miller, & Huerta, 2005). Given the potential benefits of prekindergarten programs, efforts are currently being made to increase enrollments of Latino children into high-quality programs.

Current empirical evidence suggests that young Latino children benefit cognitively from such programs. An evaluation of the public prekindergarten program in Tulsa, Oklahoma, found benefits for all racial/ethnic and SES groups (Gormley, Gayer, & Dawson, 2004). Gains for Latino students in this program were especially impressive. Latinos experienced a 79% gain in letter–word identification, a 39% gain in spelling, and a 54% gain in applied problem solving. These figures outpaced gains that naturally would have occurred during 1 year of children's development (Gormley, Gayer, & Dawson, 2004). Further research evaluating the longitudinal benefits and curricular and instructional strategies of the Oklahoma program—and others like it—is needed.

Critical to the success of prekindergarten programs for Latino children are ways in which language and culture are integrated. More specifically, a trademark of high-quality prekindergarten programs for young Latino children is the provision of DL (English and Spanish) content and instruction by school staff who are bilingual and culturally competent (Barnett, Yarosz, et al., 2007; Borman et al., 2006). This approach validates the child's cognitive and linguistic abilities while bridging home–school cultural differences, thereby establishing an environment in which parents feel comfortable and are able to communicate with teachers.

CONCLUSION

The issues covered in this chapter about the intersection of early schooling, learning, and development of bilingual children indicate that the demographic circumstances of young Latinos in the United States should serve as an impetus to develop and support schooling programs and practices that recognize the conditions and strengths of Latino children and families. Because three out of four young Latino children are exposed to Spanish in the home, the ways in which these programs integrate language in teaching and learning are critical. In terms of academic achievement, bilingual students lag behind their monolingual peers at the beginning of kindergarten, and the gap closes very little thereafter. First- and second-generation Latino children and those of Mexican and Central American origins demonstrate particularly low achievement. SES, low parent education, limited English proficiency of parents, and other home circumstances bear strongly on student performance. Home language practices strongly influence early student achievement. Research indicates that the amount of extra talk between caretakers and their children, book-reading, and parent–child interactions (e.g., reading, telling stories, singing) influence early cognitive development. Data indicate that parents who have little formal education are less likely to engage in these activities. For example, compared with Whites, Latino parents are less likely to read, tell stories, and sing to their children. For school-age emergent bilinguals, best evidence suggests that 3 to 5 years are needed to obtain oral English proficiency and 4 to 7 years to obtain academic English proficiency. Additional research is needed to determine the duration of English proficiency for 3- and 4-year-old emergent bilinguals. Also, appropriate tests and testing procedures are necessary to accurately determine language and cognitive competency of young Latino students (as well as other culturally and linguistically diverse student populations). Assessment tools and procedures should systematically link learning outcomes with various contextual features and should be used primarily to improve learning outcomes and service provision for these children. Studies in literacy development demonstrate that word- and text-level skills transfer between languages. Letter learning, phonemic awareness, word reading, and passage comprehension in Spanish are strongly correlated with parallel skills in English. Moreover, the integration of Spanish in the classroom has been shown to strengthen transfer. As the process of transfer takes time, literacy for emergent bilingual students, on average, takes longer than for native English speakers. Also, schooling program options for bilinguals differ in their goals (e.g., whether bilingual proficiency is an aim), their requirements for staff competency, and the student populations they are meant to serve. The effectiveness of a given program depends on local conditions, choices, and leveraging the cognitive benefits of bilingualism. In terms of student academic achievement, meta-analyses and best-evidence syntheses suggest that programs supporting bilingual approaches to curriculum and instruction are favorable to English-only or English-immersion programs. These programs provide sound instruction in both Spanish and English and demonstrate, on average, academic benefits of 0.2 to 0.3 standard deviations over and above English-only programs.

Driven by sociocultural concepts of language and learning, DL programs integrate native Spanish-speaking students with native English speakers in the same classroom. Educators in DL programs use English-plus-Spanish approaches to teach both languages through course content. Studies suggest that language-minority and language-majority students in DL programs perform academically at equal levels as their peers and in many cases outperform those in other programs. Further research is needed to assess the effectiveness of programs that promote English-plus-Spanish strategies for the diverse segments of the bilingual child population, by SES, parent education, and immigrant status. Finally, preliminary evidence suggests that high-quality prekindergarten programs can improve school readiness for young bilingual children and decrease achievement differences between racial and ethnic groups at kindergarten entry. Further research on the longitudinal gains these programs produce is needed.

8

POLICIES

The success of the educational interventions discussed in Chapter 7 (this volume) is contingent on the development of educational policies that target the needs of bilingual children. Unfortunately, at every level of educational policy in the United States, policies regarding the education of bilingual students have been highly restrictive, aimed at the acquisition of English at the cost of supporting any aspects of the students' heritage language or promoting bilingualism (Gandara & Hopkins, 2010). This policy stance is incongruent with the growing knowledge base addressed by the preceding chapters. In this chapter, we highlight this incongruence between research and policy related to bilingual students in the United States.

In contrast to present policy, specific policies at all levels of government should strive to provide and support rich language environments, high-quality dual-language (DL) and prekindergarten programs, and efforts to recruit and prepare highly qualified teachers. In addition, educational policies should expand federal and state-funded prekindergarten, increase bilingual student enrollments in these programs, develop parent outreach initiatives, and improve assessment procedures and accountability measures.

Regarding teacher quality, state governments must fund programs to increase the number of K–3 and prekindergarten teachers in their states who are proficient in Spanish and other primary languages of the bilingual children they serve. As a part of their training, teachers should receive instruction in second language acquisition and how content learning intersects with the process of managing two language systems. States may consider aggressively recruiting teachers within bilingual communities as a way to increase the number of linguistically and culturally competent teachers. Colleges and universities should be engaged as partners to ensure that bilingual teachers are recruited to the field of early education (pre-K–3) and that teachers receive appropriate training.

State governments should continue to expand their state-funded prekindergarten initiatives with the objective of creating voluntary universal prekindergarten systems. For bilingual children, expansion should be accompanied by curriculum development and instructional approaches that integrate both multiple languages and English. In addition, educational policies should seek to increase enrollment rates of bilingual children in the programs that fund extensive local efforts to provide information to parents on the availability of prekindergarten programs in their communities.

Educational policies should allot local education agencies the necessary support to develop DL programs. These programs should be developed on the basis of empirical evidence and strategies shown to be successful (see Center for Applied Linguistics, 2005). Such programs should be assessed continuously and, when necessary, modified to optimize learning, language development, and general academic performance of bilingual children.

THE FEDERAL COURTS AND ENGLISH LEARNERS: ESTABLISHING LEGAL RIGHTS

The United States Supreme Court decision in *Lau v. Nichols* (1974) stands as the landmark case for establishing language-minority status as a claim for discrimination. The Court's decision also called for providing support to limited-English-proficient (LEP) students and access to the curriculum:

> There is no equality of treatment merely by providing students with English instruction. Students without the ability to understand English are effectively foreclosed from any meaningful discourse. Basic English skills are at the very core of what these public schools teach. Imposition of a requirement that, before a child can effectively participate in the education program he must already have acquired those basic skills is to make a mockery of public education. We know that those who do not understand English are certain to find their classroom experiences wholly incomprehensible and in no way meaningful. (Lau v. Nichols, 1974, p. 18)

The class action lawsuit was filed against the San Francisco Unified School District on March 25, 1970, and involved 12 American-born and foreign-born Chinese students. Prior to the suit, the district initiated a pullout program in 1966 at the request of parents of LEP students. In a 1967 school census, the district identified 2,456 LEP Chinese students. By 1970, the district had identified 2,856 such students, more than half of whom (1,790) had received no special instruction. Also, the vast majority of these students (more than 2,600) were taught by teachers who did not speak Chinese. The district still argued that it had taken initial steps to serve the LEP students. In the end, the Court ruled in favor of the students and parents, and the majority opinion overruled an appeals court that had ruled in favor of the district.

The majority opinion relied on statutory, or legislative, grounds and avoided any reference to constitutional determination. A student's right to special educational services flowed from the district's obligations under Title VI of the Civil Rights Act of 1964, which prohibits discrimination on the basis of race, color, or national origin in programs or activities receiving federal financial assistance. A May 25, 1970, memorandum issued by the U.S. Department of Health, Education, and Welfare also justified the requirement of special educational services. After *Lau*, the language-minority education lawsuits were brought almost exclusively by Latino litigants. Although some cases were litigated to ensure compliance with the *Lau* requirements of "affirmative steps," most subsequent cases involved issues not addressed by *Lau*: Who are these students? What form of additional educational services must be provided?

In *Aspira of New York, Inc. v. Board of Education* (1975), a community action group brought a suit on behalf of all Latino children in the New York School District. The plaintiff argued that these students could not successfully participate in an English schooling context because of their lack of English proficiency but that they could successfully participate in a Spanish-language curriculum (Roos, 1984). The U.S. district court hearing this case adopted a language dominance procedure to identify those students eligible for non-English, Spanish-language instructional programs.

The language dominance procedure called for parallel examinations to obtain language proficiency estimates on Spanish and English standardized achievement tests. All students scoring below the 20th percentile on an English language test were given the same (or a parallel) achievement test in Spanish. Students who scored higher on the Spanish achievement test and Spanish language proficiency test were to be placed in a Spanish language program. These procedures assumed adequate reliability and validity for the language and achievement tests administered. Such an assumption was, and still is, highly questionable. However, the court argued that it acted in "reasonable manner," admitting that in the absence of better assessment procedures it was forced to follow precedent (*Lau*). A subsequent case, *Otero v. Mesa County School District No. 51* (1975), concluded that a clear relationship between low academic achievement and a lack of English proficiency must be clearly demonstrated before a court could mandate special instructional services.

In the key Fifth Circuit decision of *Castañeda v. Pickard* (1981), the court interpreted Section 1703(f) of the Equal Education Opportunities Act (EEOA) of 1974 as substantiating the holding of *Lau* that schools cannot ignore the special language needs of students. The EEOA extended Title VI of the Civil Rights Act to all educational institutions, not just those receiving federal funding. According to Section 1703(f) of the EEOA,

> No state shall deny equal educational opportunities to an individual on account of his or her race, color, sex, or national origin by—the failure of an educational agency to take appropriate action to overcome language barriers that impede equal participation by its students in its instructional programs.

Furthermore, the court then contemplated whether the statutory requirement of the EEOA that districts take "appropriate action to overcome language barriers" should be further delineated. The plaintiffs argued for a construction of "appropriate action" that would necessitate bilingual programs to incorporate bilingual students' primary language. The court concluded, however, that Section 1703(f) did not embody a congressional mandate that any particular form of remedy be uniformly adopted.

However, the court did conclude that Congress required districts to adopt an appropriate program, and by creating a cause of action in the federal court to enforce Section 1703(f), it left to federal judges the task of determining whether a given program was appropriate. While the court noted that Congress had not provided guidance in that statute or in its brief legislative history on what it intended by selecting "appropriateness" as the operative standard, it continued with reluctance and hesitancy and described a mode of analysis for a Section 1703(f) case. It became legally possible to substantiate a violation of Section 1703(f), following from *Lau*, on three grounds: (a) The program providing special language services to eligible English learners is not based on sound educational theory; (b) the program is not being implemented in an effective manner; or (c) the program, after a period of "reasonable implementation," does not produce results that substantiate language barriers are being overcome so as to eliminate achievement gaps between bilingual and English-only speaking students. It is obvious that these criteria allow a local school district to continue to implement a program with some educational theoretical support for a "reasonable" time to make judgments on its positive or negative effects.

Furthermore, in the *Castaneda* decision, the court again spoke, reluctantly but firmly, to the issue of program implementation. In particular, the court indicated that the district must provide adequate resources, including trained instructional personnel, materials, and other relevant support, that would ensure effective program implementation. Implicit in these standards is the requirement that districts staff their programs with language-minority education specialists, typically defined by state-approved credentials or professional course work (similar to devices used to judge professional expertise in other areas of professional education).

LOOKING FORWARD: THE TENTATIVE LEGACY OF *LAU*

The U.S. federal courts have played a significant role in shaping educational policy for bilingual students. Although hesitant at times, the courts have addressed issues of student identification, program implementation, resource allocation, professional staffing, and program effectiveness. Moreover, they have obligated both local and state educational agencies to language-minority education responsibilities. However, in recent years the courts' role in establishing the rights of English learners has eroded as the power of *Lau v. Nichols* has been undermined. Through the cumulative impact of three cases—*Guardians Association v. Civil Service Commission* (1983), *Alexander v. Choate* (1985), and *Alexander v. Sandoval* (2001)—the court (a) established that the language of Title VI applies to purposeful discrimination and does not extend to adverse effect, and (b) determined that plaintiffs could only sue for intentional discrimination, which has left enforcement almost entirely in the hands of the executive branch. While *Lau* is not the only source of federal legal protection for English learners, the likeliest alternatives are not a perfect substitute for *Lau* (see Moran, 2004, for a thorough discussion of these alternatives). Still, although the core elements of *Lau v. Nichols* are on increasingly shaky ground, the central finding remains uncontested: that an English-only curriculum can be exclusionary whether or not that was the intent of school officials (Gándara, Moran, & García, 2004).

FEDERAL LEGISLATION: LANGUAGE, LITERACY, AND ACCOUNTABILITY

Although court decisions have emerged that are significant regarding the education of American bilingual students, federal legislative efforts have also been significant.

Bilingual Education Act (1968–1994)

Since its inception in 1968 through its final reauthorization in 1994, the Bilingual Education Act (BEA), Title VII of the Elementary and Secondary

Education Act (ESEA) of 1965, served as the United States' primary federal legislative effort to provide equal educational opportunity to English learners. The legislation was reauthorized on five occasions (1974, 1978, 1984, 1988, and 1994). The BEA was eliminated as part of the No Child Left Behind Act (NCLB) of 2001, the most recent reauthorization of the ESEA. Under provisions of NCLB, federal funds will continue to support the education of LEP students through Title III: Language Instruction for Limited English Proficient and Immigrant Students. However, Title III differs markedly from the initial enactment of Title VII (the BEA) and all subsequent reauthorizations. Overall, while the original intent of the BEA was never one of establishing language policy, the role of language became a prominent marker as the legislation articulated the goals and nature of education for English learners.

As in *Lau v. Nichols*, the BEA stemmed from the Civil Rights Act of 1964 as part of the "war on poverty" legislation. The legislation was primarily a crisis intervention, a political strategy to funnel poverty funds to the second largest minority group in the Southwest, Mexican Americans (Casanova, 1991). The BEA intended to establish a demonstration program to meet the educational needs of low-income, emergent bilingual children. It was primarily a remedial effort, aimed at overcoming students' "language deficiencies," and these "compensatory efforts were considered to be a sound educational response to the call for equality of educational opportunity" (Navarro, 1990, p. 291). No particular program of instruction was recommended; instead, financial assistance was provided to local educational agencies "to develop and carry out new and imaginative . . . programs" (Bilingual Education Act of 1968, §702). Among the approved activities were the following programs: bilingual education, history and culture, early childhood education, and adult education for parents.

Although the aim of the BEA was never one of establishing language policy, the role of language became a prominent marker as the legislation articulated the goals and nature of education for English learners in its various reauthorizations from 1974 to 1994. In its early years, all programs funded under the BEA featured native language instruction, but reauthorization in subsequent years marked a shift toward English acquisition as a primary goal (Birman & Ginsburg, 1983). Bilingualism was viewed as a laudable goal but not the responsibility of schools. Rather, families, churches, and other institutions outside the school could foster native language maintenance (Casanova, 1991; Crawford, 1999).

ESEA Reauthorizations of 1994 and 2001: From Bilingual Education to English Only

The 1994 reauthorization of the BEA marked a return to developing English language proficiency in combination with native-language maintenance, to the extent possible. However, the 2001 reauthorization of the ESEA, or the NCLB Act as it is commonly known, focuses on the goal of "English proficiency." Illustrative of this shift is the complete elimination of the word *bilingual* from the law and any government office affiliated with the law. The federal office that oversees the provisions of the law is now referred to as the Office of English Language Acquisition, Language Enhancement, and Academic Achievement for Limited-English-Proficient Students, instead of the Office of Bilingual Education and Minority Languages Affairs. What was formerly known as the National Clearinghouse for Bilingual Education is now known as the National Clearinghouse for English Language Acquisition and Language Instruction Educational Programs. Table 8.1 summarizes key differences in how the 1994 and the 2001 reauthorizations of the ESEA address the education of LEP students.

As Table 8.1 demonstrates, significant changes are evident in the following areas: purpose, program, allocation of funds, and accountability and assessment. As a result of Title III of NCLB, federal funds are no longer federally administered via competitive grants designed to ensure equity and promote quality programs for English learners, programs that served as models to the larger nation. Instead, resources are allocated primarily through a state formula program for language instruction educational programs (LIEPs) that are based on scientifically-based research (U.S. Department of Education, 2002). LIEPs are defined as

> an instruction course in which LEP students are placed for the purpose of developing and attaining English proficiency, while meeting challenging State academic content and student academic achievement standards. A LIEP may make use of both English and a child's native language to enable the child to develop and attain English proficiency. (U.S. Department of Education, 2002, p. 20)

No Child Left Behind Act: Reading First and Early Reading First

The NCLB of 2001 added two new reading programs to the ESEA in an attempt to understand and simplify the complexities of literacy teaching and learning (Antunez, 2002). According to the U.S. Department of Education, Reading First and its preschool-level companion, Early Reading First (ERF), both focus on putting proven methods of early reading instruction in classrooms. Recent reports provide preliminary evidence to suggest that Reading First is being implemented in schools and classrooms as intended by the legislation (Center on Education Policy, 2006; U.S. Department of Education, 2006). Table 8.2 provides a comparison of key components of Reading First and ERF.

TABLE 8.1
Significant Differences in the 1994 and 2001 Reauthorization of the Elementary and Secondary Education Act of 1965

Issue	1994 Title VII: Bilingual Education Act	2001 Title III: Language Instruction, Limited English Proficient, and Immigrant Students
Eligible populations	Limited-English-proficient students. Recent immigrants who have not been attending one or more schools in any one or more states for more than 3 full years. (§7501(7)) Native Americans, Native Alaskans, Native Hawaiians, Native American Pacific Islanders.	Limited-English-proficient students. Immigrant children and youths: 3–21 years of age, not born in any state, have not been attending one or more schools in any one or more states for more than 3 full academic years. (§3301(6)) Native Americans, Native Alaskans, Native Hawaiians, Native American Pacific Islanders.
Purpose	(A) To help such children and youths develop proficiency in English and, to the extent possible, their native language; and (B) to meet the same challenging state content standards and challenging state student performance standards expected of all children. (§7111(2)) The use of a child or youth's native language and culture in classroom instruction can (A) promote self-esteem and contribute to academic achievement and learning English by limited-English-proficient children and youths. (§7102(14)) The unique status of Native American languages and language enhancement.	To help ensure that children who are limited English proficient, including immigrant children and youths, attain English proficiency, develop high levels of academic attainment in English, and meet the same challenging state academic content and student academic achievement standards as all children are expected to meet. (§3102(1)) Programs for Native Americans: develop English proficiency and, to the extent possible, proficiency in their native language. (§3211(2))

Programs	Competitive grants to local education agencies (schools, districts). State education agencies approve the grant application before submission but play no official role in the grant's implementation. Quality bilingual education programs enable children and youth to learn English and meet high academic standards including proficiency in more than one language. (§7102(9)) Priority is given to programs that provide for development of bilingual proficiency both in English and another language for all participating students. (§7116(i)(1))	To streamline language instruction educational programs into a program carried out through formula grants to state educational agencies and local educational agencies. (§3102(7)) To implement language instruction educational programs, based on scientifically based research on teaching limited-English-proficient children. (§3102(9))
Allocation of funds	Cap of 25% of funds for SAIPs (Special Alternative Instructional Programs), can be lifted if an applicant has demonstrated that developing and implementing a bilingual education program is not feasible.	95% of funds must be used for grants at the local level to teach limited-English-proficient children; each state must spend this percentage to award formula subgrants to districts.
Accountability and assessment	Local education agency is the locus of control and is granted great flexibility on how to best serve students. It sets own goals and ways of assessing them.	To hold various educational agencies accountable for increases in English proficiency and core academic content knowledge by requiring: (A) demonstrated improvements in the English proficiency of limited-English-proficient students each fiscal year; and (B) adequate yearly progress. (§3102(8))

TABLE 8.2
Reading First and Early Reading First of the No Child Left Behind (NCLB) Act

Issue	Reading First: NCLB, Title I, Part B, Subpart 1	Early Reading First: NCLB, Title I, Part B, Subpart 2
Target population	Children in kindergarten through third grade, particularly those from low-income families	Preschool-age children, particularly those from low-income families
Purpose	To provide assistance to state educational agencies and local education agencies: (1) In establishing reading programs for students kindergarten through Grade 3 that are based on scientifically reading research, to ensure that every student can read at grade level or above no later than Grade 3. (2) In preparing teachers through professional development and other support so the teachers can identify specific reading barriers facing their students and so the teachers have tools to effectively help their students to read. (3) In selecting or developing effective instructional materials, programs, learning systems, and strategies that have been proven to prevent or remediate reading failure within a state. (§1201(1))	(1) To support local efforts to enhance the early language, literacy, and prereading development of preschool-age children through strategies and professional development that are based on scientifically based reading research. (2) To provide preschool-age children with cognitive learning opportunities in high-quality language and literature-rich environments, so that children can attain the fundamental knowledge and skills necessary for optimal reading development in kindergarten and beyond. (3) To demonstrate language and literacy based on scientifically based reading research that supports age-appropriate development of oral language (vocabulary, expressive language, listening comprehension), phonological awareness (rhyming, blending, segmenting), print awareness, and alphabetic knowledge. (4) To use screening assessments to effectively identify preschool-age children who may be at risk of reading failure. (5) To integrate such scientific reading research-based instructional materials and literacy activities with existing programs. (§1221(a)(1-5))

Allocation of funds	Formula grants to states, submitting an approved application, based on proportion of children ages 5–17 who reside within the state and who are from families with incomes below the poverty line. (§1202(b)(3)(A)) Subgrants to local education agencies on a competitive basis. States give priority to local education agencies in which at least 15% of the children, or 6,500 children served, are from families with incomes below poverty line. (§1202(c)(2)(B))	Grants awarded on a competitive basis to local education agencies and public or private organizations that serve children from low-income families. (§1221(b)(1))
Required use of local funds	Authorized activities include: (1) Selecting and administering screening, diagnostic, and classroom-based instructional reading assessments. (2) Selecting and implementing a reading instruction program based on scientifically based research instruction and provides such instruction to children in kindergarten through Grade 3. (3) Procuring and implementing instructional materials that are based on scientifically based reading research. (4) Providing professional development for teachers of kindergarten through Grade 3, and special education teachers of kindergarten through Grade 12. (§1201(c)(7)(A))	Authorized activities include: (1) Providing preschool-age children with high-quality oral language and literature-rich environments in which to acquire language and prereading skills. (2) Providing professional development that is based on scientifically based research knowledge of early language and reading development. (3) Identifying and providing activities and instructional materials that are based on scientifically based reading research. (4) Acquiring, providing training for, and implementing screening reading assessments or other appropriate measures.
English learners	Called out in delineation of children who can be served by local funds in kindergarten through Grade 3, and defined as "children who are identified as having limited English proficiency." (§1202(c)(7)(A)(ii)(II)(ff))	Not specifically mentioned in the legislation.
Key definition	Essential components of reading instruction: Explicit and systematic instruction in phonemic awareness, phonics, vocabulary development, reading fluency (including oral reading skills), and reading comprehension strategies. (§1208(3))	

The Reading First program provides formula grants to states, and funds are allocated to states on the basis of the proportion of children ages 5 to 17 who reside in the state and who are from families with incomes below the poverty line. Then state education agencies award subgrants to local education agencies on a competitive basis for proposals that show promise for raising student achievement and for successful implementation of scientifically based reading programs for children from kindergarten through Grade 3. Funds can support professional development for teachers, use of diagnostic and screening tools, as well as classroom-based instructional reading assessments to measure how well children are reading and to monitor progress (U.S. Department of Education, 2008). ERF is one of only two NCLB initiatives that address preschoolers, and it focuses on preparing them to enter kindergarten with the necessary language, cognitive, and early reading skills. Unlike Reading First, ERT awards are made directly to local education agencies and public or private organizations on a competitive basis.

The Reading First legislation was, in fact, formulated from the findings of the National Reading Panel (National Institute of Child Health and Human Development, 2000). The National Reading Panel was approved in 1997 by Congress to initiate a national, comprehensive agenda for approaches to reading instruction and to guide the development of related policy (Ramirez, 2001). After public hearings, discussion, and review of the findings of a National Research Council report, *Preventing Reading Difficulties in Young Children* (Snow, Burns, & Griffin, 1998), the panel decided to focus on the following subtopics for study: alphabetics (phonemic awareness and phonics instruction), fluency, and comprehension (vocabulary instruction, text comprehension instruction, and teacher preparation and comprehension strategies instruction). In addition, studies of second language acquisition, bilingualism, and biliteracy were not included, and as such, the panel did not address issues relevant specifically to English learners.

Both Reading First and ERF call for programs to be grounded in scientifically based research, which is defined in the NCLB as "research that applies rigorous, systematic, and objective procedures to obtain valid knowledge relevant to reading development, reading instruction, and reading difficulties" (NCLB Act of 2001, §1208(6)(A)). The legislation goes on to provide more detailed guidance on the specific characteristics of the research methods. Of particular importance is the careful delineation of the essential components of reading instruction for Reading First programs and the areas of early language and reading development for ERF programs. These flow directly from the National Reading Panel study areas mentioned earlier. Reading First focuses on "explicit and systematic instruction in phonemic awareness; phonics; vocabulary development; reading fluency, including oral reading skills;

and reading comprehension strategies" (NCLB Act of 2001, §1208(3)). ERF focuses on

> (A) recognition, leading to automatic recognition, of letters of the alphabet, knowledge of letters, sounds, blending of letter sounds, and increasingly complex vocabulary; (B) understanding that written language is composed of phonemes and letters each representing one or more speech sounds that in combination make up syllables, words, and sentences; (C) spoken language, including vocabulary and oral comprehension abilities; and (D) knowledge of the purposes and conventions of print. (ESEA of 1965, §1221(a)(3))

It is important to note that neither the National Reading Panel nor the resulting Reading First or ERF legislation examines or makes recommendations specific to reading instruction for English learners. This is problematic because of (a) the number of English learners who are served by Reading First schools and (b) the fact that literacy development for English learners includes all the challenges implicit for monolingual children and, in addition, is shaped by an array of linguistic, cognitive, and academic variables (Antunez, 2002). More than one third of teachers who have emergent bilinguals in their classes reported that no time was set aside to coordinate instruction with English language staff. In fact, only 10% of teachers reported that they had weekly meetings with English language staff to coordinate reading instruction for English learners, this despite the fact that Reading First schools were significantly more likely to have adopted new materials for emergent bilinguals (43% vs. 29%; U.S. Department of Education, 2006). With regard to ERF, children who participated in these programs were more likely than children nationally to be Latino (46% vs. 21%). In addition, four out of 10 ERF parents (41%) reported that the primary language spoken in the home was one other than English. Although Snow et al. (1998) did not specifically address research related to emergent bilinguals and literacy, their report did state that learning to speak English should be a priority before the children are taught to read in English. Also, Snow et al. recommended the oral development of the home language and, when feasible, literacy development in the home language (National Institute of Child Health and Human Development, 2000). At the same time, a seminal review (August & Shanahan, 2006) of the research on language-minority children and literacy found a significant gap in the research when it comes to emergent bilinguals and text level reading, as opposed to word level reading. In fact, not much is known about how emergent literacy skills might relate to later literacy skills outcomes (August & Shanahan, 2006). Given the linguistic, cognitive, and academic variables that compound the processes of reading for emergent bilinguals, literacy instruction for these children and relevant educational policy require additional considerations and recommendations for instruction both within and beyond the areas identified in Reading First (Antunez, 2002).

No Child Left Behind Act: Accountability and English Learners

Under NCLB, states are required to ensure that all students meet standards of proficiency in math and reading by 2014. And as Congress considers reauthorization of NCLB, analyses of recent achievement data show that students designated as emergent bilinguals are among those furthest behind. In eighth grade, 51% of emergent bilingual students are behind White students in reading and math. In fourth grade, 47% of emergent bilingual students are behind in math, and 35% are behind in reading compared with their White counterparts (Fry, 2007). States are subject to a number of accountability provisions that place emphasis on the assessment of emergent bilinguals. NCLB delineates two sets of responsibilities for states, and hence districts and schools, with regard to emergent bilingual students: They are responsible for ensuring that emergent bilinguals make progress in learning English (Title III) and that emergent bilinguals become proficient in mathematics and in reading and language arts (Title I). Both Title I and Title III of NCLB include requirements for emergent bilingual students with the ultimate goal of increasing English-language proficiency and academic achievement. Table 8.3 summarizes the main provisions of each.

The provisions around whether emergent bilingual students must be assessed in English and whether the results contribute toward determination of a state's adequate yearly progress (AYP) are particularly important. Accountability provisions mandate annual assessment in English for any student who has attended school in the United States (excluding Puerto Rico) for 3 or more consecutive years and attainment of "annual measurable achievement objectives" (U.S. Department of Education, 2002). States are required to hold subgrantees accountable for making AYP. Subgrantees must report every second fiscal year and include a description of the program as well as the progress made by children in learning English, meeting state standards, and attaining English proficiency. States report every second year to the U.S. Department of Education, and that department reports every second year to Congress. Subgrantees failing to meet AYP goals must develop an improvement plan with sanctions if they continue to fail for 4 years (U.S. Department of Education, 2002). In fact, failure to meet AYP can eventually result in the loss of Title III funds, restructuring, and corrective action.

From a policy perspective, as a result of NCLB, emergent bilingual students are no longer invisible in the classroom, district, or state: Attention to this population of students has increased (Cohen & Clewell, 2007).

TABLE 8.3

Comparison of Main Provisions of Title I and Title III of the No Child Left Behind Act of 2001

	Title I	Title III
Standards	Academic content standards for all students, including limited-English-proficient (LEP) students. Student academic achievement standards for all students, including LEP students.	Develop English language proficiency standards aligned with academic content standards.
Assessments	Academic content assessments in reading, mathematics, and science in 2007–2008. Must provide for participation of all students.	See English language proficiency assessments for Title I.
Academic Assessment and LEP students	LEP students are to be assessed in a valid and reliable manner. Must be provided with reasonable accommodations when assessed, to the extent practicable, "in the language and form most likely to yield accurate data" on academic knowledge. Students who have been in schools 3 years or more generally must be assessed in English.	
State English language proficiency assessments	Must annually assess English language proficiency of LEP students, measuring oral language, reading, and writing skills in English.	
Annual measurable objectives	Annual objectives that lead to achieving proficiency in reading/language arts and math by 2014. To be deemed as making adequate yearly progress (AYP), each district and school must show that requisite percentage of each designated student group, as well as the student population as a whole, met the state proficiency goal. Must also show that at least 95% of students in each designated subgroup participated in these assessments. Must demonstrate that district and schools have met targets on other academic indicators (graduation rates in high school, attendance, etc.)	Establish objectives for improving LEP students' English language proficiency in speaking, reading, writing, and listening. States receiving funds under Title III must establish annual goals for increasing and measuring progress of LEP students in (a) learning English, (b) attaining English proficiency, and (c) meeting AYP goals in attaining academic proficiency outlined in Title I. (§3122(3)(A))

(continues)

TABLE 8.3
Comparison of Main Provisions of Title I and Title III of the No Child Left Behind Act of 2001   *(Continued)*

	Title I	Title III
Actions when annual targets/goals not achieved	Can also make AYP through "safe harbor" provision, if percentage of students considered not proficient decreased by at least 10% and the group made progress on one of the state's other academic indicators. Specific action must be taken if district and school do not meet state progress goals. If district and school do not make AYP for 2 consecutive years, they are identified for improvement. And parents must be given opportunity to transfer to another school. If district and school continue to miss AYP for additional years, this can lead to corrective action or restructuring.	If district and school receive funding under Title II and do not meet goals for 2 consecutive years, they must develop an improvement plan. If district and school have not met goals for 4 consecutive years, they must modify curriculum and method of instruction, or state must determine whether to continue to fund the district and require the district to replace personnel related to district's inability to meet goals.

Note. Data from U.S. Government Accountability Office (2006).

Unfortunately, the practice of assessing emergent bilingual students appropriately under this policy is a significant challenge. Cognitive and linguistic abilities and educational performance of children are generally obtained by measuring specific skills, typically through standardized testing. Several concerns and problematic issues have come to light over the past few decades in relation to test development and assessment practices for culturally and linguistically diverse students (see Chapter 4, this volume). Present efforts continue to strive to develop appropriate measures and procedures that take into account children's cultural and linguistic backgrounds so as to not penalize those who fall outside the cultural mainstream in the United States. The goal of these tests and procedures, in general, is to create culturally and linguistically relevant means and scores that accurately portray the abilities and concurrent performance levels of a diverse body of children.

Although important strides have been made in the development of appropriate tests and testing procedures for culturally and linguistically diverse students (Genesee 2010; Rhodes, Ochoa, & Ortiz, 2005; see Chapter 4, this volume), much research and development is still needed. Tests are still limited in their overall number as well as the domains and skills they cover (Espinosa & López, 2006). Moreover, several tests developed for specific language minority groups are merely translations of original English versions, which tend to be based on Euro-American cultural values. Their view of competence, in many cases, is simply not applicable to other groups with different backgrounds. As such, the content and construct validity of an English measure may not be the same when translated into Spanish. Furthermore, tests with appropriate content and construct validity should contain enough items to assess an identified skill and be standardized with representative samples of Latino children from diverse national origins, language backgrounds, and socioeconomic conditions.

In practice, most states have met the requirement of including at least 95% of emergent bilinguals in reading and mathematics assessments. However, a report by the U.S. Government Accountability Office (2006) noted little evidence that states' tests yield valid and reliable results for emergent bilinguals, and although most states use some form of accommodation for emergent bilinguals, more research is needed on which accommodations are most appropriate. Although the Department of Education has provided some support and training, state officials report that they need more guidance to develop valid and reliable assessments for both English language proficiency and academic content areas. Without specific guidance, states may spend time developing assessments that do not adequately track student progress. Furthermore, additional research needs to be conducted and disseminated on appropriate accommodations for emergent bilingual students (U.S. Government Accountability Office, 2006). To this end, the Department of Education initiated an emergent bilingual partnership to provide states with technical assistance and resources to make content assessments more accessible and appropriate for emergent bilingual students. In addition, experts from around the country are being brought together to develop high-quality English and native language assessments in reading and math.

IMPLICATIONS FOR FUTURE POLICY

With NCLB up for reauthorization, scholars, policymakers, researchers, and practitioners alike are weighing in on recommendations for revisions to the legislation. In 2007, 15 leaders in education—representing K–12 and higher education, school and school-system governance, civil rights, and business—came together to form the Commission on No Child Left Behind, a bipartisan, independent effort dedicated to improving NCLB. Their final report provides a summary of the main provisions of NCLB, discussion of the impact of NCLB implementation in various contexts, and recommendations for improving the legislation (Commission on No Child Left Behind, 2007). The commission made specific recommendations regarding emergent bilingual students that we summarize here.

First, the commission recommended withholding a portion of the state's administrative funding if that state has not fully developed and implemented English language proficiency standards, assessments, and annual measurable objectives. Second, the commission recommended extending the time period, from 2 years to 3 years, so that English learners can remain in the emergent bilingual subgroup for AYP purposes after attaining proficiency in English. This will help schools more accurately measure the achievement of emergent bilinguals. Third, the commission recommended that states use their allocation of funding to create and implement alternative assessments for emergent bilinguals, to develop plans for establishing universally designed assessment systems, and to further develop and implement high-quality science assessments now required under law. Fourth, the commission recommends that the U.S. Department of Education develop a common scale across states to determine English language proficiency. Finally, the commission recommends ensuring that teachers of English learners receive the training and support they need by requiring states to create an endorsement for teacher certification for those who spend more than 25% of their teaching time with English learners.

IMPLICATIONS FOR THE CLASSROOM

As the United States advances educational policy for all its students in an ever-diversifying population, it is even more important to understand the dramatic shifts in technology, globalization, and democratization. These circumstances pose a particular challenge to educators and those who look to educational agencies for help in realizing the moral imperatives of equity and social justice. García (2001a, 2001b) indicated that language will continue to be at the forefront of federal and state policy activity. As such, in this volume we have attempted to deepen readers' understanding of the education of emergent bilinguals through the lens of educational policy. Through both litigation and legislation, we have established several important conclusions regarding the responsibilities of educational agencies. Using a question-and-answer format, Exhibit 8.1 sets out some of these responsibilities and provides a practical guide for understanding the legal status of emergent bilingual students and the legal liability of the educational agencies that serve them.

CONCLUSION

Overall, this chapter has described federal education policy as it relates to emergent bilingual students and, at the same time, explored whether policy has proved to disadvantage or enhance the education of these students. For now, policy is almost characterized by a "blind spot" when it comes to the new demographic reality, particularly the growth in numbers of emergent bilinguals. Consequently, it is not surprising that policy has not delineated a clear path for practitioners (Wiese & García, 2006). If we can attend to policy that "counts," then we can predict that as more bilingual students enter the "right" kind of schools barriers to their academic, social, and economic success and mobility will fall. In that policy arena, language distinctions will blend with other features of society (García, 2001b) in which the negative effects of racial, ethnic, linguistic, and class differences are eliminated. This is, of course, a highly optimistic scenario of the future of emergent bilinguals and U.S. society in general.

To this end, the search for general principles of learning that work for all students must be redirected. This redirection considers a search for and documentation of particular implementations of general and nongeneral principles of teaching and learning that serve a diverse set of environments, in and out of school. This mission requires an understanding of how individuals with diverse sets of experiences, packaged individually into cultures, "make meaning," communicate that meaning, and extend it, particularly in the social contexts we call schools. Such a mission requires in-depth treatment of the processes associated with producing diversity, issues of socialization in and out of schools, coupled with a clear examination of how such understanding is actually transformed into pedagogy and curriculum, across the content areas, which can result in high academic performance for all students. Policy must align itself with this mission.

EXHIBIT 8.1
Legal Rights of Bilingual Students and Legal Liabilities
of Educational Agencies

Question: Is there a legally acceptable procedure for identifying language-minority students in need of special instructional treatment?
Answer: Yes. The legal obligation is to identify all students who have problems speaking, understanding, reading, or writing English because of a home language background other than English. To do this, a two-phase approach is common and acceptable. First, the parents are asked, through a home language survey or on a registration form, whether a language other than English is spoken in the child's home. If the answer is affirmative, the second phase is triggered. In the second phase, students identified through the home language survey are given an oral language proficiency test and an assessment of their reading and writing skills.

Question: Once the students are identified, are there any minimal standards for the educational program provided to them?
Answer: Yes. First, a number of courts have recognized that special training is necessary to equip a teacher to provide meaningful assistance to limited-English-proficient students. The teacher (and it is clear that it must be a teacher, not an aide) must have training in second language acquisition techniques to teach English as a second language. Second, the time spent on assisting these students must be sufficient to assure that they acquire English skills quickly enough to assure that their disadvantage in the English language classroom does not become a permanent educational disadvantage.

Question: Must students be provided with instruction in the student's native language as well as English?
Answer: At the present time, the federal obligation has not been construed to compel such a program. However, the federal mandate is not fully satisfied by an ESL (English as a Second Language) program. The mandate requires English language help plus programs to assure that students not be substantively handicapped by any delay in learning English. To do this may require either (a) a bilingual program that keeps the students up in their course work while learning English or (b) a specially designed compensatory program to address the educational loss suffered by any delay in providing understandable substantive instruction. Finally, it is legally necessary to provide the material resources necessary for the instructional components. The program must be reasonably designed to succeed. Without adequate resources, this requirement cannot be met.

Question: What minimal standards must be met if a bilingual program is to be offered?
Answer: The heart of a basic bilingual program is a teacher who can speak the language of the students and address the students' limited English proficiency. Thus, a district offering a bilingual program must take affirmative steps to match teachers with these characteristics. These might include allocation of teachers with language skills to bilingual classrooms and affirmative recruitment of bilingual teachers. Additionally, it requires the district to establish a formal system to assess teachers to ensure that they have the prerequisite skills. Finally, where there are insufficient teachers, there must be a system to ensure that teachers with most (but not all) of the skills are in bilingual classrooms, that those teachers are on track to obtain the necessary skills, and that bilingual aides are hired whenever the teacher lacks the necessary language skills.

EXHIBIT 8.1
Legal Rights of Bilingual Students and Legal Liabilities
of Educational Agencies *(Continued)*

Question: Must there be standards for removal of a student from a program? What might these be?

Answer: There must be definite standards. These generally mirror the standards for determining whether a student is in need of special language services in the first place. Thus, objective evidence that the student can compete with English-speaking peers without a lingering language disability is necessary.

Several common practices are unlawful. First, the establishment of an arbitrary cap on the amount of time a student can remain in a program fails to meet the requirement that all language-minority students be assisted. Second, it is common to have programs terminate at a certain grade level, for example, sixth grade. While programs may change to accommodate different realities, it is unlawful to deny a student access to a program merely because of grade level.

Question: Must a district develop a design to monitor the success of its program?

Answer: Yes. The district is obligated to monitor the program and to make reasonable adjustments when the evidence suggests that the program is not successful.

Monitoring is a two-part process. First, it is necessary to monitor the progress of students in the program to assure that they are making reasonable progress toward learning and that the program is providing the students with substantive instruction comparable with that given to English-proficient students. Second, any assessment of the program must include a system to monitor the progress of students after they leave the program. The primary purpose of the program is to assure that the limited-English-proficient students ultimately are able to compete on an equal footing with their English-speaking peers. This cannot be determined in the absence of such a post-reclassification monitoring system.

Question: May a district deny services to a student because there are few students in the district who speak her or his language?

Answer: No. The 1974 Equal Educational Opportunities Act and subsequent court decisions make it clear that every student is entitled to a program that is reasonably designed to overcome any handicaps occasioned by a language deficit. The number of students who speak a particular language may be considered to determine how to best address the student needs given human and fiscal resources available. Still, some form of special educational services must be provided.

Note. Reprinted from the *Handbook of Research on Literacy and Diversity* (pp. 50–51), edited by L. M. Morrow, R. Rudea, and D. Lapp, 2009, New York, NY: Guilford. Copyright 2009 by author. Reprinted with permission from author.

EPILOGUE

As stated throughout Part II of this volume, the rapid growth in the bilingual population in the United States calls for development of high-quality bilingual education programs that take into account cognitive and functional/structural neurological processes in bilingual children. We emphasized in Part I that the newest neuroscience data can be used to make a strong case for raising all children in the United States as bilinguals from very early in life, preferably starting from birth to 3 years. Children in the United States should be provided with formal bilingual education experience starting in preschool, kindergarten at the latest, for them to reap the greatest cognitive benefits of learning multiple languages. To accomplish this, we provided the reader with improved understanding of the monolingual and bilingual development processes and the relationship between bilingualism and cognition (Chapters 1–3). We then considered some of the major issues between proponents and opponents of bilingual education and provided research findings relevant to the issues (Chapter 3). By doing this, we hoped that the information will inform students, educators, administrators, and policymakers regarding research outcomes relative to successful bilingual education and policy. This should result in contributing to implementation of research-based programs that have proved successful in bilingual education and in enhancing bilingual children's experiences in the classroom and other learning environments (see Chapter 3 and especially Chapter 7).

LOOKING TO THE FUTURE: COLLABORATION IS THE KEY

Why has the educational advancement of at-risk students, including emergent bilinguals, remained relatively unchanged? Why have decades of research efforts failed to improve educational practices for and the performance patterns of children from immigrant families? How can the relative strengths of bilingual students be leveraged to buffer the influence of salient risk factors to sustain school success? Although school improvements take time, and schools and classrooms alone do not account for variations in student learning, some brief reflections on educational research, policy, and practice for bilingual students may aid in answering these questions and may provide a path for innovative collaboration among students, parents, school personnel, and researchers from diverse fields of enquiry to identify and implement more effective and meaningful practices.

To date, researchers have made satisfactory efforts to provide teachers, school administrators, and practitioners with evidence-based practices that enhance the academic engagement and learning of bilingual students. From educational research, we know that culturally knowledgeable teachers who are proficient in English and the child's native language are a particular asset, and that the strategic inclusion of the child's native language in classroom instruction can increase overall language and academic learning (August & Shanahan, 2006). We also know that screening for and closely monitoring learning problems, intensive small-group intervention, extensive and varied vocabulary instruction, and regular peer-assisted learning opportunities improve the effectiveness of literacy learning for emergent bilingual students (Gersten et al., 2007).

As stated in the introduction chapter and throughout this volume, research by cognitive psychologists and neuroscientists needs to inform educational research regarding the cognitive/intellectual abilities of emergent bilingual and balanced proficient bilingual children. Education researchers, educators, and policymakers need to find ways to utilize research outcomes to better meet the needs of bilingual children and all students in applied learning settings. Even with these efforts by researchers and their respective funders, bilingual students continue to underperform, and evidence-based practices go unimplemented in many schools or are poorly implemented in others. Why is this the case? In our perspective, at least part of the implementation problem lies within the silos we—researchers, practitioners, and policymakers—tend to work in. Time and experience show that the demonstrated added value of high-quality programs is weak when implementation potential is not sufficiently considered or evaluated. And it is difficult for researchers to consider implementation potential without collaboration from policymakers and practitioners.

Take, for example, the preparation of bilingual and culturally knowledgeable teachers. Years of data analyses and interpretation indicate that emergent bilingual children with fluently bilingual and culturally responsive teachers tend to perform better than those without (August & Shanahan, 2006; Slavin & Cheung, 2005). Yet most bilingual students do not have access to these teachers in classrooms. This is particularly detrimental during the early years of schooling when native language foundations are established. In some cases, this deficiency is due to policy initiatives constraining DL education programs (Gándara et al., 2000). In others, however, it is due simply to poor implementation.

Federal, state, and local governments, in collaboration with private foundations, nonprofit organizations, and local agencies, are tasked with producing large increases in the number of culturally knowledgeable preschool and elementary school teachers proficient in two languages (e.g., English and Spanish). And their efforts are magnified as they work collaboratively with researchers and families. The federal government should underwrite tests of programs designed to produce large increases in bilingual and culturally knowledgeable teachers; state governments should fund and experiment with successful teacher preparation programs and provide incentive pay for teachers with these credentials; local governments should support state initiatives by proposing specific strategies to develop workforce needs; and private and nonprofit organizations should serve as liaisons between organizations providing strategic fiscal support where possible (National Task Force on Early Childhood Education for Hispanics, 2007). All the while, educational researchers should document the sustained effectiveness of implemented practices using validated measurement techniques (across socioeconomic segments) to determine the relative benefit of bilingual curricular and instructional strategies.

Collaboration between these groups certainly does not come easy. Yet, in our perspective, innovative collaboration among knowledge producers (i.e., researchers), consumers (i.e., practitioners), and enactors (i.e., policymakers) is necessary to expedite the educational change needed for emergent bilingual students. It diminishes the implementation gap by applying evidence-based practice while creating research-informed best practices.

Certainly, long-standing principles in teaching and learning apply to improving opportunities for bilingual students. Increased academic learning time, improved adult–teacher ratios and teacher–student ratios, and meaningful parent involvement are ongoing concerns that deserve due consideration

(Portes, 2005). Additionally, teachers will continue to need domain-specific expertise and pedagogical skills that invite student participation and engage family and community members (Darling-Hammond & Bransford, 2005). We posit that the enhanced collaborations for which we advocate can improve the extent to which these practices are implemented as well.

We encourage practitioners, policymakers, and researchers to continue to innovate and enhance such collaborations, and we offer some recommendations. These recommendations share the common thread of seeking a cultural consciousness in our work, which serves as a glue for sustained collaboration.

To practitioners, including teachers and administrators, understand that one's values, customs, practices, symbols, and beliefs permeate one's practice—the knowledge, skills, and relationships one develops (Banks et al., 2007; Rogoff, 2003). Make an effort to understand the knowledge and skills of students and their families. This can be accomplished in many ways (García & Gonzalez, 2006; Gonzalez, Moll, & Amanti, 2005). The point is to establish trusting relationships with parents, to be aware of the tools and participation patterns they tend to use with their children in daily activities, and to incorporate these in meaningful ways in the classroom setting (Bruner, 1996).

To policymakers, adequate structure should be in place to foster meaningful exchanges and relationships between families and schools. Understanding families' cultural ways of learning requires effort and much reflection. This is true in terms of understanding one's own cultural heritage as well as less familiar cultural communities. It requires taking the perspective of others (Rogoff, 2003), which necessitates visiting and revising one's assumptions of relationships in the social world. Conflict will continue to occur when different cultural communities share time and space to engage in a shared activity, such as schooling (Banks, 1988; García Coll et al., 1996; Gonzalez et al., 2005). As different communities share space and activity within schools, understanding, predicting, and shaping family and school practice can occur to develop engaging learning environments within and outside of school (Lesgold, 2004).

Currently, there is no comprehensive theoretical model that describes ways in which sociocultural processes shape student engagement and learning (Nasir & Hand, 2006) to guide research and practice. We know that important processes occur across multiple levels (institutions, interpersonal relations, and individual development) to shape learning and that cultural histories of schools and families mediate these processes (Cole & Engeström, 1993); however, refined research designs and methods are needed to measure cultural differences to inform classroom practices of specific ways to increase student engagement and learning.

In reviewing empirical (qualitative and quantitative) studies on literacy development of bilingual students, Goldenberg, Rueda, and August (2006) conducted a synthesis of research on the influence of sociocultural contexts on literacy learning. They found only a handful of studies that attempted to link sociocultural contexts with literacy outcomes inferentially in ways beneficial to practitioners and policymakers. Most of the research was descriptive, not allowing for the sort of inferences needed to inform classroom practices broadly. Although descriptive information of the family and school histories and practices is necessary, it is not sufficient to provide practitioners and policymakers with recommended ways of fitting family and school cultural practices in the classroom to improve student performance. To date, a vast majority of cultural studies in education are able to describe cultural and historical differences in family and school practices, but very few, unfortunately, provide empirically supported ways to negotiate differences that respond to family practice while enhancing student engagement and learning over time (Banks et al., 2007). Cultural researchers tend to study how children are socialized to accept participation rules, authority, and linguistic norms, while leaving the inferential work of school and classroom input that raises student achievement to policy analysts and others who often underestimate cultural mediation (Fuller & Clark, 1994). Our recommendation to educational researchers, therefore, is to engage in both activities simultaneously through interdisciplinary and collaborative inquiry. Certainly this innovation would strengthen collaboration among families, students, and schools, as well as among policymakers, practitioners, and researchers, to provide a holistic approach to understanding the bilingual child at the level of the brain through cognitive and neuroscience research, at the level of the individual in the classroom and other social interaction settings through educational research, and at the level of society.

Emergent bilingual children (i.e., dual-language learners) should be given the proper type of education starting early in development (from birth, prekindergarten, or kindergarten) and sufficient time to become proficient in English while maintaining high ability in their home language, ultimately achieving high bilingual proficiency and balance. Children who are English monolinguals should be provided the opportunity to learn a second language from early on as well. Achieving this goal will result in children gaining (a) cognitive benefits that accrue to the bilingual brain (functional and structural plasticity), (b) social benefits of communicating in multiple languages and increased cross-cultural communication and interactions, and (c) economic benefits related to social and business interactions within today's global society and economy.

As a bilingual nation, the United States will become a more tolerant multicultural society in which diversity is welcomed and celebrated. Being a bilingual nation will also ensure the United States' continued status as a political world power as well as a global business leader.

It is our sincere hope that this book will contribute to moving us toward accomplishing these formidable goals. If so, we will have done our small part in transforming the United States into a better society and nation.

To entrenched bilingual education opponents, we say they should realize the great harm they are imposing on emergent bilingual children by denying them the opportunity to acquire the cognitive and sociocultural benefits of becoming fully bilingual. We also ask them to support providing all children in the United States with the same opportunities by supporting bilingual education as a national priority.

Finally, we hope that as racial/ethnic and language diversity continue to increase in the United States, and as immigrants become voting citizens in greater numbers, a shift toward supporting bilingual education and diversity in all areas will occur. The United States will be the better nation for it.

REFERENCES

Abedi, J., Hofstetter, C. H., & Lord, C. (2004). Assessment accommodations for English-language learners: Implications for policy-based empirical research. *Review of Educational Research, 74*, 1–28. doi:10.3102/00346543074001001

Acredolo, L. P., & Goodwyn, S. W. (1990). Sign language in babies: The significance of symbolic gesturing for understanding language development. In R. Vasta (Ed.), *Annals of child development* (Vol. 7, pp. 1–42). Greenwich, CT: JAI Press.

Adesope, O. O., Lavin, T., Thompson, T., & Ungerleider, C. (2010). A systematic review and meta-analysis on the cognitive correlates of bilingualism. *Review of Educational Research, 80*, 207–245. doi:10.3102/0034654310368803

Akhtar, N. (2004). Nativist versus constructivist goals in studying child language. *Journal of Child Language, 31*, 459–462. doi:10.1017/S0305000904006063

Akhter, N., Carpenter, M., & Tomasello, M. (1996). The role of discourse novelty in early word learning. *Child Development, 67*(2), 635–645. doi:10.2307/1131837

Alexander v. Choate, 469 U.S. 287 (1985).

Alexander v. Sandoval, 532 U.S. 275 (2001).

Allen, S. E., & Crego, M. B. (1996). Early passive acquisition in Inuktitut. *Journal of Child Language, 23*, 129–155. doi:10.1017/S0305000900010126

Altarriba, J., & Heredia, R. R. (2008). *An introduction to bilingualism: Principles and process*. Mahwah, NJ: Erlbaum.

Altus, G. T. (1953). W.I.S.C. patterns of a selective sample of bilingual school children. *Journal of Genetic Psychology, 83*, 241–248.

Alvarez, J. A., & Emory, E. (2006). Executive function and the frontal lobes: A meta-analytic review. *Neuropsychology Review, 16*, 17–42. doi:10.1007/s11065-006-9002-x

Andreou, G., & Karapetsas, A. (2004). Verbal abilities in low and highly proficient bilinguals. *Journal of Psycholinguistic Research, 33*, 357–364. doi:10.1023/B:JOPR.0000039545.16783.61

Anglin, J. M. (1993). Vocabulary development: A morphological analysis. *Monographs of the Society for Research in Child Development, 58*(10, Serial No. 238), 1–165. doi:10.2307/1166112

Antunez, B. (2002). Implementing Reading First with English language learners. In *Directions in language and education* (p. 12). Washington, DC: National Clearinghouse for English Language Acquisition and Language Instruction Educational Programs.

Arias, R., & Lakshmanan, U. (2003, April). *Code switching in a Spanish–English bilingual child: A communication resource*. Paper presented at the Fourth International Symposium on Bilingualism, Tempe, AZ.

Artiles, A. J., Rueda, R., Salazar, J. J., & Higareda, I. (2002). English-language learner representation in special education in California urban school districts. In D. J. Losen & G. Orfield (Eds.), *Race inequity in special education* (pp. 117–136). Cambridge, MA: Harvard Education Press.

Arzubiaga, A., Rueda, R., & Monzó, L. (2002). Reading engagement of Latino children. *Journal of Latinos and Education, 1*, 231–243. doi:10.1207/S1532771XJLE0104_3

Aspira of New York v. Board of Education of the City of New York, 394 F. Supp. 1161 (1975).

Atkinson, R. C., & Shiffrin, R. M. (1968). Human memory: A proposed system and its control processes. In K. W. Spence & J. T. Spence (Eds.), *The psychology of learning and motivation: Advances in research and theory* (Vol. 2, pp. 90–195). Orlando, FL: Academic Press.

Atwill, K., Blanchard, J., Gorin, J., & Burnstein, K. (2006, April). *The influence of language proficiency on cross-language transfer of phonemic awareness in kindergarten Spanish-speaking children*. Paper presented at the annual meeting of the American Education Research Association, San Francisco, CA.

Au, K. H.-P., & Mason, J. M. (1981). Social organizational factors in learning to read: The balance of rights hypothesis. *Reading Research Quarterly, 17*, 115–152. doi:10.2307/747251

August, D., Calderón, M., & Carlo, M. (2002). *Transfer of skills from Spanish to English: A study of young learners*. Washington, DC: Center for Applied Linguistics.

August, D., Calderón, M., Carlo, M., & Nuttall, M. (2006). Developing literacy in English-language learners: An examination of the impact of English-only versus bilingual instruction. In P. D. Mccardle & E. Hoff (Eds.), *Childhood bilingualism: Research on infancy through school age* (pp. 146–171). Clevedon, England: Multilingual Matters.

August, D., & Hakuta, K. (1997). *Improving schooling for language-minority children*. Washington, DC: National Academy Press.

August, D., & Shanahan, T. (Eds.). (2006). *Developing literacy in second language learners: Report of the National Literacy Panel on language minority youth and children*. Mahwah, NJ: Erlbaum.

Bain, B. (1974). Bilingualism and cognition: Toward a general theory. In S. T. Carey (Ed.), *Bilingualism, biculturalism, and education: Proceedings from the conference at College Universitaire Saint Jean* (pp. 119–128). Edmonton, Alberta, Canada: University of Alberta.

Baker, C. (2000). *The care and education of young bilinguals: An introduction for professionals*. Clevedon, England: Multilingual Matters.

Baker, K. A., & de Kanter, A. A. (1981). *Effectiveness of bilingual education: A review of the literature*. Washington, DC: U.S. Department of Education.

Baker, K. A., & Pelavin, S. (1984, April). *Problems in bilingual education*. Paper presented at the annual meeting of the American Education Research Association, New Orleans, LA.

Baldwin, D. A., Markman, E. M., Bill, B., Desjardins, R. N., Irwin, J. M., & Tidball, G. (1996). Infants' reliance on social criteria for establishing word–object relations. *Child Development, 67,* 3135–3153. doi:10.2307/1131771

Balkan, L. (1970). *Les effets ju bilinguisme francais-anglais sur les aptitudes intellectuelles* [The effects of French-English bilingualism on the intellectual capacities]. Brussels, Belgium: AIMAV.

Ballantyne, A. O., Spilkin, A. M., & Trauner, D. A. (2007). The revision decision: Is change always good? A comparison of CELF-R and CELF-3 test scores in children with language impairment, focal brain damage, and typical development. *Language, Speech, and Hearing Services in Schools, 38,* 182–189. doi:10.1044/0161-1461(2007/019)

Bandura, A. (1971). *Psychological modeling: Conflicting theories.* Chicago, IL: Aldine-Atherton.

Bandura, A. (1977). Self-efficacy: Toward a unifying theory of behavioral change. *Psychological Review, 84,* 191–215. doi:10.1037/0033-295X.84.2.191

Bandura, A. (2006). Toward a psychology of human agency. *Perspectives on Psychological Science, 2,* 164–180. doi:10.1111/j.1745-6916.2006.00011.x

Banks, J. (1988). The influence of ethnicity and class on cognitive styles: Implications for research and education. In W. J. Lonner & V. O. Tyler Jr. (Eds.), *Cultural and ethnic factors in learning and motivation: Implications for education.* Seattle, WA: Western Washington University.

Banks, J., Au, K. H., Ball, A. F., Bell, P., Gordon, E. W., Gutiérrez, K. D., . . . Zhou, M. (2007). *Learning in and out of school in diverse environments: Life-long, life-wide, life-deep.* Seattle, WA: LIFE Center.

Barnett, W. S., Jung, K., Wong, V., Cook, T., & Lamy, C. (2007, March). *Effects of five state prekindergarten programs on early learning: Five -state prekindergarten study.* Paper presented at the annual meeting of the Society for Research in Child Development, Boston, MA.

Barnett, W. S., Yarosz, D. J., Thomas, J., Jung, K., & Blanco, D. (2007). Two-way and monolingual English immersion in preschool education: An experimental comparison. *Early Childhood Research Quarterly, 22,* 277–293.

Baron-Cohen, S., Tager-Flusberg, H., & Cohen, D. J. (Eds.). (2000). *Understanding other minds: Perspectives from developmental cognitive neuroscience* (2nd ed.). Oxford, England: Oxford University Press.

Bartsch, K., & Wellman, H. M. (1995). *Children talk about the mind.* New York, NY: Oxford University Press.

Bates, E., O'Connell, B., & Shore, C. (1987). Language and communication in infancy. In J. D. Osofsky (Ed.), *Handbook of infant development* (2nd ed., pp. 149–203). New York, NY: Wiley.

Bates, E., & Snyder, L. (1985). The cognitive hypothesis in language development. In I. Uzgiris & J. McV. Hunt (Eds.), *Research with scales of psychological development in infancy* (pp. 168–206). Champaign, IL: University of Illinois Press.

Beal, C. R. (1990). Development of knowledge about the role of inference in text comprehension. *Child Development, 61,* 1011–1023. doi:10.2307/1130872

Becker, K. A. (2003). *History of the Stanford-Binet intelligence scales: Content and psychometrics* (Stanford-Binet Intelligence Scales, 5th Edition Assessment Service Bulletin No. 1). Itasca, IL: Riverside.

Bee, H., & Boyd, D. (2010). *The developing child* (12th ed.). Allyn & Bacon: Boston, MA.

Benedict, H. (1979). Early lexical development: Comprehension and production. *Journal of Child Language, 6,* 183–200. doi:10.1017/S0305000900002245

Ben-Zeev, S. (1972). *The influence of bilingualism on cognitive development and cognitive strategy.* Unpublished dissertation, University of Chicago, Chicago, IL.

Berk, L. E. (2008). *Infants & children* (6th ed.). Boston, MA: Pearson.

Berko, J. (1958). The child's learning of English morphology. *Word, 14,* 150–177.

Berko Gleason, J. (2005). *The development of language* (6th ed.). Boston, MA: Pearson Education.

Berko Gleason, J., & Bernstein Ratner, N. (2008). *The development of language* (7th ed.). Boston, MA: Allyn & Bacon.

Berry, C. S. (1922). Classification by tests of intelligence of 10,000 first grade children. *The Journal of Educational Research, 6,* 185–203.

Bhatnagar, J. (1980). Linguistic behaviour and adjustment of immigrant children in French and English schools in Montreal. *International Journal of Applied Psychology, 29,* 141–158. doi:10.1111/j.1464-0597.1980.tb00887.x

Bialystok, E. (1997). Effects of bilingualism and biliteracy on children's emerging concepts of print. *Developmental Psychology, 33,* 429–440. doi:10.1037/0012-1649.33.3.429

Bialystok, E. (1999). Cognitive complexity and attentional control in the bilingual mind. *Child Development, 70,* 636–644. doi:10.1111/1467-8624.00046

Bialystok, E. (2000). Symbolic representation across domains in preschool children. *Journal of Experimental Child Psychology, 76,* 173–189. doi:10.1006/jecp.1999.2548

Bialystok, E. (2001). Metalinguistic aspects of bilingual processing. *Annual Review of Applied Linguistics, 21,* 169–181. doi:10.1017/S0267190501000101

Bialystok, E., Craik, F. I. M., Grady, C., Chau, W., Ishii, R., Gunji, A., & Pantev, C. (2005). Effect of bilingualism on cognitive control in the Simon task: Evidence from MEG. *NeuroImage, 24,* 40–49. doi:10.1016/j.neuroimage.2004.09.044

Bialystok, E., Craik, F. I. M., Klein, R., & Viswanathan, M. (2004). Bilingualism, aging, and cognitive control: Evidence from the Simon task. *Psychology and Aging, 19,* 290–303. doi:10.1037/0882-7974.19.2.290

Bialystok, E., Majumder, S., & Martin, M. M. (2003). Developing phonological awareness: Is there a bilingual advantage? *Applied Psycholinguistics, 24,* 27–44. doi:10.1017/S014271640300002X

Bilingual Education Act, Pub. L. No. 90-247, 81 Stat. 816 (1968).

Bilingual Education Act, Pub. L. No. 93-380, 88 Stat. 503 (1974).

Bilingual Education Act, Pub. L. No. 95-561, 92 Stat. 2268 (1978).

Bilingual Education Act, Pub. L. No. 98-511, 98 Stat. 2370 (1984).

Bilingual Education Act, Pub. L. No. 100-297, 102 Stat. 279 (1988).

Bilingual Education Act, Pub L. No. 103-382, 108 Stat. 3518 (1994).

Binet, A., & Simon, T. (1905). Upon the necessity of establishing a scientific diagnosis of inferior states of intelligence. *L'Année Psychologique, 11*, 163–191. doi:10.3406/psy.1904.3675

Binet, A., & Simon, T. (1911/1916). The development of intelligence in the child. In H. H. Goddard (Ed.) & E. S. Kite (Trans.), *Development of intelligence in children: The Binet-Simon scale* (pp. 182–273). Baltimore, MD: Williams & Wilkins. (Original work published 1908)

Birman, B. F., & Ginsburg, A. L. (1983). Introduction: Addressing the needs of language minority children. In K. A. Baker & A. A. D. Kanter (Eds.), *Bilingual education: A reappraisal of federal policy* (pp. ix–xxi). Lexington, MA: D. C. Heath.

Bloom, K. (1998). The missing link's missing link: Syllabic vocalizations at 3 months of age. *Behavioral and Brain Sciences, 21*, 514–515. doi:10.1017/S0140525X98251260

Bloom, L. (1970). *Language development: Form and function in emerging grammars.* Cambridge, MA: MIT Press.

Bloom, L. (1973). *One word at a time: The use of single word utterances before syntax.* The Hague, the Netherlands: Mouton.

Bochner, S., & Jones, J. (2003). *Child language development: Learning to talk* (2nd ed.). London, England: Whurr.

Bohannon, J. N., & Bonvillian, J. D. (2008). Theoretical approaches to language acquisition. In J. K. Gleason (Ed.), *The development of language* (6th ed., pp. 254–314). Boston, MA: Allyn & Bacon.

Bohannon, J. N., & Marquis, A. (1977). Children's control of adult speech. *Child Development, 48*, 1002–1008. doi:10.1111/j.1467-8624.1977.tb01259.x

Borghese, P., & Gronau, R. C., (2005). Convergent and discriminant validity of the universal nonverbal intelligence test with limited English proficient Mexican-American elementary students. *Journal of Psychoeducational Assessment, 23*, 128–139. doi:10.1177/073428290502300202

Borman, G. D., Hewes, G. H., Reilly, M., & Alvarado, S. (2006). *Comprehensive school reform for Latino elementary-school students: A meta-analysis* (Commissioned by the National Task Force on Early Childhood Education for Hispanics). Madison, WI: University of Wisconsin.

Bowen, W. G., & Bok, D. (1998). *The shape of the river: Long-term consequences of considering race in college and university admissions.* Princeton, NJ: Princeton University Press.

Brakke, K. E., & Savage-Rumbaugh, E. S. (1995). The development of language skills in bonobo and chimpanzee: I. Comprehension. *Language & Communication, 15*, 121–148. doi:10.1016/0271-5309(95)00001-7

Braswell, J., Daane, M., & Grigg, W. (2003). *The nation's report card: Mathematics highlights 2003* (NCES No. 2004451). Washington, DC: U.S. Department of Education, National Center for Education Statistics.

Brigham, C. C. (1923). *A study of American intelligence.* Princeton, NJ: Princeton University Press.

Brooker, L. (2002). "Five on the first of December!": What can we learn from case studies of early childhood literacy? *Journal of Early Childhood Literacy, 2,* 291–313. doi:10.1177/14687984020023003

Brown, A. L., Bransford, J. D., Ferrara, R. A., & Campione, J. C. (1983). Learning, remembering, and understanding. In P. H. Mussen (Series Ed.), J. H. Flavell & E. M. Markman (Vol. Eds.), *Handbook of child psychology: Vol. 3. Cognitive development* (pp. 77–166). New York, NY: Wiley.

Brown, G. L. (1922). Intelligence as related to nationality. *The Journal of Educational Research, 5,* 324–327.

Brown, R., & Bellugi, U. (1964). Three processes in the child's acquisition of syntax. *Harvard Educational Review, 34,* 133–151.

Brown, R. (1973). *A first language: The early stages.* Cambridge, MA: Harvard University Press.

Bruner, J. (1996). *The culture of education.* Cambridge, MA: Harvard University Press.

Buriel, R., & Cardoza, D. (1988). Sociocultural correlates of achievement among three generations of Mexican American high school seniors. *American Educational Research Journal, 25,* 177–192.

Bus, A. G., van IJzendoorn, M. H., & Pellgrini, A. D. (1995). Joint book reading makes for success in learning to read: A meta-analysis on intergenerational transmission of literacy. *Review of Educational Research, 65,* 1–21.

Caesar, L. G., & Kohler, P. D. (2007). The state of school-based bilingual assessment: Actual practice versus recommended guidelines. *Language, Speech, and Hearing Services in Schools, 38,* 190–200. doi:10.1044/0161-1461(2007/020)

Campbell, J. M., & McCord, D. M. (1999). Measuring social competence with the Wechsler picture arrangement and comprehension subtests. *Assessment, 6,* 215–223. doi:10.1177/107319119900600302

Capps, R. (2001). *Hardship among children of immigrants: Findings from the 1999 national survey of America's families.* Washington, DC: Urban Institute.

Capps, R., Fix, M. E., Murray, J., Ost, J., Passel, J. S., & Hernandez, S. H. (2005). *The new demography of America's schools: Immigration and the No Child Left Behind Act.* Retrieved from http://www.urban.org/url.cfm?ID=311230

Carlisle, J. F., Beeman, M., Davis, L. H., & Spharim, G. (1999). Relationship of metalinguistic capabilities and reading achievement for children who are becoming bilingual. *Applied Linguistics, 20,* 459–478.

Carlisle, J. F., Beeman, M., & Shah, P. P. (1996). The metalinguistic capabilities and English literacy of Hispanic high school students: An exploratory study. *Yearbook of the National Reading Conference, 45,* 306–316.

Carlson, S. M., & Meltzoff, A. N. (2008). Bilingual experience and executive functioning in young children. *Developmental Science, 11*, 282–298. doi:10.1111/j.1467-7687.2008.00675.x

Carreira, M. (2000). Validating and promoting Spanish in the United States: Lessons from linguistic science. *Bilingual Research Journal, 24*, 333–352.

Casanova, U. (1991). Bilingual education: Politics or pedagogy. In O. García (Ed.), *Bilingual education* (Vol. 1, pp. 167–182). Amsterdam, the Netherlands: John Benjamins.

Castañeda v. Pickard, 648 F. 2nd 289 (5th Cir. 1981).

Casteel, M. A. (1993). Effects of inferences necessity and reading goal on children's inferential generation. *Developmental Psychology, 29*, 346–357. doi:10.1037/0012-1649.29.2.346

Cazabon, M., Lambert, W., & Hall, G. (1999). *Two-way bilingual education: A report on the Amigos Program*. Washington, DC: Center for Applied Linguistics.

Center for Applied Linguistics. (2004). *Directory of two-way bilingual immersion programs in the United States*. Washington, DC: Author. Retrieved from http://www.cal.org/jsp/TWI/Schoollistings.jsp

Center for Applied Linguistics. (2005, March). *Guiding principles for dual language education*. Washington, DC: Author.

Center on Education Policy. (2006). *Keeping watch on Reading First*. Washington, DC: Author.

Charles, D. C. (1987). The emergence of educational psychology. In J. A. Glover & R. R. Roning (Eds.), *Historical foundations of educational psychology* (pp. 17–38). New York, NY: Plenum Press.

Chater, N., & Manning, C. D. (2006). Probabilistic models of language processing and acquisition. *Trends in Cognitive Sciences, 10*, 335–344.

Chee, M. W. L., Weekes, B., Lee, K. M., Soon, C. S., Schreiber, A., Hoon, J. J., & Chee, M. (2000). Overlap and dissociation of semantic processing of Chinese characters, English words, and pictures: Evidence from fMRI. *NeuroImage, 12*, 392–403. doi:10.1006/nimg.2000.0631

Chomsky, N. (1957). *Syntactic structures*. The Hague, the Netherlands: Mouton.

Chomsky, N. (1959). A review of B. F. Skinner's *Verbal behavior*. *Language, 35*, 26–58. doi:10.2307/411334

Chomsky, N. (1968). *Language and mind*. San Diego, CA: Harcourt Brace Jovanovich.

Chomsky, N. (1980). *Rules and representations*. Oxford, England: Basil Blackwell.

Chomsky, N., & Place, U. (2000). The Chomsky–Place correspondence 1993–1994. *Analysis of Verbal Behavior, 17*, 7–38.

Christenson, S. L. (2004). The family–school partnership: An opportunity to promote learning and competence of all students. *School Psychology Review, 33*, 83–104.

Christian, D. (1994). *Two-way bilingual education: Students learning through two languages*. Washington, DC: Center for Applied Linguistics.

Christian, D. (1997). *Directory of two-way bilingual*. Washington, DC: Center for Applied Linguistics.

Christian, D., Genesee, F., Lindholm-Leary, K., & Howard, L. (2004). *Project 1.2 two-way immersion* (Final progress report). Berkeley, CA: University of California, Center for Research on Education, Diversity & Excellence.

Clahsen, H., Hadler, M., & Weyerts, H. (2004). Speeded production of inflected words in children and adults. *Journal of Child Language, 31*, 683–712. doi:10.1017/S0305000904006506

Clifford, R. M., Barbarin, O., Chang, F., Early, D., Bryant, D., Howes, C., . . . Pianta, R. (2005). What is pre-kindergarten? Characteristics of public pre-kindergarten programs. *Applied Developmental Science, 9*, 126–143. doi:10.1207/s1532480xads0903_1

Cobb, B., Vega, D., & Kronauge, C. (2005, April). *Effects of an elementary dual language immersion school program on junior high school achievement of native Spanish speaking and native English speaking students*. Paper presented at the annual meeting of the American Education Research Association, Montreal, Quebec, Canada.

Cohen, C. C. de, & Clewell, B. C. (2007). *Putting English language learners on the educational map* (Policy brief). Washington, DC: Urban Institute.

Cole, M., & Cole, S. R. (2001). *The development of children*. New York, NY: Worth.

Cole, M., & Engeström, Y. (1993). A cultural–historical approach to distributed cognition. In G. Salomon (Ed.), *Distributed cognitions: Psychological and educational considerations* (pp. 1–43). New York, NY: Cambridge University Press.

Cole, M., Engeström, Y., & Vasquez, O. A. (1997). *Mind, culture, and activity: Seminal papers from the laboratory of comparative human cognition*. New York, NY: Cambridge University Press.

Cole, S., & Barber, E. (2003). *Increasing faculty diversity: The occupational choices of high-achieving minority students*. Cambridge, MA: Harvard University Press.

Collier, V. P. (1987). Age and rate of acquisition of second language for academic purposes. *TESOL Quarterly, 21*, 617–641. doi:10.2307/3586986

Collier, V. P. (1989). How long? A synthesis of research on academic achievement in a second language. *TESOL Quarterly, 23*, 509–531. doi:10.2307/3586923

Collier, V. P. (1995). *Acquiring a second language for school: Directions in language and education* (Vol. 1, No. 4). Washington, DC: National Clearinghouse for Bilingual Education.

Commission on No Child Left Behind. (2007). *Beyond No Child Left Behind: Fulfilling the promise to our nation's children*. Washington, DC: Aspen Institute.

Corballis, M. C. (2009). The evolution of language. *Annals of the New York Academy of Sciences, 1156*, 19–43. doi:10.1111/j.1749-6632.2009.04423.x

Costa, A., Hernandez, M., & Sebastián-Gallés, N. (2008). Bilingualism aids conflict resolution: Evidence from the ANT task. *Cognition*, *106*, 59–86. doi:10.1016/j.cognition.2006.12.013

Crain, S., & Thornton, R. (1998). *Investigations in universal grammar: A guide to experiments on the acquisition of syntax*. Cambridge, MA: MIT Press.

Crawford, J. (1999). *Bilingual education: History, politics, theory, and practice* (4th ed.). Los Angeles, CA: Bilingual Education Services.

Crawford, J. (2000). *At war with diversity: U.S. language policy in an age of anxiety*. Clevedon, England: Multilingual Matters.

Cremin, J. (1957). *The republic and the school: Horace Mann: On the education of free men*. New York, NY: Teachers College.

Cummins, J. (1976). The influence of bilingualism on cognitive growth: A synthesis of research finding and explanatory hypotheses. *Working Papers on Bilingualism*, *9*, 1–43.

Cummins, J. (1977). Cognitive factors associated with the attainment of intermediate levels of bilingual skill. *Modern Language Journal*, *61*, 3–12. doi:10.2307/325360

Cummins, J. (1979). Linguistic interdependence and the educational development of bilingual children. *Review of Educational Research*, *49*, 222–251.

Cummins, J. (1980). The cross-lingual dimensions of language proficiency: Implications for bilingual education. *TESOL Quarterly*, *14*, 175–187. doi:10.2307/3586312

Cummins, J. (1981a). *California State Department of Education, schooling and language minority students: A theoretical framework*. Los Angeles, CA: Los Angeles Evaluation, Assessment and Dissemination Center.

Cummins, J. (1981b). *The role of primary language development in promoting educational success for language minority students*. California state department of education, schooling and language minority students: A theoretical framework. Los Angeles, CA: Los Angeles Evaluation, Assessment and Dissemination Center.

Cummins, J. (1984). *Bilingualism and special education: Issues in assessment and pedagogy*. San Diego, CA: College-Hill Press.

Cummins, J. (1989). A theoretical framework for bilingual special education. *Exceptional Children*, *56*, 111–119.

Cummins, J. (1991). Interdependence of first- and second-language proficiency in bilingual children. In E. Bialystok (Ed.), *Language processing in bilingual children* (pp. 12–27). New York, NY: Cambridge University Press. doi:10.1017/CBO9780511620652.006

Cummins, J. (1993). Review of bilingualism, multiculturalism, and second language learning: The McGill conference in honour of Wallace E. Lambert. *Canadian Journal of Experimental Psychology*, *47*, 611–614. doi:10.1037/h0084954

Cummins, J. (1998). Immersion education for the millennium: What have we learned from 30 years of research on second language immersion? In M. R. Childs & R. M. Bostwick (Chairs), *English through two languages: Research and practice*. Symposium conducted at the Second Katoh Gakuen International Symposium on Immersion and Bilingual Education, Katoh Gakuen, Japan.

Cummins, J. (1999). Paradigms in bilingual education research: Does theory have a place? *Educational Researcher, 28*(7), 26–41.

Cummins, J. (2000). *Language, power, and pedagogy: Bilingual children in the crossfire.* Clevedon, England: Multilingual Matters.

Dapretto, M., & Bjork, E. L. (2000). The development of word retrieval abilities in the second year and its relation to early vocabulary growth. *Child Development, 71*(3), 635–648. doi:10.1111/1467-8624.00172

Darcy, N. T. (1946). The effect of bilingualism upon the measurement of intelligence source. *The Journal of Genetic Psychology, 3*(7), 21–44.

Darling-Hammond, L., & Bransford, J. (Eds.). (2005). *Preparing teachers for a changing world: What teachers should learn and be able to do.* San Francisco, CA: Jossey-Bass.

Darsie, M. L. (1926). The mental capacity of American-born Japanese children. *Comparative Psychological Monographs, 3*(5), 89.

Davis, L. H., Carlisle, J. F., & Beeman, M. (1999). Hispanic children's writing in English and Spanish when English is the language of instruction. *Yearbook of the National Reading Conference, 48,* 238–248.

de Villiers, J. G., & de Villiers, P. A. (1973). A cross-sectional study of the acquisition of grammatical morphemes in child speech. *Journal of Psycholinguistic Research, 2,* 267–278. doi:10.1007/BF01067106

de Villiers, P. A., & de Villiers, J. G. (1979). *Early language.* Cambridge, MA: Harvard University Press.

DeBaryshe, B. D. (1995). Maternal belief systems: Linchpin in the home reading process. *Journal of Applied Developmental Psychology, 16,* 1–20. doi:10.1016/0193-3973(95)90013-6

DeCasper, A. J., Lecanuet, J.-P., Busnel, M.-C., Granier-Deferre, C., & Maugeais, R. (1994). Fetal reactions to recurrent maternal speech. *Infant Behavior and Development, 17,* 159–164. doi:10.1016/0163-6383(94)90051-5

Dehaene-Lambertz, G., Hertz-Pannier, L., & Dubois, J. (2006). Nature and nurture in language acquisition: Anatomical and functional brain-imaging studies in infants. *Trends in Neurosciences, 29,* 367–373. doi:10.1016/j.tins.2006.05.011

Demos, V. (1988). Ethnic mother tongue maintenance among Greek orthodox Americans. *International Journal of the Sociology of Language, 69,* 39–71. doi:10.1515/ijsl.1988.69.73

Derwing, B. (1973). *Transformational grammar as a theory of language acquisition.* Cambridge, England: Cambridge University Press.

Dews, S., Winner, E., Kaplan, J., Rosenblatt, E., Hunt, M., Lim, K., . . . Smarsh, B. (1996). Children's understanding of the meaning and functions of verbal irony. *Child Development, 67,* 3071–3085. doi:10.2307/1131767

Diamond, A. (1991). Frontal lobe involvement in cognitive changes during the first year of life. In K. R. Gibson & A. C. Petersen (Eds.), *Brain maturation and cog-*

nitive development: Comparative and cross-cultural perspectives (pp. 127–180). New York, NY: Aldine de Greuter.

Diaz, R. M. (1985). Bilingual cognitive development: Addressing three gaps in current research. *Child Development, 56*, 1376–1388. doi:10.2307/1130458

Dickson, V. E. (1917). The relation of mental testing to school administration: With special reference to children entering school. *Normal Seminar Bulletin*. July, 1.

diSibio, M., & Whalen, T. (2000). Using the WPPSI-R with bilingual children: Implications for practice. *The California School Psychologist, 5*, 5–17.

Dolson, D. P. (1985). The effects of Spanish home language use on the scholastic performance of Hispanic pupils. *Journal of Multilingual and Multicultural Development, 6*, 135–155. doi:10.1080/01434632.1985.9994192

Dominey, P. F. (2005). Emergence of grammatical constructions: Evidence from stimulation and grounded agent experiments. *Connection Science, 17*, 289–306. doi:10.1080/09540090500270714

Dopke, S. (2000). *Cross-linguistic structures in simultaneous bilingualism*. Amsterdam, PA: Benjamin.

Draganski, B., Gaser, C., Busch, V., Schuierer, G., Bogdahn, U., & May, A. (2004, January 22). Changes in grey matter induced by training: Newly honed juggling skills show up as a transient feature on a brain-imaging scan. *Nature, 427*, 311 312. doi:10.1038/427311a

Dressler, C., & Kamil, M. (2006). First- and second-language literacy. In D. August & T. Shanahan (Eds.), *Report of the National Literacy Panel on language minority youth and children* (pp. 176–222). Mahwah, NJ: Erlbaum.

Duffy, J. D., & Campbell, J. J., III. (2001). Regional prefrontal syndromes: A theoretical and clinical overview. In S. P. Salloway, P. F. Malloy, & J. D. Duffy (Eds.), *The frontal lobes and neuropsychiatric illness* (pp. 113–123). Washington, DC: American Psychiatric Publishing.

Duke, L. M., & Kaszniak, A. W. (2000). Executive control functions in degenerative dementias: A comparative review. *Neuropsychology Review, 10*, 75–99. doi:10.1023/A:1009096603879

Dulay, H., & Burt, M. (1974). Natural sequences in child second language acquisition. *Language Learning, 24*, 37–53. doi:10.1111/j.1467-1770.1974.tb00234.x

Duncan, G. J., & Magnuson, K. A. (2005). Can family socioeconomic resources account for racial and ethnic test score gaps? *The Future of Children, 15*(1), 35–54. doi:10.1353/foc.2005.0004

Duncan, S. E., & De Avila, E. A. (1979). Bilingualism and cognition: Some recent findings. *NABE Journal, 4*, 15–50.

Duquette, G. (1991). Cultural processing and minority language children with needs and special needs. In G. Duquette & L. Malve (Eds.), *Language, culture, and cognition* (pp. 54–66). Philadelphia, PA: Multilingual Matters.

Durán, B. J., & Weffer, R. E. (1992). Immigrants' aspirations, high school process, and academic outcomes. *American Educational Research Journal, 29*, 163–181.

Durgunoglu, A. Y., Nagy, W. E., & Hancin-Bhatt, B. J. (1993). Cross-language transfer of phonological awareness. *Journal of Educational Psychology, 85*, 453–465. doi:10.1037/0022-0663.85.3.453

Eimas, P. D., Siqueland, E. R., Jusczyk, P., & Vigorito, J. (1971, January 22). Speech perception in early infancy. *Science, 171*, 303–306. doi:10.1126/science.171.3968.303

Elementary and Secondary Education Act of 1965, Title II, Pub. L. No. 89-10, 27 Stat. (1965).

Enard, W., Khaitovich, P., Klose, J., Zollner, S., Heissig, F., Giavalisco, P., . . . Paabo, S. (2002, April 12). Intra-and interspecific variation in primate gene expression patterns. *Science, 296*, 340–343. doi:10.1126/science.1068996

Enard, W., Przeworski, M., Fisher, S. E., Lai, C. S., Wiebe, V., Kitano, T., . . . Paabo, S. (2002, August 22). Molecular evolution of FOXP2, a gene involved in speech and language. *Nature, 418*, 869–872. doi:10.1038/nature01025

English Language Education for Children in Public Schools of 2000, Ariz. Rev. Stat. §15-75.

English Language Education for Immigrant Children of 1998, Cal. Educ. Code § 300.

Equal Educational Opportunities Act of 1974, Pub. L. No. 93-380, 88 Stat. 514 (1974).

Ercikan, K., & Roth, W.-M. (2006). What good is polarizing research into qualitative and quantitative? *Educational Researcher, 35*(5), 14–23. doi:10.3102/0013189X035005014

Ervin, S. M. (1964). Imitation and structural change in children's language. In E. Lenneberg (Ed.), *New directions in the study of language* (pp. 163–189). Cambridge, MA: MIT Press.

Espinosa, L. M. (2010a). Assessment of young English language learners. In E. E. García & E. C. Frede (Eds.), *Young English language learners: Current research and emerging directions for practice and policy* (pp. 119–142). New York, NY: Teachers College Press.

Espinosa, L. M. (2010b). Classroom teaching and instruction: Best practices for young English language learners. In E. E. García & E. C. Frede (Eds.), *Young English language learners: Current research and emerging directions for practice and policy* (pp. 143–164). New York, NY: Teachers College Press.

Espinosa, L. M., & López, M. (2006). *Assessment considerations for young English language learners across different levels of accountability* Philadelphia, PA: National Early Childhood Accountability Task Force.

Fan, J., McCandliss, B. D., Sommer, T., Roz, A., & Posner, M. I. (2002). Testing the efficiency and independence of attentional networks. *Journal of Cognitive Neuroscience, 14*, 340–347. doi:10.1162/089892902317361886

Fantini, A. E. (1985). *Language acquisition of a bilingual child.* Clevedon, England: Multilingual Matters.

Feingold, G. A. (1924). Intelligence of the first generation of immigrant groups. *Journal of Educational Psychology, 15*, 65–82. doi:10.1037/h0073889

Field, T. (1982). *Emotion and early interaction.* Hillsdale, NJ: Erlbaum.

Figueroa, L. (2005, April). *The development of pre-reading knowledge in English and Spanish: Latino English language learners in a dual-language education context*. Paper presented at the annual meeting of the American Education Research Association, Montreal, Quebec, Canada.

Filler, L. (1965). *Horace Mann: On the crisis in education*. Yellow Springs, OH: Antioch Press.

Fischer, C. S., Hout, M., Sánchez Jankowski, M., Lucas, S. R., Swidler, A., & Voss, K. (1996). *Inequality by design: Cracking the Bell Curve myth*. Princeton, NJ: Princeton University Press.

Fischer, K. W. (1980). A theory of cognitive development: The control and construction of hierarchies of skills. *Psychological Review, 87*, 477–531. doi:10.1037/0033-295X.87.6.477

Fisher, R. A. (1930). *The Genetical Theory of Natural Selection*. Oxford, England: Oxford University Press.

Fishman, J. A. (1966). *The ethnic group school and mother tongue maintenance: Language loyalty in the United States*. The Hague, the Netherlands: Mouton.

Flavell, J. H. (1979). Metacognition and cognitive monitoring: A new area of cognitive-developmental inquiry. *The American Psychologist, 34*, 906–911. doi:10.1037/0003-066X.34.10.906

Flavell, J. H. (1981). Cognitive monitoring. In W. P. Dickson (Ed.), *Children's oral communication skills* (pp. 35–60). New York, NY: Academic Press.

Flavell, J. H. (2000). Development of children's knowledge about the mental world. *International Journal of Behavioral Development, 24*, 15–23. doi:10.1080/016502500383421

Flavell, J. H. (2004). Theory-of-mind development: Retrospect and prospect. *Merrill-Palmer Quarterly, 50*, 274–290. doi:10.1353/mpq.2004.0018

Flavell, J. H., & Miller, P. H. (1998). Social cognition. In W. Damon (Series Ed.), D. Kuhn & R. S. Seigler (Vol. Eds.), *Handbook of child psychology: Vol. 2. Cognition, perception, and language* (5th ed., pp. 851–898). New York, NY: Wiley.

Flavell, J. H., Miller, P. H., & Miller, S. A. (1993). *Cognitive development* (3rd ed.). Englewood Cliffs, NJ: Prentice Hall.

Flavell, J. H., Miller, P. H., & Miller, S. A. (2002). *Cognitive development* (4th ed.). Englewood Cliffs, NJ: Prentice Hall.

Frey, W. H. (2006). *Diversity spreads out: Metropolitan shifts in Hispanic, Asian, and Black populations since 2000* (Metropolitan Policy Program: Living Cities Census Series). Washington, DC: Brookings Institute.

Frisch, K. V., & Lindauer, M. (1956). The "language" and orientation of the honey bee. *Annual Review of Entomology, 1*, 45–58. doi:10.1146/annurev.en.01.010156.000401

Frost, J. (2000). From "epi" through "meta" to mastery: The balance of meaning and skill in early reading instruction. *Scandinavian Journal of Educational Research, 44*, 125–144. doi:10.1080/713696670

Fry, R. (2007, June 6). *How far behind in math and reading are English language learners?* Washington, DC: Pew Hispanic Center.

Fuller, B., & Clark, P. (1994). Raising school effects while ignoring culture? Local conditions and the influence of classroom tools, rules, and pedagogy. *Review of Educational Research, 64*, 119–157.

Gabiña, J. J., Gorostidi, R., Iruretagoiena, R., Olaziregi, I., & Sierra, J. (1986). *EIFE: Influence of factors on the learning of Basque.* Vitoria-Gasteiz, Spain: Eusko Jaurlaritzaren Argitalpen Zerbitzu Nagusia.

Galton, F. (1869). *Hereditary genius.* London, England: Macmillan.

Galton, F. (1883). *Inquiries into human faculty and its development.* London, England: Macmillan.

Galton, F. (1904). Eugenics: Its definition, scope, and aims. *The American Journal of Sociology, 10*(1), 1–25. doi:10.1086/211280

Gándara, P. & Hopkins, M. (2010). *Forbidden languages: English learners and restrictive language policies.* New York, NY: Teachers College Press.

Gándara, P., Maxwell-Jolly, J., García, E., Asato, J., Gutiérrez, K., Stritikus, T., & Curry, J. (2000). *The initial impact of Proposition 227 on the instruction of English learners.* Santa Barbara, CA: Linguistic Minority Research Institute. Retrieved from http://www.uclmrinet.ucsb.edu

Gándara, P., Moran, R., & García, E. E. (2004). Legacy of *Brown: Lau* and language policy in the United States. *Review of Research in Education, 28*(1), 27–46. doi:10.3102/0091732X028001027

Ganger, J., & Brent, M. R. (2004). Reexamining the vocabulary spurt. *Developmental Psychology, 40*, 621–632. doi:10.1037/0012-1649.40.4.621

García, E. E. (Ed.). (1983). *The Mexican-American child: Language, cognition, and social development.* Tempe, AZ: Arizona State University, Center for Bilingual Education.

García, E. E. (2001a). *Hispanic education in the United States: Raices y alas.* Lanham, MD: Rowman & Littlefield.

García, E. E. (2001b). *Understanding and meeting the challenge of student diversity* (3rd ed.). Boston, MA: Houghton Mifflin.

García, E. E. (2002). Bilingualism in schooling in the United States. *International Journal of the Sociology of Language, 155/156*, 1–92. doi:10.1515/ijsl.2002.028

García, E. E. (2005). *Teaching and learning in two languages: Bilingualism and schooling in the United States.* New York, NY: Teachers College Press.

García, E. E. (2008). Bilingual education in the United States. In J. Altarriba & R. R. Heredia (Eds.), *An introduction to bilingualism: Principles and processes* (pp. 30–48). Mahwah, NJ: Erlbaum.

García, E. E., & Carrasco, R. (1981). An analysis of bilingual mother–child discourse. In R. Duran (Ed.), *Latino discourse* (pp. 46–61). Norwood, NJ: Ablex.

García, E. E., & Cuellar, D. (2006). Who are these linguistically and culturally diverse students? *Teachers College Record, 108*, 2220–2246. doi:10.1111/j.1467-9620.2006.00780.x

García, E. E., & Frede, E. C. (2010). *Young English language learners: Current research and emerging directions for practice and policy*. New York, NY: Teachers College Press.

García, E. E., & González, D. (2006). *Pre-K and Latinos: The foundation for America's future*. Washington, DC: Pre-K Now Research Series. Retrieved from http://www.preknow.org//resource/reports/preknowreports.cfm

García, E. E., & Jensen, B. T. (2006). Dual-language programs in the US: An alternative to monocultural, monolingual education. *Language Magazine*, 5(6), 30–37.

García, E. E., & Jensen, B. T. (2007a). Advancing school readiness for young Hispanic children through universal prekindergarten. *Harvard Journal of Hispanic Policy*, 19, 25–37.

García, E. E., & Jensen, B. T. (2007b). *Language development and early education of young Hispanic children in the United States*. Tempe, AZ: National Task Force on Early Childhood Education for Hispanics. Draft available online at http://www.ecehispanic.org/work/lang_dev_6August2007.pdf

García, E. E., Jensen, B. T., & Cuéllar, D. (2006). Early academic achievement of Hispanics in the United States: Implications for teacher preparation. *New Educator*, 2, 123–147. doi:10.1080/15476880600657215

García, E. E., Jensen, B. T., Miller, L. S., & Huerta, T. (2005). *Early childhood education of Hispanics in the United States*. Tempe, AZ: National Task Force on Early Childhood Education for Hispanics. Retrieved from http://www.ecehispanic.org/work/white_paper_Oct2005.pdf

García, E. E., & Miller, L. S. (2008). Findings and recommendations of the National Task Force on Early Childhood Education for Hispanics. *Child Development Perspectives*, 2(2), 53–58. doi:10.1111/j.1750-8606.2008.00042.x

García, G. E. (1991). Factors influencing the English reading test performance of Spanish speaking Hispanic children. *Reading Research Quarterly*, 26, 371–392. doi:10.2307/747894

García Coll, C., Lamberty, G., Jenkins, R., McAdoo, H., Crnic, K., Wasik, B., & Vazquez Garcia, H. (1996). An integrative model for the study of developmental competencies in minority children. *Child Development*, 67, 1891–1914. doi:10.2307/1131600

Gardner, H. (1999). *Intelligence reframed: Multiple intelligences for the 21st century*. New York, NY: Basic Books.

Gardner, R. A., & Gardner, B. T. (1969, August). Teaching sign language to a chimpanzee. *Science*, 165, 664–672. doi:10.1126/science.165.3894.664

Garretson, O. K. (1928). A study of the causes of retardation among Mexican children. *Journal of Educational Psychology*, 19, 31–40. doi:10.1037/h0073861

Genesee, F. (Ed.). (1999). *Program alternatives for linguistically diverse students*. Berkeley, CA: University of California, Center for Research on Education, Diversity and Excellence.

Genesee, F. (2003, April). *The capacity of language faculty: Contributions from studies of simultaneous bilingual acquisition*. Paper presented at the Fourth International Symposium on Bilingualism, Tempe, AZ.

Genesee, F. (2004). What do we know about bilingual education for majority language students? In T. K. Bhatia & W. Ritchie (Eds.), *Handbook of bilingualism and multiculturalism* (pp. 547–576). Malden, MA: Blackwell.

Genesee, F. (2010). Dual language development in preschool children. In E. García & E. Frede (Eds.), *Enhancing the knowledge base for serving young English language learners* (pp. 59–79). New York, NY: Columbia University, Teachers College Press.

Genesee, F., Geva, E., Dressler, C., & Kamil, M. (2006). Synthesis: Cross-linguistic relationships. In D. August & T. Shanahan (Eds.), *Report of the National Literacy Panel on language minority youth and children* (pp. 147–168). Mahwah, NJ: Erlbaum.

Genesee, F., Lindholm-Leary, K., Saunders, W., & Christian, D. (2005). English language learners in US schools: An overview of research findings. *Journal of Education for Students Placed at Risk, 10*, 363–385. doi:10.1207/s15327671espr1004_2

Genesee, F., & Nicoladis, E. (2009). Bilingual first language acquisition. In E. Hoff & M. Shate (Eds.), *Blackwell handbook of language development* (pp. 324–344). Malden, MA: Wiley-Blackwell.

Genishi, C. (1981). Code switching in Chicano six-year olds. In R. Duran (Ed.), *Latino language and communicative behavior* (pp. 133–152). Norwood, NJ: Ablex.

Gersten, R., (1985). Structured immersion for language minority students: Results of a longitudinal evaluation. *American Educational Research Association, 7*, 187–196.

Gersten, R., Baker, S. K., Shanahan, T., Linan-Thompson, S., Collins, P., & Scarcella, R. (2007). *Effective literacy and language instruction for English learners in the elementary grades: An IES practice guide*. Washington, DC: U.S. Department of Education, Institute of Education Sciences.

Geva, E. (2006). Second-language oral proficiency and second-language literacy. In D. August & T. Shanahan (Eds.), *Report of the National Literacy Panel on language minority youth and children* (pp. 126–139). Mahwah, NJ: Erlbaum.

Geva, E., & Genesee, F. (2006). First-language oral proficiency and second language literacy. In D. August & T. Shanahan (Eds.), *Report of the National Literacy Panel on language minority youth and children* (pp. 185–195). Mahwah, NJ: Erlbaum.

Geva, E., & Ryan, E. B. (1993). Linguistic and memory correlates of academic skills in first and second languages. *Language Learning, 43*, 5–42. doi:10.1111/j.1467-1770.1993.tb00171.x

Geva, E., Yaghoub-Zadeh, Z., & Schuster, B. (2000). Part IV: Reading and foreign language learning: Understanding individual differences in word recognition skills of ESL children. *Annals of Dyslexia, 50*, 121–154. doi:10.1007/s11881-000-0020-8

Giardini, G., & Root, W. T. (1923). A comparison of the Detroit first grade tests given in Italian and English. *Psychological Clinic, 15*, 101–108.

Gierl, M. J., & ElAtia, S. (2007). [Review of the book *Adapting Educational and Psychological tests for cross-cultural assessment*]. *Applied Psychological Measurement, 31*, 74–78. doi:10.1177/0146621606288556

Gingrich, N. (2007, April 2). *The Lantern.* Retrieved from http://azbilingualed.org/NEWS_2007/bilingual_education_gingrich_condemnationwrong.htm

Glass, G. V., McGaw, B., & Smith, M. L. (1981). *Meta-analysis in social research.* Beverly Hills, CA: Sage.

Gleitman, L., & Wanner, E. (1982). Language acquisition: The state of the state of the art. In E. Wanner & L. Gleitman (Eds.), *Language acquisition: The state of the art* (pp. 3–48). Cambridge, MA: Cambridge University Press.

Goldenberg, C. (1987). Low income Hispanic parents' contributions to their first-grade children's word recognition skills. *Anthropology & Education Quarterly, 18*, 149–179. doi:10.1525/aeq.1987.18.3.05x1130l

Goldenberg, C. N., & Gallimore, R. (1991). Local knowledge, research knowledge, and educational change: A case study of early Spanish reading improvement. *Educational Researcher, 20*(8), 2–14.

Goldenberg, C. N., Gallimore, R., Reese, L., & Garnier, H. (2001). Cause or effect? A longitudinal study of immigrant Latino parents' aspirations and expectations, and their children's school performance. *American Educational Research Journal, 38*, 547–582. doi:10.3102/00028312038003547

Goldenberg, C. N., Reese, L., & Gallimore, R. (1992). Effects of literacy materials from school on Latino children's home experiences and early reading achievement. *American Journal of Education, 100*, 497–536. doi:10.1086/444026

Goldenberg, C. N., Rezaei, A., & Fletcher, J. (2005, April). *Home use of English and Spanish and Spanish-speaking children's oral language and literacy achievement.* Paper presented at the annual meeting of the American Educational Research Association, Montreal, Quebec, Canada.

Goldenberg, C., Rueda, R., & August, D. (2006). Synthesis: Sociocultural contexts and literacy development. In D. August & T. Shanahan (Eds.), *Report of the National Literacy Panel on language minority youth and children* (pp. 249–268). Mahwah, NJ: Erlbaum.

Goldin-Meadow, S. (2000). Beyond words: The importance of gestures to researchers and learners. *Child Development, 71*, 231–239. doi:10.1111/1467-8624.00138

Goldin-Meadows, S., & Mylander, C. (1990a). Beyond the input given: The child's role in the acquisition of Language. *Language, 66*, 323–355. doi:10.2307/414890

Goldin-Meadow, S., & Mylander, C. (1990b). The role of parental input in the development of a morphological system. *Journal of Child Language, 17*, 527–563. doi:10.1017/S0305000900010874

Goldman, S. R., Reyes, M., & Varnhagen, C. K. (1984). Understanding fables in first and second language. *NABE Journal, 8*, 835–866.

Goldman-Rakic, P. S. (1987). Circuitry of primate prefrontal cortex and regulation of behavior by representational memory. In F. Plum (Ed.), *Handbook of physiology: The nervous system* (pp. 373–417). Bethesda, MD: American Physiological Society.

Goldstein, B. C., Harris, K. C., & Klein, M. D. (1993). Assessment of oral storytelling abilities of Latino junior high school students with learning handicaps. *Journal of Learning Disabilities, 26,* 138–143.

Golinkoff, R. (1983). The preverbal negotiation of failed messages: Insights into the transition period. In R. Golinkoff (Ed.), *The transition from prelinguistic to linguistic verbal communication* (pp. 57–78). Hillsdale, NJ: Erlbaum.

Goncz, B., & Kodzepeljic, D. (1991). Cognition and bilingualism revisited. *Journal of Multilingual and Multicultural Development, 12,* 137–163. doi:10.1080/01434632.1991.9994455

Gonzalez, N., Moll, L., & Amanti, C. (2005). *Funds of knowledge: Theorizing practices, households, communities, and classrooms.* Mahwah, NJ: Erlbaum.

Goodenough, F. (1926). Racial differences in the intelligence of school children. *Journal of Experimental Psychology, 9,* 388–397. doi:10.1037/h0073325

Gormley, W. T., Gayer, T., & Dawson, B. (2004). *The effects of universal pre-K on cognitive development.* Washington, DC: Georgetown University, Public Policy Institute.

Gormley, W. T., Gayer, T., Phillips, D., & Dawson, B. (2005). The effects of universal pre-K on cognitive development. *Developmental Psychology, 41,* 872–884. doi:10.1037/0012-1649.41.6.872

Gorrell, J. J., Bregman, N. J., McAllister, H. A., & Lipscomb, T. J. (1982). A comparison of spatial and role-taking in monolingual and bilingual children. *The Journal of Genetic Psychology, 140,* 3–10.

Gottardo, A. (2002). The relationship between language and reading skills in bilingual Spanish-English speakers. *Topics in Language Disorders, 22*(5), 46–70. doi:10.1097/00011363-200211000-00008

Gould, S. J. (1993). *The mismeasure of man.* New York, NY: Norton.

Graham, V. T. (1925). The intelligence of Italian and Jewish children. *Journal of Abnormal and Social Psychology, 20,* 371–376. doi:10.1037/h0073438

Green, J., Camilli, G., & Elmore, P. (Eds.). (2006). *Handbook of complementary methods for research in education.* Washington, DC: American Educational Research Association.

Greene, J. P. (1997). A meta-analysis of the Rossell and Baker review of bilingual education research. *Bilingual Research Journal, 21,* 103.

Greene, J. P. (1998). *A meta-analysis of the effectiveness of bilingual education.* Claremont, CA: Thomas Rivera Policy Institute.

Greenspan, A. (2007). *The age of turbulence: Adventures in a new world.* New York, NY: Penguin Press.

Grosjean, F. (1982). *Life with two languages.* New York, NY: Cambridge University Press.

Gross, D., Conrad, B., Fogg, L., Willis, L., & Garvey, C. (1993). What does the NCATS (Nursing Child Assessment Teaching Scale) measure? *Nursing Research, 42*, 260–265.

Grossman, W. M. (2002, October 5). Designed for life: Interview with Don Norman. *New Scientist, 176*(2363), 46.

Guardians Association v. Civil Service Commission, 463 U.S. 582 (1983).

Haier, R. J., Chueh, D., Touchette, P., Lott, I., Buchsbaum, M., Machmillan, D., . . . Sosa, E. (1995). Brain size and cerebral glucose metabolic rate in non-specific mental retardation and Down syndrome. *Intelligence, 20*, 191–210. doi:10.1016/0160-2896(95)90032-2

Hakuta, K. (1986). *Mirror of language: The debate on bilingualism.* New York, NY: Basic Books.

Hakuta, K. (1990). Language and cognition in bilingual children. In A. Padilla, H. Fairchild, & C. Valadez (Eds.), *Bilingual education: Issues and strategies* (pp. 47–59). Newbury Park, CA: Sage.

Hakuta, K. (2007). English language learners with reference to the state of New Mexico public schools. In *Essential elements for successful schools: Expert briefs on the essential factors that need to be present in successful schools serving at-risk students, English learners, and students with disabilities in urban, suburban, and rural schools* (pp. 21–25). Palo Alto, CA: American Institute for Research. Retreived from http://www.nmschoolfunding.org/pdf/New%20Mexico%20Research%20 Briefs.pdf

Hakuta, K., & Diaz, R. M. (1984). The relationship between bilingualism and cognitive ability: A critical discussion and some new longitudinal data. In K. E. Nelson (Ed.), *Children's language* (pp. 319–344). Hillsdale, NJ: Erlbaum.

Hakuta, K., Ferdman, B. M., & Diaz, R. M. (1987). Bilingualism and cognitive development: Three perspectives. In S. Rosenberg (Ed.), *Advances in applied psycholinguistics: Vol. 2. Reading, writing and language learning* (pp. 284–319). Cambridge, England: Cambridge University Press.

Hakuta, K., & García, E. (1989). Bilingualism and education. *American Psychologist, 44*, 374–379. doi:10.1037/0003-066X.44.2.374

Hakuta, K., Goto Butler, Y., & Witt, D. (2000). *How long does it take English learners to attain proficiency?* (University of California Linguistic Minority Research Institute Policy Report 2000-1). Santa Barbara, CA: University of California.

Hall, S. (1891). Notes on the study of infants. *Pedagogical Seminary, 1*, 127–138.

Hancock, D. R. (2002). The effects of native language books on the pre-literacy skill development of language minority kindergartners. *Journal of Research in Childhood Education, 17*, 62–68. doi:10.1080/02568540209594999

Hansen, D. A. (1989). Locating learning: Second language gains and language use in family, peer, and classroom contexts. *NABE Journal, 13*, 161–180.

Harry, B., & Klingner, J. (2006). *Why are so many minority students in special education? Understanding race and disability in schools*. New York, NY: Teachers College Press.

Hart, B., & Risley, T. R. (1995). *Meaningful differences in the everyday experience of young American children*. Baltimore, MD: Paul H. Brookes.

Hart, B., & Risley, T. R. (1999). *Learning to talk: The social world of children*. Baltimore, MD: Brookes.

Haught, B. B. (1931). The language difficulty of Spanish-American children. *Journal of Applied Psychology, 15*, 92–95. doi:10.1037/h0074256

Hauser, M. D., Chomsky, N., & Fitch, W. (2002, November 22). The faculty of language: What is it, who has it, and how did it evolve? *Science, 298*, 1569–1579. doi:10.1126/science.298.5598.1569

Heath, S. B. (1983). *Ways with words: Language, life, and work in communities and classrooms*. New York, NY: Cambridge University Press.

Heath, S. B. (1986). Sociocultural contexts of language development. In California State Department of Education (Ed.), *Beyond language: Social and factors in schooling language minority students* (pp. 143–186). Los Angeles, CA: California State University, Evaluation, Dissemination, and Assessment Center.

Hébert, R., Bilodeau, M., Foidart, D., Leger, R., Saindon, C., Schaubroeck, G., & Laurencelle, Y. (1976). *Rendement Academique et Langue d'Enseignement Chez les Éléves Franco-Manitobains* [Academic results and language teaching of French-Manatobians (bilinguals)]. Saint-Boniface, Manitoba, Canada: Centre de Recherches du College Universitaire de Saint-Boniface.

Heckman, J., & Masterov, D. (2004). *The productivity argument for investing in young children*. Chicago, IL: Committee for Economic Development.

Hepper, P. G. (1996). Fetal memory: Does it exist? What does it do? *Acta Paediatrica, 85* (Suppl. 416), 16–20. doi:10.1111/j.1651-2227.1996.tb14272.x

Hernandez, D. (2006). *Young Hispanic children in the U.S.: A demographic portrait based on Census 2000* (A report to the National Task Force on Early Childhood Education for Hispanics). New York, NY: Foundation for Child Development.

Hernandez, D. J., Denton, N. A., & Macartney, S. E. (2007, April). Children in immigrant families—The U.S. and 50 states: National origins, language, and early education. In *Child trends: Children in America's newcomer families* (Publication No. #2007-11). Washington, DC: Child Trends and Center for Social and Demographic Analysis.

Hernandez, D. J., Denton, N. A., & Macartney, S. E. (2008). Children in immigrant families: Looking to America's future. *Social Policy Report, 22*(3), 1–24.

Hernandez, P. J., Macartney, S., & Denton, N. A., (2010). Young English language learners: A demographic portrait. In E. E. García & E. C. Frede, *Young English language learners: Current research and emerging directions for practice and policy* (pp. 10–41). New York, NY: Teachers College Press.

Herrnstein, R. J., & Murray, C. (1994). *The bell curve*. New York, NY: Free Press.

Hilgard, E. (1996). History of educational psychology. In D. C. Berliner & R. C. Calfee (Eds.), *Handbook of educational psychology* (pp. 990–1004). New York, NY: Macmillan.

Hill, H. (1936). The effect of bilingualism on the measured intelligence of elementary school children of Italian parentage. *Journal of Experimental Education, 5*, 75–78.

Hinton, L. (1998). Language loss and revitalization in California: Overview. *International Journal of the Sociology of Language, 132*, 83–93. doi:10.1515/ijsl.1998.132.83

Hoff, E. (2005). *Language development* (3rd ed.). Belmont, CA: Wadsworth/Thomson Learning.

Hoff-Ginsberg, E. (1997). *Language development*. Pacific Grove, CA: Brooks/Cole.

Hopstock, P. J., & Stephenson, T. G. (2003). *Native languages of LEP students: Descriptive study of services to LEP students and LEP students with disabilities* (Special Topic Report No. 1). Arlington, VA: Development Associates and U.S. Department of Education, Office of English Language Acquisition.

Howard, E. R., Sugarman, J., & Christian, D. (2003). *Trends in two-way immersion education: A review of the research*. Washington, DC: Center for Applied Linguistics.

Huerta, A. (1977). The development of code-switching in a young bilingual. *Working Papers in Sociolinguistics, 21*, 1–16.

Huerta-Macías, A., & Quintero, E. (1992). Code-switching, bilingualism, and biliteracy: A case study. *Bilingual Research Journal, 16*(3–4), 69–90.

Hulk, A., & van der Linden, E. (1996). Language mixing in a French–Dutch bilingual child. In E. Kellerman, B. Weltens, & T. Bongaerts (Eds.), *Eurosia 6: A selection of papers* (pp. 89–101). Utrecht, the Netherlands: Vereniging voor Toegepaste Taalwetenschap.

Ianco-Worral, A. D. (1972). Bilingualism and cognitive development. *Child Development, 43*, 1390–1400. doi:10.2307/1127524

Ingram, D. (1986). Phonological development: Production. In P. Fletcher & M. Garman (Eds.), *Language acquisition* (2nd ed., pp. 223–239). Cambridge, England: Cambridge University Press.

Jacobs, L. A. (1999). Equal opportunity, natural inequalities, and racial disadvantage: The Bell Curve and its critics. *Philosophy of the Social Sciences, 29*, 120–144.

Jacoby, R., & Glauberman, N. (Eds.). (1995). *The Bell Curve debate: History, documents, opinions*. New York, NY: Random House.

Jensen, A. R. (1969). How much can we boost IQ and scholastic achievement? *Harvard Educational Review, 39*, 1–123.

Jensen, A. R. (1975, August–September). *Test bias and construct validity*. Paper presented at the 83rd Annual Convention of the American Psychological Association, Chicago, IL.

Jensen, A. R. (1998). *The g factor: The science of mental ability*. London, England: Praeger.

Jensen, B. T. (2007). The relationship between Spanish use in the classroom and the mathematics achievement of Spanish-speaking kindergartners. *Journal of Latinos and Education, 6*, 267–280.

Jensen, B. T. (2008a). Raising questions for binational research in education: An exploration of Mexican primary school structure. In E. Szecsy (Ed.), *Second Binational Symposium: Resource book*. Tempe, AZ: Arizona State University. Retrieved from http://simposio.asu.edu/docs/2007/cdrom/book/jensen_PDF.pdf

Jensen, B. T. (2008b, March). *Understanding differences in binational reading development: Comparing Mexican and U.S Hispanic students*. Paper presented at the annual meeting of the American Educational Research Association, New York City, NY.

Jerger, S., & Damian, M. F. (2005). What's in a name? Typicality and relatedness effects in children. *Journal of Experimental Child Psychology, 92*, 46–75.

Jiménez, R. T. (1997). The strategic reading abilities and potential of five low-literacy Latina/o readers in middle school. *Reading Research Quarterly, 32*, 224–243. doi:10.1598/RRQ.32.3.1

Jiménez, R. T., García, G. E., & Pearson, D. P. (1996). The reading strategies of bilingual Latina/o students who are successful English readers: Opportunities and obstacles. *Reading Research Quarterly, 31*, 90–112. doi:10.1598/RRQ.31.1.5

Johansson, B., Wedenberg, E., & Westin, B. (1992). Fetal heart rate response to acoustic stimulation in the relation to fetal development and hearing impairment. *Acta Obstetricia et Gynecologica Scandinavica, 71*, 610–615. doi:10.3109/00016349209006229

Jonassen, D. H. (1985). Learning strategies: A new educational technology. *Programmed Learning and Educational Technology, 22*, 26–34.

Jordan, R. H. (1921). *Nationality and school progress*. Bloomington, IL: Public School Publishing.

Juan-Espinosa, M., Garcia, L. F., Colom, R., & Abad, F. J., (2000). Testing the age related differenciation hypothesis through the Wechsler's scales. *Personality and Individual Differences, 29*, 1069–1075. doi:10.1016/S0191-8869(99)00254-8

Kail, R. V., (2010). *Children and their development* (5th Ed.). Upper Saddle River, NJ: Pearson Education Inc.

Kelley, E., Jones, G., & Fein, D. (2004). Intellectual and neuropsychological assessment. In G. Goldstein, S. R. Beers, & M. Hersen (Eds.), *Comprehensive handbook of psychological assessment* (pp. 191–215). New York, NY: Wiley.

Kelley, T. L. (1919). Communications and discussions: The measurement of overlapping. *Journal of Educational Psychology, 10*, 229–232. doi:10.1037/h0075771

Kessler, C., & Quinn, M. E. (1987). Language minority children's linguistic and cognitive creativity. *Journal of Multilingual and Multicultural Development, 8*, 173–186. doi:10.1080/01434632.1987.9994284

Kim, K. H. S., Relkin, N. R., Lee, K.-M., & Hirsch, J. (1997). Distinct cortical areas associated with native and second languages. *Nature, 388*, 171–174.

Kincheloe, J., Steinberg, S., & Gresson, A. D. (Eds.). (1996). *Measured lies: The Bell Curve examined.* New York, NY: St. Martin's Press.

Kinzler, K. D., Dupoux, E., & Spelke, E. S. (2007). The native language of social cognition. *Proceedings of the National Academy of Sciences USA, 104*, 12577–12580. doi:10.1073/pnas.0705345104

Kisilevsky, B. (2003, May 13). Fetus heart races when mom reads poetry: New findings reveal fetuses recognize mothers' voice in-utero. *ScienceDaily.* Retrieved from http://www.sciencedaily.com/releases/2003/05/030513080440.htm

Kisilevsky, B. S., Hains, S. M. J., Lee, K., Xie, X., Huang, H., Ye, H. H., . . . Wang, Z. (2003). Effects of experience on fetal voice recognition. *Psychological Science, 14*, 220–224. doi:10.1111/1467-9280.02435

Klitgaard, R. (1985). *Choosing elites.* New York, NY: Basic Books.

Koch, H. L., & Simmons, R. (1928). A study of the test performance of American, Mexican and Negro children. *Psychological Monographs, 35*, 1–116.

Kohnert, K., & Bates, E. (2002). Balancing bilinguals: II. Lexical comprehension and cognitive processing in children learning Spanish and English. *Journal of Speech, Language, and Hearing Research, 45*, 347–359. doi:10.1044/1092-4388(2002/027)

Kondo, K. (1998). The paradox of US language policy and Japanese language education in Hawaii. *International Journal of Bilingual Education and Bilingualism, 1*, 47–64. doi:10.1080/13670059808667673

Kosslyn, S. M., & Rosenberg, R. S. (2006). *Psychology: The brain, the person, the world* (3rd ed.). Boston, MA: Pearson.

Kosslyn, S. M., & Rosenberg, R. S. (2007). *Psychology in context* (3rd ed.). Boston, MA: Pearson.

Kovács, A. M., & Mehler, J. (2009, July 31). Flexible learning of multiple speech structures in bilingual infants. *Science, 325*, 611–612. doi:10.1126/science.1173947

Krashen, S. (1997). *Why bilingual education?* Charleston, WV: ERIC Clearinghouse on Rural Education and Small Schools. (ERIC Document Reproduction Service No. EDO-RC-96-8)

Krashen, S. (2002). The comprehension hypothesis and its rivals. In *Selected papers from the 11th international symposium on English teaching/4th Pan-Asian conference* (pp. 395–404). Taipei, Republic of China: Crane.

Krause, J., Croft, D. P., & James, R. (2007). Social network theory in the behavioral sciences: Potential applications. *Behavioral Ecology and Sociobiology, 62*, 15–27. doi:10.1007/s00265-007-0445-8

Kucer, S. B., & Silva, C. (1999). The English literacy development of bilingual students within a transitional whole language curriculum. *Bilingual Research Journal, 23*, 347–371.

Kuhl, P. K. (2004). Early language acquisition: Cracking the speech code. *Nature Reviews Neuroscience, 5*, 831–843. doi:10.1038/nrn1533

Kuhl, P. K., Conboy, B. T., Padden, D., Nelson, T., & Pruitt, J. (2005). Early speech perception and later language development: Implications for the "critical period." *Language Learning and Development, 1*, 237–264. doi:10.1207/s15473341lld0103&4_2

Kuhn, D. (1999). Metacognitive development. In L. Balter & C. S. Tamis-LeMonda (Eds.), *Child psychology: A handbook of contemporary issues* (pp. 259–286). Philadelphia, PA: Psychology Press.

Kumar, S., Filipski, A., Swarna, V., Walker, A., & Hedges, S. B. (2005). Placing confidence limits on the molecular age of the human-chimpanzee divergence. *Proceedings of the National Academy of Sciences USA, 102*, 18842–18847. doi:10.1073/pnas.0509585102

LaCroix, S. (2008). *The bilingual assessment of cognitive abilities in French and English* (Doctoral dissertation, University of British Columbia, Vancouver, BC, Canada). Retrieved from https://circle.ubc.ca/handle/2429/2575

Lambert, W. E. (1973, November). *Culture and language as factors in learning and education.* Paper presented at the Fifth Annual Learning Symposium on Cultural Factors in Learning, Bellingham, WA.

Lambert, W. E., & Anisfeld, E. (1969). A note on the relation of bilingualism and intelligence. *Canadian Journal of Behavioural Science, 1*, 123–128. doi:10.1037/h0082691

Lanauze, M., & Snow, C. E. (1989). The relation between first- and second-language writing skills: Evidence from Puerto Rican elementary school children in bilingual programs. *Linguistics and Education, 1*, 323–339. doi:10.1016/S0898-5898(89)80005-1

Landry, R. G. (1974). A comparison of second language learners and monolinguals on divergent thinking tasks at the elementary school level. *Modern Language Journal, 58*, 10–15. doi:10.2307/323983

Lau v. Nichols, 414 U.S. 563 (1974).

Lazarin, M. (2005). *To the extent practicable: Inclusion on English language learners in assessment and accountability systems under the No Child Left Behind Act.* Washington, DC: National Council of La Raza.

Lee, J., Grigg, W., & Dion, G. (2007). *The nation's report card: Mathematics 2007.* Washington, DC: U.S. Department of Education, Institute of Education Sciences, National Center for Education Statistics.

Lee, J., Grigg, W., & Donahue, P. (2007). *The nation's report card: Reading 2007.* Washington, DC: U.S. Department of Education, Institute of Education Sciences, National Center for Education Statistics.

Lesaux, N., & Geva, E. (2006). Synthesis: Development of literacy in language minority students. In D. August & T. Shanahan (Eds.), *Report of the National Literacy Panel on language minority youth and children* (pp. 171–189). Mahwah, NJ: Erlbaum.

Lesaux, N., Koda, K., Siegel, L., & Shanahan, T. (2006). Development of literacy. In D. August & T. Shanahan (Eds.), *Report of the National Literacy Panel on language minority youth and children* (pp. 75–122). Mahwah, NJ: Erlbaum.

Lesgold, A. (2004). Contextual requirements for constructivist learning. *International Journal of Educational Research, 41*, 495–502. doi:10.1016/j.ijer.2005.08.014

Lewis, L. B., Antone, L., & Johnson, J. S. (1997). Effects of prosodic stress and serial position on syllable omission in first words. *Developmental Psychology, 35*, 45–59.

Lieberman, P. (1991). *Uniquely human.* Cambridge, MA: Harvard University Press.

Lieberson, S., Dalto, G., & Johnston, M. E. (1975). The course of mother tongue diversity in nations. *American Journal of Sociology, 81*, 34–61. doi:10.1086/226033

Liedtke, W. W., & Nelson, L. D. (1968). Concept formation and bilingualism. *Alberta Journal of Educational Research, 14*, 225–232.

Liegéois, F., Baldeweg, T., Connelly, A., Gadian, D. G., Mishkin, M., & Vargha-Khadem, F. (2003). Language fMRI abnormalities associated with FOXP2 gene mutation. *Nature Neuroscience, 6*, 1230–1237. doi:10.1038/nn1138

Light, R. J., & Smith, P. V. (1969). Social allocation models of intelligence. *Harvard Educational Review, 39*, 484–510.

Light, R. J., & Smith, P. V. (1971). Accumulating evidence: Procedures for resolving contradictions among different research studies. *Harvard Educational Review, 41*, 429–471.

Lindholm, K. J. (1999, April). *Two-way bilingual education: Past and future.* Paper presented at the meeting of the American Education Research Association, Montreal, Quebec, Canada.

Lindsey, K. A., Manis, F. R., & Bailey, C. E. (2003). Prediction of first-grade reading in Spanish-speaking English-language learners. *Journal of Educational Psychology, 95*, 482–494. doi:10.1037/0022-0663.95.3.482

Long, K. K., & Padilla, A. M. (1970). *Evidence for bilingual antecedents of academic success in a group of Spanish-American college students.* Unpublished research report, Western Washington State College, Bellingham, WA.

Lopez, D. E. (1978). Chicano language loyalty in an urban setting. *Sociology and Social Research, 62*, 267–278.

López, M., Barrueco, S., & Miles, J. (2006). *Latino infants and families: A national perspective of protective and risk factors for development* (A report to the National Task Force on Early Childhood Education for Hispanics). Tempe, AZ: Arizona State University.

Lust, B. (2006). *Child language: Acquisition and growth.* Cambridge, England: Cambridge University Press

Lyn, H. (2007). Mental representation of symbols as revealed by vocabulary errors in two bonobos (*Pan paniscus*). *Animal Cognition, 10*, 461–475. doi:10.1007/s10071-007-0086-3

Macnamara, J. (1964, Summer). The commission on Irish: Psychological aspects. *Studies*, 164–173.

Madsen, I. N. (1924). Some results with the Stanford Revision of the Binet-Simon tests. *School and Society, 19*, 559–562.

Maguire, E. A., Gadian, D. G., Johnsrude, I. S., Good, C. D., Ashburner, J., Frachowiak, R. S. J., & Frith, C. D. (2000). Navigational-related structural change in the hippocampi of taxi drivers. *Proceedings of the National Academy of Sciences USA, 97*, 4398–4403. doi:10.1073/pnas.070039597

Mandler, J. M. (2004). Thought before language. *Trends in Cognitive Sciences, 8*, 508–513. doi:10.1016/j.tics.2004.09.004

Mann, C. (1922). Failures due to language deficiency. *Psychological Clinic, 13*, 230–237.

Maratsos, M. (2000). More overregularizations after all: New data and discussion on Marcus, Pinker, Ullman, Hollander, Rosen & Xu. *Journal of Child Language, 27*, 183–212. doi:10.1017/S0305000999004067

Marcus, G. F., Pinker, S., Ullman, M., Hollander, M., Rosen, T. J., & Xu, F. (1992). Overregularization in language acquisition. *Monographs of the Society for Research in Child Development, 57*(4, Serial No. 228). doi:10.2307/1166115

Marian, V. (2008). Bilingual research methods. In J. Altarriba & R. R. Heredia (Eds.), *An introduction to bilingualism: Principles and processes* (pp. 13–34). Mahwah, NJ: Erlbaum.

Maverick, M. (1997). *Texas iconoclast.* Fort Worth, TX: Texas Christian University Press.

McClure, E. (1981). Formal and functional aspects of the code-switched discourse of bilingual children. In R. Duran (Ed.), *Latino language and communicative behavior* (pp. 47–63). Norwood, NJ: Ablex.

McDonough, L. (2002). Basic-level nouns: First learned but misunderstood. *Journal of Child Language, 29*, 357–377.

McGhee-Bidlack, B. (1991). The development of noun definitions: A meta-linguistic analysis. *Journal of Child Language, 18*, 417–434. doi:10.1017/S0305000900011132

McKee, C., & McDaniel, D. (2004). Multiple influences on children's language performance. *Journal of Child Language, 31*, 489–492. doi:10.1017/S0305000904006130

McLaughlin, B. (1987). *Theories of second-language learning.* London, England: Arnold.

Mechelli, A., Crinion, J. T., Noppeney, U., O'Doherty, J., Ashburner, J., Frackowiak, R. S., & Price, C. J. (2004, October 14). Structural plasticity in the bilingual brain: Proficiency in a second language and age at acquisition affect grey-matter density. *Nature, 431*, 757. doi:10.1038/431757a

Menke, M. R. (2010). *The acquisition of Spanish vowels by native English-speaking students in Spanish immersion programs.* (Doctoral dissertation). Available from ProQuest Dissertations and Theses database. (UMI No. 3411865).

Menyuk, P. (1964). Comparison of grammar of children with functionally deviant and normal speech. *Journal of Speech and Hearing Research, 7*, 109–121.

Miller, J. F., Heilmann, J., Nockerts, A., Iglesias, A., Fabiano, L., & Francis, D. J. (2006). Oral language and reading in bilingual children. *Learning Disabilities Research & Practice, 21*, 30–43. doi:10.1111/j.1540-5826.2006.00205.x

Miller, L. S. (1995). *An American imperative: Accelerating minority educational advancement*. New Haven, CT: Yale University Press.

Mitchell, D., Destino, T., & Karam, R. (1997). *Evaluation and English language development programs in Santa Ana Unified School District: A report on data system reliability and statistical modeling of program impacts*. Riverside, CA: University of California, California Educational Research Cooperative.

Mitchell, P. (1997). *Introduction to theory of mind: Children, autism and apes*. London, England: Arnold.

Miyake, A., Friedman, N. P., Emerson, M. J., Witzki, A. H., Howerter, A., & Wager, T. D. (2000). The unity and diversity of executive functions and their contributions to complex "frontal lobe" tasks: A latent variable analysis. *Cognitive Psychology, 41*, 49–100. doi:10.1006/cogp.1999.0734

Moerk, E. L. (1983). A behavioral analysis of controversial topics in first language acquisition. *Journal of Psycholinguistic Research, 12*, 129–155. doi:10.1007/BF01067408

Monzó, L., & Rueda, R. (2001). *Constructing achievement orientations toward literacy: An analysis of sociocultural activity in Latino home and community contexts* (CIERA Report No. 1-011). Ann Arbor, MI: Center for the Improvement if Early Reading Achievement.

Moon, C., Cooper, R. P., & Fifer, W. P. (1993). Two-day-olds prefer their native language. *Infant Behavior and Development, 16*, 495–500. doi:10.1016/0163-6383(93)80007-U

Moore, C., Angelopoulos, M., & Bennett, P. (1999). Word learning in the context of referential and salience cues. *Developmental Psychology, 35*, 60–68. doi:10.1037/0012-1649.35.1.60

Moran, R. F. (2004). Undone by law: The uncertain legacy of Lau v. Nichols. *UC Linguistic Minority Research Institute Newsletter, 13*, 1–5. Retrieved from http://www.lmri.ucsb.edu/publications/newsletters/index.php

Morrow, L. M., Rueda, R., & Lapp, D. (2009). *Handbook of Research on Literacy and Diversity*. New York, NY: Guilford.

Moshman, D. (1998). Cognitive development beyond childhood. In W. Damon (Series Ed.), D. Kuhn & R. S. Seigler (Vol. Eds.), *Handbook of child psychology: Vol. 2. Cognition, perception, and language* (5th ed., pp. 947–978). New York, NY: Wiley.

Mowrer, O. H. (1960). *Learning theory and the symbolic processes*. New York, NY: Wiley. doi:10.1037/10772-000

Müller, N. (1998). Transfer in bilingual first language acquisition. *Bilingualism: Language and Cognition, 1*, 151–171. doi:10.1017/S1366728998000261

Murdoch, K. (1920). A study of race differences in New York City. *School & Society, 11*, 147–150.

Murphy, J., & Dodd, B. (2010). A diagnostic challenge: Language difficulties and hearing impairment in a secondary-school student from a non-English-speaking background. *Child Language Teaching and Therapy, 26*, 207–220. doi:10.1177/0265659009349977

Nagy, W. E., García, G. E., Durgunoglu, A. Y., & Hancin-Bhatt, B. (1993). Spanish–English bilingual students' use of cognates in English reading. *Journal of Reading Behavior, 25*, 241–259.

Nagy, W. E., McClure, E. F., & Mir, M. (1997). Linguistic transfer and the use of context by Spanish–English bilinguals. *Applied Psycholinguistics, 18*, 431–452. doi:10.1017/S0142716400010924

Náñez, J. E., Sr. (2010). Bilingualism and cognitive processing in young children. In E. García & E. Frede (Eds.), *Enhancing the knowledge base for serving young English language learners* (pp. 80–99). New York, NY: Columbia University Teachers Press.

Náñez, J. E., Sr. & Padilla, R. V. (1993). Processing of simple and choice reaction time tasks by Chicano adolescents. *Hispanic Journal of Behavioral Sciences, 15*, 498–509. doi:10.1177/07399863930154005

Náñez, J. E., Sr., & Padilla, R. V. (1995). Bilingualism and processing of elementary cognitive tasks by Chicano adolescents. *The Bilingual Research Journal, 19*, 249–260.

Náñez, J. E., Sr., Padilla, R. V., & Lopez-Maez, L. (1992). Bilinguality, intelligence, and cognitive information processing. In R. V. Padilla & A. H. Benavides (Eds.), *Critical perspectives on bilingual education research* (pp. 43–69). Tempe, AZ: Bilingual Press/Editorial Bilingue.

Nasir, N. S., & Hand, V. M. (2006). Exploring sociocultural perspectives on race, culture, and learning. *Review of Educational Research, 76*, 449–475. doi:10.3102/00346543076004449

National Association for the Education of Young Children. (2005). *Screening and assessment of young English-language learners.* Washington, DC: National Association for the Education of Young Children.

National Center for Education Statistics. (1995). *Approaching kindergarten: A look at preschoolers in the United States: National household survey.* Washington, DC: U.S. Department of Education, Office of Educational Research and Improvement.

National Center for Education Statistics. (2001). *User's manual for the ECLS-K base year public-use data files and electronic codebook* (NCES 2001-029, Rev.). Washington, DC: Author.

National Center for Education Statistics. (2003). *Status and trends in the education of Hispanics* (NCES 2003-007). Washington, DC: U.S. Government Printing Office.

National Clearinghouse for English Language Acquisition. (2006). The growing numbers of limited English proficient students (1993-94-2003/04). Washington, DC: U.S. Department of Education, Office of English Language Acquisition.

National Institute of Child Health and Human Development, National Reading Panel. (2000). *Teaching children to read: An evidence-based assessment of the scientific research literature on reading and its implications for reading instruction.* Bethesda, MD: National Institute of Child Health and Human Development.

National Task Force on Early Childhood Education for Hispanics. (2007). *Para nustros niños: Report of expanding and improving early education for Hispanics—Main report*. Tempe, AZ: National Task Force on Early Childhood Education for Hispanics. Retrieved from http://www.ecehispanic.org/work/expand_Main Report.pdf

Navarro, R. A. (1990). The problems of language, education, and society: Who decides? In E. E. García & R. V. Padilla (Eds.), *Advances in bilingual education research* (pp. 289–313). Tucson, AZ: University of Arizona Press.

Neisser, V. (1967). *Cognitive psychology*. New York, NY: Appleton-Century-Crofts.

Nelson, K. E. (1973). Structure and strategy in learning to talk. *Monographs of the Society for Research in Child Development, 38*(1–2, Serial No. 149), 1–135.

Nelson, K. E. (1977). Facilitating children's acquisition of syntax. *Developmental Psychology, 13*, 101–107.

Nelson, K. E. (1981). Individual differences in language development: Implications for development and language. *Developmental Psychology, 17*, 170–187. doi:10.1037/0012-1649.17.2.170

Nemser, W. (1971). Approximate systems of foreign language learners. *International Review of Applied Linguistics, 9*, 115–123. doi:10.1515/iral.1971.9.2.115

Nicoladis, E. (2002). What's the difference between "toilet paper" and "paper toilet"? French–English bilingual children's crosslinguistic transfer in compound nouns. *Journal of Child Language, 29*, 843–863. doi:10.1017/S0305000902005366

Nicoladis, E. (2003). Cross-linguistic transfer in deverbal compounds of preschool bilingual children. *Bilingualism: Language and Cognition, 6*, 17–31. doi:10.1017/S1366728903001019

Ninio, A., & Snow, C. (1999). The development of pragmatics: Learning to use language appropriately. In W. Ritchie & T. Bhatia (Eds.), *Handbook of child language acquisition* (pp. 347–386). New York, NY: Academic Press.

No Child Left Behind Act of 2001, Pub. L. 107-110, 115 Stat. 1425.

Nord, C. W., Lennon, J., Liu, B., & Chandler, K. (1999). *Home literacy activities and signs of children's emerging literacy, 1993 and 1999* (NCES 2000-026). Washington DC: US Department of Education, Office of Educational Research and Improvement, National Center for Education Statistics. Retrieved from http://nces.ed.gov/pubs2000/2000026.pdf

Nyborg, H., & Jensen, A. R. (2000). Black–White differences on various psychometric tests: Spearman's hypothesis tested on American armed services veterans. *Personality and Individual Differences, 28*, 593–599. doi:10.1016/S0191-8869(99)00122-1

Oller, D. K., & Eilers, R. E. (1988). The role of audition in infant babbling. *Child Development, 59*, 441–449. doi:10.2307/1130323

Osgood, C. E. (1953). *Method and theory in experimental psychology*. New York, NY: Oxford University Press.

Otero v. Mesa County School District No. 51, 408 F. Supp. 162 (1975).

Ovando, C., Collier, V., & Combs, V. (2006). *Bilingual and ESL classrooms: Teaching in multicultural contexts* (4th ed.). New York, NY: McGraw-Hill.

Oviatt, S. L. (1980). The emerging ability to comprehend language: An experimental approach. *Child Development, 51,* 97–106. doi:10.2307/1129595

Padilla, A. M., & Liebman, E. (1975). Language acquisition in the bilingual child. *Bilingual Review: La Revista Bilingue, 2,* 34–55.

Paradis, J., & Navarro, S. (2003). Subject realization and crosslinguistic interference in the bilingual acquisition of Spanish and English: What is the role of the input? *Journal of Child Language, 30,* 371–393. doi:10.1017/S0305000903005609

Paredes Scribner, A. (2002). Best assessment and intervention practices with second language learners. In A. Thomas & J. Grimes (Eds.), *Best practices in school psychology IV* (pp. 1485–1500). Bethesda, MD: National Association of School Psychologists.

Passingham, R. E. (1982). *The human primate.* Oxford, England: Freeman.

Patterson, N., Richter, D. J., Gnerre, S., Lander, E. S., & Reich, D. (2006, June 29). Genetic evidence for complex speciation of humans and chimpanzees. *Nature, 441,* 1103–1108. doi:10.1038/nature04789

Peal, E., & Lambert, W. E. (1962). The relation of bilingualism to intelligence. *Psychological Monographs: General and Applied, 76*(27, Whole No. 546), 1–23.

Peña, E. D., & Quinn, R. (1997). Task familiarity: Effects on the test performance of Puerto Rican and African American children. *Language, Speech, and Hearing Services in Schools, 28,* 323–332.

Peréa, F. C., & García Coll, C. (2008). The social and cultural contexts of bilingualism. In J. Altarriba & R. R. Heredia (Eds.), *An introduction to bilingualism: Principles and processes* (pp. 199–241). Mahwah, NJ: Erlbaum.

Peregoy, S. F. (1989). Relationships between second language oral proficiency and reading comprehension of bilingual fifth grade students. *NABE Journal, 13,* 217–234.

Peregoy, S. F., & Boyle, O. F. (1991). Second language oral proficiency characteristics of low, intermediate and high second language readers. *Hispanic Journal of Behavioral Sciences, 13,* 35–47. doi:10.1177/07399863910131003

Pérez, E. (1981). Oral language competencies improves reading skills of Mexican American third graders. *The Reading Teacher, 35*(1), 24–27.

Peterson, J. (1923). The comparative abilities of white and negro children. *Comparative Psychology Monographs, 1*(5), 1–141.

Petitto, L. A., Holowka, S., Sergio, L. E., & Ostry, D. (2001, September 6). Language rhythms in baby hand movements. *Nature, 413,* 35–36. doi:10.1038/35092613

Petitto, L. A., & Marentette, P. F. (1991, March 22). Babbling in the manual mode: Evidence for the ontogeny of language. *Science, 251,* 1493–1496. doi:10.1126/science.2006424

Petitto, L. A., Zatorre, R. J., Gauna, K., Nikelski, E. J., Dostie, D., & Evans, A. C. (2000). Speech-like cerebral activity in profoundly deaf people processing signed languages: Implications for the neural basis of human language. *Proceedings of the National Academy of Sciences USA, 97,* 13961–13966. doi:10.1073/pnas.97.25.13961

Piaget, J. (1950). *The psychology of intelligence.* New York, NY: Harcourt, Brace.

Piaget, J. (1954). *The construction of reality in the child.* New York, NY: Basic Books. doi:10.1037/11168-000

Piaget, J. (1972). Intellectual evolution from adolescence to adulthood. *Human Development, 15,* 1–12. doi:10.1159/000271225

Piaget, J., & Inhelder, B. (1969). *The psychology of the child.* New York, NY: Basic Books.

Pinker, S. (1984). *Language learnability and language development.* Cambridge, MA: Harvard University Press.

Pinker, S. (1987). The bootstrapping problem in language acquisition. In B. MacWhinney (Ed.), *Mechanisms of language acquisition* (pp. 399–441). Hillsdale, NJ: Erlbaum.

Pinker, S. (1994). *The language instinct: How the mind creates language.* New York, NY: Morrow.

Pinker, S. (2007). *The stuff of thought: Language as a window into human nature.* New York, NY: Wiley.

Pinker, S., & Bloom, P. (1990). Natural language and natural selection. *Behavioral and Brain Sciences, 13,* 707–784.

Pinker, S., & Jackendoff, R. (2005). The faculty of language: What's special about it? *Cognition, 95,* 201–236. doi:10.1016/j.cognition.2004.08.004

Pintner, R. (1932). *Pintner Intelligence Test: Manual of direction.* New York, NY: Teachers College, Columbia University, Bureau of Publications.

Pintner, R., & Keller, R. (1922). Intelligence tests of foreign children. *Journal of Educational Psychology, 13,* 214–222. doi:10.1037/h0075026

Poplack, S. (1980). Sometimes I'll start a sentence in Spanish y termino en español: Toward a typology of code switching. *Linguistics, 18,* 581–618. doi:10.1515/ling.1980.18.7-8.581

Porter, R. P. (1990). *Forked tongue: The politics of bilingual education.* New York, NY: Basic Books.

Portes, A., & Hao, L. (1998). E pluribus unum: Bilingualism and loss of language in the second generation. *Sociology of Education, 71,* 269–294.

Portes, A., & Hao, L. (2002). The price of uniformity: Language, family and personality adjustment in the immigrant second generation. *Ethnic and Racial Studies, 25,* 889–912. doi:10.1080/0141987022000009368

Portes, P. (2005). *Dismantling educational inequality: A cultural–historical approach to closing the achievement gap.* New York, NY: Peter Lang.

Powers, S., & Lopez, R. L. (1985). Perceptual, motor, and verbal skills of monolingual and bilingual Hispanic children: A discriminant analysis. *Perceptual and Motor Skills, 60*, 999–1002.

Prabhakaran, V., Smith, J. A. L., Desmond, J. E., Glover, G. H., & Gabrieli, D. E. (1997). Neural substrates of fluid reasoning: An fMRI study of neocortical activation during performance of the Raven's Progressive Matrices test. *Cognitive Psychology, 33*, 43–63. doi:10.1006/cogp.1997.0659

Pray, L. (2005). How well do commonly used language instruments measure English oral-language proficiency? *Bilingual Research Journal, 29*, 387–409. doi:10.1080/15235882.2005.10162841

Premack, D. (1976). *Intelligence in ape and man.* Hillsdale, NJ: Erlbaum.

Pressey, S. L., & Pressey, L. W. (1918). A group point scale for measuring general intelligence, with first results from 1,100 school children. *Journal of Applied Psychology, 2*, 250–269. doi:10.1037/h0074629

Pucci, S. L., & Ulanoff, S. H. (1998). What predicts second language reading success? A study of home and school variables. *International Review of Applied Linguistics, 121–122*, 1–18.

Quiroga, T., Lemos-Britton, Z., Mostafapour, E., Abbott, R. D., & Berninger, V. W. (2002). Phonological awareness and beginning reading in Spanish-speaking ESL first graders: Research into practice. *Journal of School Psychology, 40*, 85–111. doi:10.1016/S0022-4405(01)00095-4

Raikes, H., Pan, B. A., Luze, G., Tamis-LeMonda, S. C., Brooks-Gunn, J., Constantine, J., . . . Rodriguez, E. (2006). Mother–child bookreading in low-income families: Correlates and outcomes during the first three years of life. *Child Development, 77*, 924–953. doi:10.1111/j.1467-8624.2006.00911.x

Ramey, C. T., & Ramey, S. (1998). Early intervention and early experience. *American Psychologist, 53*, 109–120. doi:10.1037/0003-066X.53.2.109

Ramirez, A. (1985). *Bilingualism through schooling.* Albany, NY: State University of New York Press.

Ramirez, J. D. (2001, March). *Bilingualism and literacy: Problem or opportunity? A synthesis of reading research on bilingual students.* Paper presented at the Research Symposium on High Standards in Reading for Students in Diverse Language Groups: Research, Policy, and Practice, Washington, DC.

Ramierz, J. D., Pasta, D. J., Yuen, S. D., Billings, D. K., & Ramey, D. R. (1991). *Final report: Longitudinal study of structured English immersion strategy, early-exit and late-exit transitional bilingual education programs for language-minority children. Volume II.* (Contract no. 300-87-0156). San Mateo, CA: Aguirre International.

Ramirez, J. D., Yuen, S. D., & Ramey, D. R. (1991). *Executive summary, final report: Longitudinal study of structured English immersion strategy, early-exit and late-exit transitional bilingual education programs for language-minority children.* San Mateo, CA: Aguirre International.

Ramirez, R. (2004). *We the people: Hispanics in the United States, Census 2000 special reports*. Washington, DC: U.S. Census Bureau. Retrieved from http://www.census.gov/prod/2004pubs/censr-18.pdf

Ramist, L., Lewis, C., & McCamley-Jenkins, L. (1994). *Student group differences in predicting college grades: Sex, language, and ethnic group*. New York, NY: College Board.

Raven, J. (1936). *Mental tests used in genetic studies: The performance of related individuals on tests mainly educative and mainly reproductive*. Unpublished master's thesis, University of London, England.

Raven, J. (1989). The Raven progressive matrices: A review of national norming studies and ethnic and socioeconomic variation within the United States. *Journal of Educational Measurement, 26*, 1–16. doi:10.1111/j.1745-3984.1989.tb00314.x

Reardon, S. F. (2003). *Sources of educational inequality: The growth of racial/ethnic and socioeconomic test score gaps in kindergarten and first grade* (Working Paper No. 03-05R). University Park, PA: Pennsylvania State University, Population Research Institute.

Reardon, S. F., & Galindo, C. (2006a, April). *K–3 academic achievement patterns and trajectories of Hispanics and other racial/ethnic groups*. Paper presented at the meeting of the American Educational Research Association, San Francisco, CA.

Reardon, S. F., & Galindo, C. (2006b). *Patterns of Hispanic students' math and English literacy test scores* (Report to the National Task Force on Early Childhood Education for Hispanics). Tempe, AZ: Arizona State University.

Reardon, S., & Galindo, C. (2007). Patterns of Hispanic students' math skill proficiency in early elementary grades. *Journal of Latinos and Education, 6*(3), 1–23.

Reese, L., Garnier, H., Gallimore, R., & Goldenberg, C. (2000). Longitudinal analysis of the antecedents of emergent Spanish literacy and middle-school English reading achievement of Spanish-speaking students. *American Educational Research Journal, 37*, 633–662.

Repacholi, B., & Slaughter, V. (Eds.). (2003). *Individual differences in theory of mind*. New York, NY: Psychology Press.

Revelle, G. L., Wellman, H. M., & Karabenick, J. D. (1985). Comprehension monitoring in preschool children. *Child Development, 56*, 654–663. doi:10.2307/1129755

Reyes, I. (2001). *The development of grammatical and communicative competence in bilingual Spanish speaking children*. Unpublished doctoral dissertation, University of California, Berkeley.

Reyes, R. (1998). *A native perspective on the school reform movement: A hot topic paper*. Portland, OR: Northwest Regional Educational Laboratory, Comprehensive Center, Region X and Washington, DC: U.S. Department of Education, Office of Educational Research and Improvement, Educational Resources Information Center.

Reynolds, A. (2003). The added value of continuing early intervention into the primary grades. In A. Reynolds, M. Wang, & H. Walberg (Eds.), *Early childhood programs for a new century* (pp. 163–196). Washington, DC: CWLA Press.

Reynolds, A., & Temple, J. (2005). Priorities for a new century of early childhood programs. *Infants and Young Children, 18,* 104–118. doi:10.1097/00001163-200504000-00004

Reynolds, A. J., Temple, J. A., Robertson, D. L., & Mann, E. A. (2002). Age 21 cost–benefits analysis of the Title I Chicago child–parent centers. *Educational Evaluation and Policy Analysis, 24,* 267–303. doi:10.3102/01623737024004267

Reznick, J. S., & Goldfield, B. A. (1992). Rapid change in lexical development in comprehension and production. *Developmental Psychology, 28,* 406–413. doi:10.1037/0012-1649.28.3.406

Rhodes, R., Ochoa, S. H., & Ortiz, S. (2005). *Assessing culturally and linguistically diverse students: A practical guide.* New York, NY: Guilford.

Ricciardelli, L. A. (1992). Bilingualism and cognitive development in relation to threshold theory. *Journal of Psycholinguistic Research, 21,* 301–316. doi:10.1007/BF01067515

Rigg, M. (1928). Some further data on the language handicap. *Journal of Educational Psychology, 19,* 252–256. doi:10.1037/h0071878

Risley, T. R., & Hart, B. (2006). Promoting early language development. In N. F. Watt, C. C. Ayoub, R. H. Bradley, J. E. Puma, & W. A. Lebeouf (Eds.), *The crisis in young mental health: Vol. 4. Early intervention programs and policies* (pp. 291–317). Westport, CT: Praeger.

Robin, K. B., Frede, E. C., & Barnett, W. S. (2006). *Is more better? The effects of full-day vs. half-day preschool on early school achievement.* New Brunswick, NJ: National Institute for Early Education Research.

Rock, D. A., & Stenner, A. J. (2005). Assessment issues in the testing of children at school entry. *The Future of Children, 15*(1), 15–34. doi:10.1353/foc.2005.0009

Rodriguez, J. L., Díaz, R. M., Duran, D., & Espinosa, L. (1995). The impact of bilingual preschool education on the language development of Spanish-speaking children. *Early Childhood Research Quarterly, 10,* 475–490. doi:10.1016/0885-2006(95)90017-9

Rogoff, B. (1990). *Apprenticeship in thinking: Cognitive development in social context.* Oxford, England: Oxford University Press.

Rogoff, B. (2003). *The cultural nature of human development.* New York, NY: Oxford University Press.

Rolstad, K., Mahoney, K., & Glass, G. V. (2005). The big picture: A meta-analysis of program effectiveness research on English language learners. *Educational Policy, 19,* 572–594. doi:10.1177/0895904805278067

Roos, P. (1984, July). *Legal guidelines for bilingual administrators.* Austin, TX: Society of Research in Child Development.

Rosenthal, M. K. (1982). Vocal dialogues in the neonatal period. *Developmental Psychology, 18*, 17–21. doi:10.1037/0012-1649.18.1.17

Rossell, C. H., & Baker, K. (1996). The educational effectiveness of bilingual education. *Research in the Teaching of English, 30*(1), 7–74.

Royer, J. M., & Carlo, M. S. (1991). Transfer of comprehension skills from native to second language. *Journal of Reading, 34*, 450–455.

Rueda, R. (2007, April). *Motivation, learning, and assessment of English learners*. Paper presented at the School of Education, California State University Northridge, Northridge, CA.

Rueda, R., August, D., & Goldenberg, C. (2006). The sociocultural context in which children acquire literacy. In D. August & T. Shanahan (Eds.), *Report of the National Literacy Panel on language minority youth and children* (pp. 319–339). Mahwah, NJ: Erlbaum.

Rueda, R., MacGillivray, L., Monzó, L., & Arzubiaga, A. (2001). Engaged reading: A multi-level approach to considering sociocultural features with diverse learners. In D. McInerny & S. Van Etten (Eds.), *Research on sociocultural influences on motivation and learning* (pp. 233–264). Greenwich, CT: Information Age.

Rueda, R., & Yaden, D. (2006). The literacy education of linguistically and culturally diverse young children: An overview of outcomes, assessment, and large-scale interventions. In B. Spodek & O. N. Saracho (Eds.), *Handbook of research on the education of young children* (2nd ed., pp. 167–186). Mahwah, NJ: Erlbaum.

Rumbaugh, D. M. (1977). *Language learning by a chimpanzee: The Lana project*. New York, NY: Academic Press.

Rummelhart, D., & McClelland, J. (1987). Learning the past tense of English verbs: Implicit rules or parallel distributed processing. In B. MacWhinney (Ed.), *Mechanisms of language acquisition* (pp. 195–248). Hillsdale, NJ: Erlbaum.

Rushton, J. P. (1995). *Race, evolution, and behavior: A life history perspective*. New Brunswick, NJ: Transaction.

Rushton, J. P. (1998). [Review of the book *The g Factor: The Science of Mental Ability*, by A. R. Jensens]. *Politics and the Life Sciences, 17*, 230–233.

Rushton, J. P., & Čvorović, J. (2009). Data on the Raven's Standard Progressive Matrices from four Serbian samples. *Personality and Individual Differences, 46*, 483–486. doi:10.1016/j.paid.2008.11.020

Rushton, J. P., & Jensen, A. R. (2005). Thirty years of research on race differences in cognitive ability. *Psychology, Public Policy, and Law, 11*, 235–294. doi:10.1037/1076-8971.11.2.235

Saer, D. J. (1923). The effect of bilingualism on intelligence. *The British Journal of Psychology, 14*, 25–38.

Saffran, J. R., Loman, M., & Robertson, R. (2000). Infant memory for musical experiences. *Cognition, 77*, B15–B23. doi:10.1016/S0010-0277(00)00095-0

Saffran, J. R., & Thiessen, E. D. (2003). Pattern induction by infant language learners. *Developmental Psychology, 39*, 484–494. doi:10.1037/0012-1649.39.3.484

Samuelson, L. K. (2002). Statistical regularities in vocabulary guide language acquisition in connectionist models and 15–20 month olds. *Developmental Psychology, 38*, 1016–1037. doi:10.1037/0012-1649.38.6.1016

Sandoval, J. (1982). The WISC-R factoral validity for minority groups and Spearman hypothesis. *Journal of School Psychology, 20*, 198–204. doi:10.1016/0022-4405(82)90049-8

Sansavini, A., Bertoncini, J., & Giovanelli, G. (1997). Newborns discriminate the rhythm of multisyllibic stressed words. *Developmental Psychology, 33*, 3–11. doi:10.1037/0012-1649.33.1.3

Saunders, W. M., & O'Brien, G. (2006). Oral language. In F. Genesee, K. Lindholm-Leary, W. M. Saunders, & D. Christian (Eds.), *Educating English language learners: A synthesis of research evidence* (pp. 14–63). New York, NY: Cambridge University Press.

Schaefer, G., & Plummert, K. (1998). Rapid word learning by 15-month-olds under tightly controlled conditions. *Child Development, 69*, 309–320.

Scheffner Hammer, C., & Miccio, A. (2004). Home literacy experiences of Latino families. In B. H. Wasik (Ed.), *Handbook of family literacy* (pp. 216–241). Mahwah, NJ: Erlbaum.

Scheffner Hammer, C., Miccio, A., & Wagstaff, D. (2003). Home literacy experiences and their relationship to bilingual preschoolers' developing English literacy abilities: An initial investigation. *Language, Speech, and Hearing Services in Schools, 34*, 20–30. doi:10.1044/0161-1461(2003/003)

Schlesinger, A. M., Jr. (1991). *The disuniting of America: Reflections on a multicultural society.* New York, NY: Macmillan.

Schneider, W., & Bjorklund, D. F. (1998). Memory. In W. Damon (Series Ed.), D. Khun & R. S. Seigler (Vol. Eds.), *Handbook of child psychology: Vol. 2. Cognition, perception, and language* (5th ed., pp. 467–521). New York, NY: Wiley.

Schoneberger, T. (2000). A departure from cognitivism: Implications of Chomsky's second revolution in linguistics. *Analysis of Verbal Behavior, 17*, 57–73.

Selinker, L. (1972). Interlanguage. *International Review of Applied Linguistics, 10*, 209–231. doi:10.1515/iral.1972.10.1-4.209

Sénéchal, M., & Cornell, E. (1993). Vocabulary acquisition through shared reading experiences. *Reading Research Quarterly, 28*, 360–375. doi:10.2307/747933

Sénéchal, M., LeFevre, J., Hudson, E., & Lawson, P. (1996). Knowledge of storybooks as a predictor of young children's reading skill: A 5-year longitudinal study. *Child Development, 73*, 445–460. doi:10.1111/1467-8624.00417

Shaffer, D., & Kipp, K. (2007). *Developmental psychology: Childhood and adolescence* (7th ed.). Belmont, CA: Wadsworth/Thomson Learning.

Shaffer, D., & Kipp, K. (2010). *Developmental psychology: Childhood and adolescence* (8th ed.). Belmont, CA: Wadsworth, Cengage Learning.

Shannon, S. M. (1995). The hegemony of English: A case study of one bilingual classroom as a site of resistance. *Linguistics and Education, 7*, 175–200. doi:10.1016/0898-5898(95)90022-5

Shatz, M., & Gelman, R. (1973). The development of communication skills: Modifications in the speech of young children as a function of listener. *Monographs of the Society for Research in Child Development, 38*(5, Serial No. 152). doi:10.2307/1165783

Shaoying, G., & Darling, P. (2004). A review of the research on the critical period in second language acquisition. *Psychological Science (China), 27,* 711–714.

Sheldon, W. H. (1924). The intelligence of Mexican children. *School and Society, 19,* 139–142.

Shockley, W. (1971a). Hardy-Weinber law generalized to estimate hybrid variance for Negro populations and reduce racial aspects of the environment–heredity uncertainty. *Proceedings of the National Academy of Sciences USA, 68*(7), 1390.

Shockley, W. (1971b). Letters. *Scientific American, 224*(1), 6. doi:10.1038/scientific american0171-6

Shockley, W. (1971c). Models, mathematics, and the moral obligation to diagnose the origin of negro IQ deficits. *Review of Educational Research, 41,* 369–377.

Shockley, W., (1971d). Negro I.Q. deficit: Failure of a "Malicious Coincidence" model warrants new research proposals. *Review of Educational Research, 41,* 227–248.

Shogren, E. (1995, October 31). Gingrich assails American bilingualism as "dangerous." *Los Angeles Times.* Retrieved from http://articles.latimes.com/1995-10-31/news/mn-63269_1_official-language

Shonkoff, J., & Phillips, D. (2000). *From neurons to neighborhoods: The science of early childhood development.* Washington, DC: National Academy Press.

Siegel, D. J., Minshew, N. J., & Goldstein, G. (1996). Wechsler IQ profiles in diagnosis of high-functioning autism. *Journal of Autism and Developmental Disorders, 26,* 389–406. doi:10.1007/BF02172825

Sierra, I., & Olaziregi, J. (1989). EIFE 2. *La enseñanza del euskara: Influencia de algunos factores* [The education for Euskara: Some factors of influence]. Vitoria, Spain: Gobierno Vasco.

Siren, K. A. (1991). *Coarticulation in the speech of children and adults: Developmental trends and associated linguistic factors.* Unpublished doctoral dissertation, University of Kansas.

Skinner, B. F. (1957). *Verbal behavior.* East Norwal, CT: Appleton-Century-Crofts. doi:10.1037/11256-000

Slavin, R. E. (1986). Best-evidence synthesis: An alternative to meta analysis and traditional reviews. *Educational Researcher, 15*(9), 5–11.

Slavin, R. E., & Cheung, A. (2005). A synthesis of research on language of reading instruction for English language learners. *Review of Educational Research, 75,* 247–284. doi:10.3102/00346543075002247

Smith, M. L. (2006). Multiple methodology in education research. In J. L. Green, G. Camili, & P. B. Elmore (Eds.), *Handbook of complementary methods in education research* (pp. 457–475). Mahwah, NJ: Erlbaum.

Snow, C. (1977). Mother's speech research: From input to interaction. In C. Snow & C. Ferguson (Eds.), *Talking to children: Language input and acquisition* (pp. 31–49). Cambridge, MA: Cambridge University Press.

Snow, C. (1999). Social perspectives on the emergence of language. In B. MacWhinney (Ed.), *The emergence of language* (pp. 257–276). Mahwah, NJ: Erlbaum.

Snow, C. E., Burns, M. S., & Griffin, P. (1998). *Preventing reading difficulties in young children* (Committee on the Prevention of Reading Difficulties in Young Children). Washington, DC: National Academy Press.

Snow, C. E., & Goldfield, B. A. (1983). Turn the page please: Situation-specific language learning. *Journal of Child Language, 10,* 551–569. doi:10.1017/S0305000900005365

Sontag, L. W., & Wallace, R. O. (1935). The movement response of the human fetus to sound stimuli. *Child Development, 6,* 253–258.

Spearman, C. (1927). *The abilities of man.* New York, NY: Macmillan.

Sperling, G. (1960). The information available in brief visual presentations. *Psychological Monographs, 74*(1, Whole No. 498), 1–29.

Spoerl, D. T. (1944). The academic and verbal adjustment of college age bilingual students. *Journal of Genetic Psychology, 64,* 139–157.

Staats, A. (1971). Linguistic-mentalistic theory versus an explanatory S-R learning theory of language development. In D. Slobin (Ed.), *The ontogenesis of grammar* (pp. 103–150). New York, NY: Academic Press.

Stern, D., Beebe, B., Jaffe, J., & Bennett, S. (1977). The infant's stimulus world during social interaction: A study of caregiver behaviors with particular reference to repetition and timing. In H. Schaffer (Ed.), *Studies in mother–infant interaction* (pp. 177–202). London, England: Academic Press.

Suddendorf, T., & Corballis, M. C. (1997). Mental time travel and the evolution of the human mind. *Genetic, Social, and General Psychology Monographs, 123,* 133–167.

Suddendorf, T., & Corballis, M. C. (2007). The evolution of foresight: What is mental time travel, and is it unique to humans? *Behavioral and Brain Sciences, 30,* 299–313. doi:10.1017/S0140525X07001975

Sugarman, J., & Howard, L. (2001, September). Two-way immersion shows promising results: Findings from a new study. *ERIC/CCL Language Links: An Online Newsletter from the ERIC Clearinghouse on Languages and Linguistics.* Retrieved from http://www.cal.org/resources/archive/langlink/0901.html

Symonds, P. M. (1924). The intelligence of Chinese in Hawaii. *School & Society, 19,* 442.

Tabors, P. O. (1997). *One child, two languages: A guide for preschool educators of children learning English as a second language.* Baltimore, MD: Brookes.

Tabors, P. O., & Snow, C. E. (2002). Young bilingual children and early literacy development. In S. B. Neuman & D. K. Dickinson (Eds.), *Handbook of early literacy research* (pp. 159–178). New York, NY: Guilford Press.

Taylor, I. (1990). *Psycholinguistics: Learning and using language*. Englewood Cliffs, NJ: Prentice Hall.

Taylor, M., & Gelman, S. A. (1988). Adjectives and nouns: Children's strategies for learning new words. *Child Development, 59*, 411–419. doi:10.2307/1130320

Temple, J. A., & Reynolds, A. J. (2007). Benefits and costs of investments in preschool education: Evidence from the child–parent centers and related programs. *Economics of Education Review, 26*, 126–144. doi:10.1016/j.econedurev.2005.11.004

Terman, L. M. (1916). *The measurement of intelligence: An explanation of and a complete guide for the use of the Stanford revision and extension of the Binet-Simon Intelligence Scale*. New York, NY: Houghton Mifflin. doi:10.1037/10014-000

Terman, L. M. (1919). *The intelligence of school children: How children differ in ability the use of mental tests in school grading and the proper education of exceptional children*. Boston, MA: Houghton Mifflin.

Terrace, H. S. (1987) *Nim: A chimpanzee who learned sign language*. New York, NY: Columbia University Press.

Terrace, H. S., Petitto, L .A., Sanders, R. J., & Bever. T. G. (1979). Can an ape create a sentence? *Science, 206*, 891–902. doi:10.1126/science.504995

Tharp, R. G., & Gallimore, R. (1989). Rousing schools to life. *American Educator, 13*(2), 20–25, 46–52.

Thomas, D. G., Campos, J. J., Shucard, D. W., Ramsay, D. S., & Shucard, J. (1981). Semantic comprehension in infancy: A signal detection approach. *Child Development, 52*, 798–803. doi:10.2307/1129079

Thompson, G. G. (1952). *Child psychology*. Boston, MA: Houghton Mifflin.

Thorpe, W. H. (1961). *Birdsong*. Cambridge, England: Cambridge University Press.

Tinbergen, N. (1951). *The study of instinct*. Oxford, England: Clarendon.

Tomasello, M. (1995). Language is not an instinct. *Cognitive Development, 10*, 131–156.

Tomasello, M. (2003). *Constructing a language: A usage-based theory of language acquisition*. Cambridge, MA: Harvard University Press.

Towell, R., & Hawkins, R. (1994). *Approaches to second language acquisition*. Clevedon, England: Multilingual Matters.

Tse, L. (1998). Ethnic identity formation and its implications for heritage language development. In S. Krashen, L. Tse, & J. McQuillan (Eds.), *Heritage language development* (pp. 15–29). Culver City, CA: Language Education Associates.

Tucker, G. R. (1991). Developing a language-competent American society: The role of language planning. In A. G. Reynolds (Ed.), *Bilingualism, multiculturalism, and second language learning* (pp. 65–79). Hillsdale, NJ: Erlbaum.

Tyack, D. (1974). *The one best system: A history of American urban education*. Cambridge, MA: Harvard University Press.

U.S. Census Bureau. (1970). *Statistical abstract of the United States* (90th ed.). Washington, DC: Government Printing Office.

U.S. Census Bureau. (2000). *Statistical abstract of the United States* (120th ed.). Washington, DC: Government Printing Office.

U.S. Census Bureau. (2006). *Statistical abstract of the United States* (126th ed.). Washington, DC: Government Printing Office.

U.S. Census Bureau. (2007, March 7). *Facts for features: Cinco de Mayo* (No. CB07-FFSE.02). Washington, DC: Government Printing Office.

U.S. Census Bureau. (2008). *Statistical abstract of the United States* (128th ed.). Washington, DC: Government Printing Office.

U.S. Department of Education. (2006). *Reading First implementation evaluation: Interim report*. Washington, DC: Author.

U.S. Department of Education. (2008). *Reading First*. Retrieved from http://www.ed.gov/programs/readingfirstr/index.html

U.S. Department of Education, Office of Elementary and Secondary Education. (2002). *Outline of programs and selected changes in the No Child Left Behind Act of 2001*. Washington, DC: Author.

U.S. Government Accountability Office. (2006). *No Child Left Behind Act: Assistance from education could help states better measure progress of students with limited English proficiency* (No. GAO-06-815). Washington, DC: Author.

Veltman, C. (1983). *Language shift in the United States*. Amsterdam, the Netherlands: Mouton.

Veltman, C. (1988). Modeling the language shift process of Hispanic immigrants. *International Migration Review, 22*, 545–562. doi:10.2307/2546345

Verhoeven, L.T. (1991). Acquisition of biliteracy. *AILA Review, 8*, 61–74.

Villemarette-Pittman, N. R., Stanford, M. S., & Greve, K. W. (2003). Language and executive function in self-reported impulsive aggression. *Personality and Individual Differences, 34*, 1533–1544. doi:10.1016/S0191-8869(02)00136-8

Vygotsky, L. S. (1978). *Mind in society: The development of higher mental processes*. Cambridge, MA: Harvard University Press.

Wang, S. L. (1926). A demonstration of the language difficulty involved in comparing racial groups by means of verbal intelligence tests. *Journal of Applied Psychology, 10*, 102. doi:10.1037/h0074356

Waxman, S. R., & Markow, D. A. (1998). Object properties and object kind: Twenty-one-month-old infants' extension of novel adjectives. *Child Development, 69*, 1313–1329. doi:10.2307/1132268

Weisner, T. S. (Ed.). (2005). *Discovering successful pathways in children's development: Mixed methods in the study of childhood and family life*. Chicago, IL: University of Chicago Press.

Wellman, H. M., Cross, D., & Watson, J. (2001). Meta-analysis of theory-of-mind development: The truth about false belief. *Child Development, 72*, 655–684. doi:10.1111/1467-8624.00304

Wellman, H. M., & Gelman, S. A. (1998). Knowledge acquisition in foundation domains. In W. Damon (Series Ed.), D. Kuhn & R. S. Seigler (Vol. Eds.), *Handbook of child psychology: Vol. 2. Cognition, perception, and language* (pp. 523–573). New York, NY: Wiley.

Welsh, M. C. (2002). Developmental and clinical variations in executive functions. In D. L. Molfese & V. J. Molfese (Eds.), *Developmental variations in learning: Applications to social, executive function, language, and reading skills* (pp. 139–185). Mahwah, NJ: Erlbaum.

Werker, J. F., & Desjardins, R. N. (1995). Listening to speech in the first year of life: Experimental influences on phoneme perception. *Current Directions in Psychological Science, 4,* 76–81. doi:10.1111/1467-8721.ep10772323

Whitehurst, G. J., & Lonigan, C. J. (1998). Child development and emergent literacy. *Child Development, 69,* 848–872.

Wiese, A., & García, E. E. (2006). Educational policy in the United States regarding bilinguals in early childhood education. In B. Spodek & O. N. Saracho (Eds.), *Handbook of research on the education of young children* (2nd ed., pp. 361–374). Mahwah, NJ: Erlbaum.

Wilkinson, K. M., & Mazzitelli, K. (2003). The effect of "missing" information on children's retention of fast-mapped labels. *Journal of Child Language, 30,* 47–73. doi:10.1017/S0305000902005469

Wilkinson, K. M., Ross, E., & Diamond, A. (2003). Fast mapping of multiple words: Insights into when "the information provided" does and does not equal "the information perceived." *Applied Developmental Psychology, 24,* 739–762. doi:10.1016/j.appdev.2003.09.006

Wilkinson, L. C., Milosky, L. M., & Genishi, C. (1986). Second language learners' use of requests and responses in elementary classrooms. *Topics in Language Disorders, 6*(2), 57–70. doi:10.1097/00011363-198603000-00007

Willig, A. C. (1985). A meta-analysis of selected studies on the effectiveness of bilingual education. *Review of Educational Research, 55,* 269–317.

Winsler, A., Diaz, R. M., Espinosa, L., & Rodríguez, J. L. (1999). When learning a second language does not mean losing the first: Bilingual language development in low-income, Spanish-speaking children attending bilingual preschool. *Child Development, 70,* 349–362. doi:10.1111/1467-8624.t01-1-00026

Wong Fillmore, L. (1976). *The second time around: Cognitive and social strategies in second language acquisition.* Unpublished doctoral dissertation, Stanford University, Palo Alto, CA.

Wong Fillmore, L. (1991). When learning a second language means losing the first. *Early Childhood Research Quarterly, 6,* 323–346. doi:10.1016/S0885-2006(05)80059-6

Woodward, A. L., Markman, E. M., & Fitzsimmons, C. M. (1994). Rapid word learning in 13- and 18-month-olds. *Developmental Psychology, 30,* 553–566. doi:10.1037/0012-1649.30.4.553

Woodworth, R. S. (1910). Racial differences in mental traits. *American Association for the Advancement of Science, 31*, 171–186.

Yang, C. D. (2004). Universal grammar, statistics or both? *Trends in Cognitive Sciences, 8*, 451–456. doi:10.1016/j.tics.2004.08.006

Yerkes, R. M. (Ed.). (1921). Psychological examining in the United States Army. *Memoirs of the National Academy of Sciences, 15*, 1–890.

Yeung, K. T. (1921). The intelligence of Chinese children in San Francisco and vicinity. *Journal of Applied Psychology, 5*, 267–274. doi:10.1037/h0074283

Yip, V., & Matthews, S. (2000). Syntactic transfer in a Cantonese–English bilingual child. *Bilingualism: Language and Cognition, 3*, 193–208. doi:10.1017/S136672890000033X

Yoakum, C. S., & Yerkes, R. M. (1920). *Army mental tests*. New York, NY: Henry Holt. doi:10.1037/11054-000

Young, K. (1922). *Mental differences in certain immigrant groups*. Eugene, OR: University of Oregon Press.

Yzquierdo McLean, Z. (1995). History of bilingual assessment and its impact on best practices used today. *New York State Association for Bilingual Education Journal, 10*, 6–12. Retrieved from http://qcpages.qc.cuny.edu/ECP/bilingualcenter/Newsletters/HistoryV2-4.pdf

Zaidel, E., Zaidel, D. W., & Sperry, R. W. (1981). Left and right intelligence: Case studies of Raven's Progressive Matrices following brain bisection and hemidecortication. *Cortex, 17*, 167–186.

Zelazo, P. D., Carter, A., Reznick, S., & Frye, D. (1997). Early development of executive function: A problem-solving framework. *Review of General Psychology, 1*, 198–226. doi:10.1037/1089-2680.1.2.198

Zentella, A. C. (1997). *Growing up bilingual: Puerto Rican children in New York*. Malden, MA: Blackwell.

Zhang, J., Webb, D. M., & Podlaha, O. (2002). Accelerated protein evolution and origins of human-specific features: FOXP2 as an example. *Genetics, 162*, 1825–1835.

Zigler, E., Gilliam, W. S., & Jones, S. M. (2006). *A vision for universal preschool education*. New York, NY: Cambridge University Press.

Zimmerman, B. J., & Whitehurst, G. J. (1979). Structure and function: A comparison of two views of the development of language and cognition. In G. J. Whitehurst & B. J. Zimmerman (Eds.), *The functions of language and cognition* (pp. 1–20). New York, NY: Academic Press.

Zukow-Goldring, P. (2001). Perceiving referring actions: Latino and EuroAmerican infants and caregivers comprehending speech. In K. L. Nelson, A. Aksu-Koc, & C. Johnson (Eds.), *Children's language* (Vol. 11, pp. 139–165). Hillsdale, NJ: Erlbaum.

Zúñiga, V., & Hernández-León, R. (Eds.). (2005). *New destinations: Mexican immigration in the United Status*. New York, NY: Russell Sage.

INDEX

Capps, R., 12, 106
Carlo, M., 139–140, 144
Carlson, S. M., 59
Carpenter, M., 30
Castañeda v. Pickard, 160
CDS (child-directed speech), 50, 51
CECER-DLL (Center for Early Care and Education Research: Dual Language Learners), 3–4
CELF (Clinical Evaluation of Language Fundamentals), 96
Census Bureau, 11, 12, 57, 62, 106
Center for Applied Linguistics, 146, 148
Center for Early Care and Education Research: Dual Language Learners (CECER-DLL), 3–4
Cheung, A., 143–144
Chicago Title I Child–Parent Centers, 74–75
Child-directed speech (CDS), 50, 51
Childhood development
    in bilinguals, 98–99
    early achievement in, 103–106
    and language development, 31–34
    prekindergarten, 153–154
    social context of, 115–118
Child language, 47–49
Children in Immigrant Families (D. J. Hernandez, N. A. Denton, & S. E. Macartney), 12
Chimpanzees, 21–23, 53–54
Chinese students, 159
Chomsky, N., 30, 41, 43–44
Christian, D., 147, 149, 151–152
Civil Rights Act, 138, 159, 160, 162
Classical conditioning, 42–43
Classroom environment
    experimental, 8
    implications of education policies on, 174–175
    native language instruction in, 145
    naturalistic observation in, 7
Clinical Evaluation of Language Fundamentals (CELF), 96
Clinical Evaluation of Language Fundamentals-Revised (CELF-R), 96
Code switching, 126–128
Cognates, 133, 142

Cognition. *See also specific headings*
    defined, 35
    and language, 39, 46
Cognitive behaviorism, 45–46
Cognitive development, 35–38
    defined, 35
    and executive function, 36
    heterogeneity vs. homogeneity in, 36–37
    and language development, 39–41
    and literacy, 118–122
    and maternal book-reading, 136–137
    theoretical approaches to, 39–41, 46–47
    and theory of mind, 37–38
Cognitive egocentrism, 37
Cognitive processes, 60
    and information processing, 47
    and internal mental processes, 45
    in language development, 48–49
    and lexical comprehension, 140–141
    and second language acquisition, 63–64
Cognitive psychology, 6–9
Cognitive structures, 133
Cognitive system, 43–44
Cognitive theories. *See* Theoretical approaches
Collaboration, 7–8, 180–184
College graduates, 113
Commission on No Child Left Behind, 174
Competence, 41, 45, 46
Comprehensive school reform (CSR), 145
Computer-Based Academic Assessment System (CAAS), 144
Conceptual–intentional components, 44
Constructivist perspective, 40, 46–47
Context, sociocultural. *See* Sociocultural context
Contrastive analysis hypothesis, 124
Conversational abilities, 33
Cooing, 25–26
Coolidge, Calvin, 72
Corballis, M. C., 20, 53
Costa, A., 59
Cost effectiveness, 74–75, 153–154
Crawford, J., 72
Croft, D. P., 53

preference for, 60
rejection of, 74
in second language acquisition, 63–64
and two-way bilingual immersion,
69–71
"Homesigning," 28
Homogeneity, 36–37
Howard, E. R., 150
Howard, L., 149, 151–152
Huerta, A., 126
Human capital, 113–114

Illocutionary intent, 33
Imitation, 43, 45
Immersion models, 66, 67, 75
Immigrant groups, 12–13
bilingual education of, 62–63
IQ testing of, 84–85, 88–89
Immigration
in early 20th century U.S., 81–82
effects of, on literacy, 119
global growth of, 69
IQ testing to support legislation on,
85–91
Immigration Restriction Act, 72, 88
Individual differences, 97–98, 113–114
Infants
bilingual development in, 59
interactions with mother, 51
language acquisition in, 23–26
sensitivity of, to language, 59–60
vocalizations of, 49–50
Innateness, 44, 49, 61
Innateness hypothesis, 40
Instruction design, 132
Intellectual differences, 82–85
Intelligence assessment, 79–100
bilingual psychometrics for, 94–98
fairness in, 98–99
physical traits in, 80–81
psychological research on, 81–91
psychometrics for, 91–94
sensory-perceptual traits in, 80–81
Interactionist perspective, 37, 42, 44–51
Interdependence hypothesis, 124–125
Intergenerational bias, 111
Intergenerational educational advance-
ment, 113–114
Intergenerational language shift, 71–72
Interlanguage theories, 123–124

Internal structures, 45–47
IQ testing
administration of, 91
debate on racial/ethnic differences,
92–94
of immigrant groups, 84–85, 88–89
methodological problems with, 81, 98
of racial and ethnic groups, 82–83
for support of immigration legislation,
85–91
of U.S. Army recruits, 79, 87, 88
Italians, 83–84

Jackendoff, R., 52–53
Jacoby, R., 94
James, R., 53
James, William, 6, 116
Jensen, A. R., 83n1, 91–93,
Jensen, B. T., 134–135
Jensenism, 93, 94
Jews, 83
Johnston, M. E., 73
Jones, G., 29
Jung, K., 74, 75, 150–151

Kamil, M., 142
Karabenick, J. D., 34
Karapetsas, A., 70
Kelley, E., 29
Kelley, T. L., 83
Key School, 147
Kim, K. H. S., 61, 92, 99
Kincheloe, J., 94
Kinzler, K. D., 60
Kipp, K., 25, 28, 30–34, 39–40, 61, 91
Kohnert, K., 140–141
Krashen, S., 72–74
Krause, J., 53

Laboratory environment, 7
LAD (language acquisition device), 43
Lambert, W. E., 58, 64, 89, 90, 98
Language
and cognition, 39
and education, 133–139
evolution of, 53–54
federal legislation on, 161–174
infant sensitivity to, 59–60
prestige of, 73
production of, 53–54

ABOUT THE AUTHORS

Eugene E. García, PhD, is presently vice president for education partnerships at Arizona State University. He was dean of the Mary Lou Fulton College of Education from 2002–2006. Before joining the faculty at Arizona State Universoty, he was dean of the Graduate School of Education at the University of California, Berkeley. From 2004–2008 he chaired the National Task Force on Early Education for Hispanics funded by the Foundation for Child Development and four additional foundations. His most recent book is *Teaching and Learning in Two Languages: Bilingualism and Schooling in the United States*. His research can be viewed at http://www.ecehispanic.org.

José E. Náñez Sr., PhD, is a President's Professor of psychology and the executive director for community outreach in the Office of the Senior Vice-President for Educational Outreach and Student Services, Arizona State University. He earned his PhD in experimental child psychology from the Institute of Child Development, University of Minnesota at Minneapolis. His early research involved infant perceptual and cognitive development. Recent research includes exploration of alternative measures for identifying gifted Latino children and adolescents. Dr. Náñez has contributed to numerous book chapters and journal articles on dual language learners, most recently contributing a chapter to *Enhancing the Knowledge Base for Serving Young English Language Learners*, edited by E. García and E. Frede. His cutting-edge collaborative neuroscience research explores perceptual learning and neuroplasticity and has been published in top-tier international journals, including *Nature*, *Nature Neuroscience*, *Nature Reviews Neuroscience*, *Proceedings of the National Academy of Science*, *PLoS ONE*, and *Current Biology*. His current research interests include the relationship between bilingualism and neuroplasticity.